PROBLEM SOLVING STRATEGIES FOR WRITING

THIRD EDITION

PROBLEM SOLVING STRATEGIES FOR WRITING

THIRD EDITION

LINDA FLOWER

CARNEGIE-MELLON UNIVERSITY

HARCOURT BRACE JOVANOVICH, PUBLISHERS

San Diego   New York   Chicago   Austin   Washington, D.C.
London   Sydney   Tokyo   Toronto

Copyrights and Acknowledgments

63 Figure 4-1 from *Birds of North America*, illustrated by Arthur Singer. © 1966 by Western Publishing Company, Inc. Used by permission. **171** Excerpt from Emily Van Ness, "How to Buy a House on Your Own . . . with a Little Help from Uncle Sam," *Ms.* magazine, March 1979. Reprinted by permission of Emily Sheean Van Ness. **203–05** Excerpt from *This Is Photography*, by Thomas Miller and Wyatt Brummitt. Case Hoyt Corp., 1945. Reprinted by permission. **254** Figure 12-3 from *The Common Sense of Science*, by Jacob Bronowski. Harvard University Press, 1953. Reprinted by permission.

ISBN: 0-15-571974-2

Library of Congress Catalog Card Number: 88-80628

Printed in the United States of America

Preface

There are many reasons to improve a textbook, but I think the three major changes that mark this Third Edition are also a reflection of some exciting developments in the field of rhetoric and composition itself. These additions draw, first, on our new theoretical understanding of how writers operate within a discourse community; second, on a new research-based view of the revision process; and finally, on the pedagogy of translating such ideas into a structured sequence of assignments. Let me sketch out the goals behind each of these additions.

Writing is, on the one hand, a very peronal, individual, cognitive process. However, this personal, problem-solving event always happens within a social context, and in this new edition I have tried to place cognition more firmly in context and to help writers see that as they write, they are in fact a part of a larger discourse community. This recognition is especially important for students entering college, the community of people who read and write academic discourse. We know that this academic community has high expectations: it expects a writer to read and use information with care, to synthesize not just summarize, to think through issues in an analytical way, and, on top of that, to draw on the writer's own ideas—to make a contribution to the conversation. In our research at the Center for the Study of Writing at Berkeley and Carnegie Mellon, we have begun to see why many students have trouble entering this new discourse community, as they try to figure out its expectations and build their own uncertain representation of the task.

In this edition I have tried to help writers become more aware of how context shapes writing, and to help them see, in turn, how entering a new discourse is also a "problem" they can solve. In trying to turn theory into practical advice, I am indebted to the instructors in the freshman composition course at Carnegie Mellon. For the past three years, we have been experimenting with ways to help students investigate the various discourse communities to which they belong or to which they aspire. What we learned is reflected in the extended sequence of assignments found in the chapters mentioned below.

Chapter 1 introduces students to the way writers always operate within a discourse community. It uses the metaphor of "entering a conversation" to show how learning to enter the "academic discourse" community is a particularly important problem for student writers. It contains the case history of Harry, an enterprising student whose attempt to write an English paper, an economics project, and a magazine article on the same topic reveal some of the expectations and assumptions of these different audiences.

Chapter 5 shows students how to look at language and uncover their assumptions about assignments. It contains a new, step-by-step section on how to explore a rhetorical problem and a "thought" experiment which helps students to look at some of their own assumptions about what academic assignments call for and what teachers expect.

Chapter 8 picks up this theme, offering a set of assignments on the topic of "academic discourse." What are its features? How do its conventions vary in different disciplines? What problems does it pose for students trying to enter the "conversation"? The assignments include a number of tools for gathering information about how people talk and write in college and for building a research paper or an argument. A new section also shows students how to turn a problem analysis into a more familiar thesis and support paper. It walks writers through the process of exploring a problem in order to develop and then test a *tentative thesis*, and it provides a glossary of terms teachers often use to discuss a thesis.

The second major change in the Third Edition is an attempt to translate research into teaching. Chapter 11, on revision, has been updated to reflect some suggestive discoveries about the ways experienced writers not only detect more problems in texts, but turn to diagnosis in order to understand those problems and to plan a revision. (I am happy to mention that this study, done with my colleagues John R. Hayes, Karen Schriver, Linda Carey, and James Stratman, won the 1987 NCTE Braddock Award.)

A section in Chapter 11 outlines a three-step-process for Detecting Problems, Diagnosing Problems, and Revising the Text, drawing attention to the strategies and goals that are unique to each of these steps. The chapter then demonstrates this thinking process, showing the development of a student's paper on black awareness on campus—a process that included the use of feedback from both teacher and peers.

The third change to this edition is in response to valuable suggestions from teachers who have used the book. In addition to including new student examples, glossaries of new terms, and checklists for assessing one's process or paper, I have developed a sequence of assignments, leading from Chapter 1 to Chapter 8, which build on one another. These assignment sequences focus on two areas. One is process—studying one's own process or that of others and becoming aware of the strategies writers use. The second is language and discourse itself—studying the conventions of different communities (such as history, sports, or music), but paying special attention to the features of academic writing. These assignments combine library work with more inventive kinds of research—such a guessing who wrote certain Mystery Texts, analyzing conversations and class discussions, and watching how people read and interpret texts from inside and outside their field.

These additions to *Problem-Solving Strategies for Writing* reflect some exciting changes and fresh ideas developing in our field. But they also reflect the original outlook of this book, which was perhaps best stated in the preface to the first edition.

This book, appropriately enough, started as an attempt to solve a problem. I was asked to design a writing program for a group of pragmatists—students who would attend a noncredit course if they felt it would make a difference in the academic and professional writing they were doing outside the course. They expected substantive instruction in *how* to write, not just in how to analyze a piece of writing. I soon realized that their questions were the same ones I wanted to answer for myself: What are the principles that underlie the act of effective writing? What are some of the more intelligent strategies for tackling common writing problems? I also found that my traditional background in literary criticism and rhetorical analysis of the final text simply hadn't told me enough about how good writers actually went about producing the thoughtful and effective prose I admired.

My growing awareness of these gaps in our knowledge led me into two quite different kinds of research. I wanted first of all to translate some of the product-based wisdom of rhetoric and composition into a more process-based approach to writing. Instead of defining what a well-organized essay looks like, I wanted to show how one would go about the process of making it organized. And I wanted to offer my students the best principles that were known on writing for readers in the real world. Such writing, as I conceive it, goes beyond traditional persuasions and means helping readers to comprehend and remember fully what you have to say. This book, then, is a process-based rhetoric: an attempt to look at the traditional topics of invention or discovery, arrangement, and style—as well as audience analysis and persuasion—from the writer's point of view. Many rhetoricians from Aristotle on, and especially the creators of the "new" rhetoric, have looked at their art as a process of discovery, deliberation, and choice. This rhetorical tradition of teaching writing as intellectual discovery has a great deal to offer students. One of the goals of this book was to translate our knowledge of effective written products into a description of the process that could produce them.

Translation, however, was finally not enough. In trying to offer my students (and myself) more than traditional "good advice" about writing, I discovered how little we really know about the thinking process writers go through. And we know even less about the differences in how good and poor writers handle this process. It seemed that the only obvious response to this problem was research on composing itself. John R. Hayes, of Carnegie-Mellon University, had also become interested in this problem. As a cognitive psychologist studying creativity and problem-solving, he too was asking such questions as "What do writers actually do?" and "How can they learn to do it better?" At that time he had just started a book *(The Complete Problem Solver)* based on a university-wide course he had developed that focused on general problem-solving skills. We were curious:

Were there useful connections between writing and other basic thinking processes such as decision-making, learning, and remembering?

Cognitive psychology is, of course, a young field—a reaction, in part, against the assumptions of behaviorism. In the tradition of William James, it is concerned with the process of cognition and, like the field of English, with the nature and process of creative thought. Many of the ideas in this book, then, are the result of my happy and continuing research collaboration with John Hayes and have been influenced by the example of his constantly inquiring mind. Our objective has been to make unconscious actions a little more conscious: to give writers a greater awareness of their own intellectual processes, and therefore the power and possibility of conscious choice.

This book combines traditional rhetorical concerns with current research in composition—in an effort to create a rhetoric of the writing process. This means offering writers a set of principles and strategies for planning discourse, for generating and organizing ideas, and for designing and editing their prose for a reader. More broadly, it means showing writers how their own intellectual processes are an important part of effective writing.

This book is written for people with realistic reasons for writing; students writing themes, term papers, and reports on academic subjects; professionals writing memos and reports as a part of their job; and people in any field who simply have something to say. It is also written for people who want to know *why*. Many approaches to composition offer the student a wealth of practical but largely ad hoc advice on how to compose. I have tried to speak to writers who want to know the principle behind the practice and who, like me, would like to understand more of their own thinking processes.

The first chapter of the book is an overview of the kinds of writing people do. It looks at examples of academic, professional, and personal writing and introduces two major concepts that run throughout the book: writing for the reader and hierarchical organization.

From this point on, the book focuses on the writing process itself. The second chapter looks at familiar theories and models of the writing process, such as the inspiration method, and helps the reader to analyze his or her own strategies for writing. Chapter 4 shows how writers construct their own internal, mental representations of meaning. Most of the rest of the book, Chapters 3, 5–7, and 9–12, is organized around a set of steps or major tasks the writer must handle: planning, generating ideas, and organizing ideas; understanding readers and designing with them in mind; and evaluating and editing one's prose. For each step, I have offered the writer a variety of strategies, such as brainstorming and talking to the reader, as ways to generate ideas. These steps are summarized at the beginning of Chapter 3.

Chapter 8 does digress, however to discuss one of the basic processes that underlies most expository writing; analyzing a problem. It returns to the art of discovering problems (raised in Chapter 1) in a more formal way and leads the student through the stages of problem analysis, moving from awareness of a problematic situation to a problem definition to a thesis. Many approaches to composition start with the injunction to "find a thesis." In essence, the chapter describes the process of analysis and exploration that can lead to creating such a thesis.

The book concludes with two case studies on research writing in Chapter 13. They cover the process of doing research and developing arguments when writing research papers, consulting reports, and proposals.

The goal of this organization is to introduce the writer, in a systematic way, to distinctive parts of the writing process. Often parts of this process, such as planning or designing for a reader, are tasks writers could handle but simply tend to ignore. Second, I have tried to offer a variety of effective strategies and to suggest the power of knowing alternative ways of coping with the problem of writing.

A practical note to instructors: In order to keep the book as concise as possible, I have placed many items in the Instructor's Manual, including additional exercises, more detailed assignments, some evaluation sheets both student and instructor can use, a brief introduction to formats for reports, and a discussion of ways to teach heuristic strategies in the classroom. It is rarely enough to tell a person about a new strategy he or she might find useful; the real results come from instructors who can help students actively experience a new way of doing things.

I want to thank all the reviewers of this edition. They not only asked good questions, but gave me some valuable suggestions and answers. They are Mary Baron, University of Alaska-Fairbanks; Deborah Brandt, University of Wisconsin-Madison; John Carson, Robert Morris College; Beverley Furlow, Pima Community College; Jake Gaskins, Southeast Missouri State University; and Leroy Perkins, University of Alaska-Fairbanks.

At Harcourt Brace Jovanovich I have appreciated the efforts of Chris Cohn, Bruce Daniels, Kay Faust, Avery Hallowell, and Pat Zelinka. As always, Bill McLane has been a wise advisor, an editor who is as interested in students as he is in new ideas. For me, the stimulation in working with my colleagues in Carnegie Mellon's freshman writing course and at the Center for the Study of Writing has been invaluable. By turning our research to the problem students face as they enter new discourse communities and by taking our discoveries directly back into the classroom, we have found our students telling us new things about writing and about how to teach it. Finally, and most of all, I want to thank Tim Flower. He is the sort of friend every writer needs—a good listener and advisor when you are in trouble and a source of energy and constant inspiration when you see your way clear.

Contents

chapter eight

Analyzing A Problem and Building A Thesis   135

chapter nine

Designing for a Reader   157

chapter ten

Writing Reader-Based Prose   187

chapter eleven

Revising for Purpose and Editing for Style   213

chapter twelve

Editing for a Clear Organization   239

chapter thirteen

Two Case Studies: Research Writing   259

Index   289

To my father, Oren W. Stevenson,
with appreciation

chapter one

Writing
to Make Things Happen

THIS IS A BOOK ABOUT HOW to write: how to say what you mean and how to deal with your reader. It is also about writing in the real world and handling the problems people face when they need to write academic papers, persuasive reports, concise memos, and essays that can open a reader's eyes. In writing this book I have imagined you, the reader, as a person who writes to make something happen, whether your audience is a professor, an employer, or a peer. I have assumed that, whatever your goals are, you are interested in discovering better ways to achieve them.

Your goal as a writer might often be as basic as making your words say what you really mean. Or it might be as complicated as persuading another person to change his or her mind. In either case, your success will depend in part on the skills and writing strategies you bring to the task. So in this book we will focus on three kinds of strategies.

1. The strategies you have for *composing itself.* That is, the techniques you have for getting started, for generating ideas, for organizing them, and for reviewing what you have written. The kind of composing strategies you use has a large impact on how efficiently you write—how long it takes you to produce a page that satisfies you. Even more importantly, these strategies can also determine how well you explore and use your own knowledge as you write. Some writers have a large repertory of powerful writing strategies on which to draw; other people appear always to be at the mercy of their inspiration.

2. The strategies you have for *adapting your writing to the needs of a reader.* Good writing is intensely functional. It goes beyond mere correctness to meet the needs of the reader. Some of these

needs are practical ones. Mr. H. is reading your paper because he needs to know X so he can do Y—and only you can tell him. But many readers are not so highly motivated. They become impatient if they cannot readily comprehend and remember a written text. Writers meet these readers' needs by making their prose easy to read, their points easy to see, and their arguments logically presented. Good writers do not simply express themselves; they plan their writing around a goal they share with a reader and design it to be understood and remembered.

3. The strategies you have for *evaluating and editing* your own writing. Good writers are their own editors. This means they can test their own writing for effectiveness from the reader's point of view. If it doesn't meet that goal, they can draw on editing techniques that bring it closer.

In brief, the goal of this book is to help you gain more control of your own composing process: to become more efficient as a writer and more effective with your readers.

WHY TAKE A PROBLEM-SOLVING APPROACH TO WRITING?

How do people become good writers? How do they develop the skills of composing, adapting to a reader, and evaluating and editing their own work? The popular mythology of writing gives us two answers. First, it tells us that the ability to write is simply a question of talent. Some people are just born with "a way with words"; others aren't, and that's that. Secondly, the myth says that the process of writing depends on inspiration. If a writer is lucky or talented—or waits long enough—inspiration will come, paragraphs will flow, and the paper will write itself.

Like all myths, this one is right about some things. There are real differences among writers, and inspiration, if you can get it, is a fine composing method. However, there are two problems with this myth. One is that it leads capable people to give up too soon. It assumes that people can't really *learn how* to write except for learning rather mechanical skills such as correct use of grammar and punctuation. So, the myth says, if you weren't born with talent or don't feel inspired, there's nothing much you can do. Secondly, in addition to being discouraging, this myth is just plain wrong about what actually happens when people write.

If we looked at composing as a thinking process, we would find that it has much in common with the problem-solving processes people use every day when they are planning a trip, taking an exam, making a decision, or trying to make a diplomatic request. The general research on problem solving in the past twenty years has discovered a great deal about the special strategies that successful artists, scientists, inventors, and business managers use to go about solving problems in their work. These experts in their field are characterized by two things: a great deal of knowledge about their topic and a large repertory of powerful strategies for attacking their problems. Good writers share these qualities. They are people who have developed better ways to entertain the problem of writing.

In this book, we will look at some of this research, in part because it has uncovered some very effective strategies that anyone can use. But more than that, it will let you see the principle behind the practice and give you some insight into the logic of the strategies you are learning. In the long run, this sort of knowledge about why things work is the best knowledge, because it lets you continue to teach yourself.

The special strength of a problem-solving approach is really a frame of mind or an attitude—one that may be quite different from other ways you have approached writing. As a problem solver your first concern is not with the finished product—with fitting into a format or convention, with following the rules of grammar, or even with producing a polished style. Instead, your attention is squarely focused on your own goals as a writer, on what you want to do and say. The formal features of a finished text *do* matter, but they matter because they can help you achieve your goals as a writer. Problem solving is a goal-directed frame of mind.

Moreover, concentrating on goals and figuring out how to reach them seems to let people marshal quite surprising skills and knowledge they didn't know they had. It is easy and, in fact, quite normal to feel a little uncertain and helpless when you are facing a new piece of writing. And speaking from experience, I can also say that it is quite normal to write first drafts that even your typewriter doesn't want to read. However, a problem solver takes a very practical, "let's see what we can do" attitude toward these stumbling blocks. This attitude not only gets the process going, it lets you use more of the real powers you do have. A problem-solving approach assumes that if you know what you want to do, you can usually find a way to do it.

A second reason to approach writing as a problem solver takes us back to the fact that expert and novice writers often use different strategies. A problem-solving approach assumes that there is often a "better" way and that writers can substantially expand their repertory of strategies. There is no guarantee that any given strategy will do the job—some problems are hard. But an awareness of your own decisions and a knowledge of alternatives gives you the incalculable power of conscious choice.

In my own work as a teacher and a researcher, I need to write a good deal. If I can't show what I've learned, my research will not be of much use to anyone. And like many students, I have to write to the demands of schedules, eagle-eyed editors, and the readers in my field. So when I sit down to write, it feels good to know that there are strategies and principles behind this process—that it's not just a game of chance I play with my muse. However, I didn't begin to actively enjoy writing—to feel secretly excited about the time I spend thinking at the typewriter—until I stopped seeing my writing as a polished finished product. With that "finished product" perspective, the only way to succeed was to sound as elegant and authoritative as the published writers I was reading. And somehow I never did. The pleasure came when I began concentrating on what I wanted to accomplish and trying to figure out how to do it. For me, problem solving turns composing into a goal-directed journey—writing my way to where I want to be.

A WRITER'S GOALS

In the real world of college and work, people write because they want to make something happen. They want to make their own ideas come together or to make other people sit up and take notice. These complex goals demand intelligent strategies. Compare this goal-directed process with the simpler theme-writing process many people remember from school when they had to toss off a five-paragraph theme on a topic such as "My Summer Vacation." The writing strategy they used then may have been rather simple: Try to use big words, sound important, and concentrate on avoiding grammatical errors. The problem with this strategy, of course, is that it often produces nothing more than hot air. And it doesn't help people do the kind of serious, practical, and idea-packed writing that is expected by college professors and colleagues at work. In real-world writing, correctness is naturally important, but your ideas and your reader are even more important. This book is about the kind of writing people do when they *know* something they want to *communicate* to a *reader* who wants or needs to hear it.

One of the most common yet most demanding kinds of real-world writing people do is expository writing, or writing that analyzes and explains. In college, as well as in business and professions, people do expository writing—also called analytical writing—whenever they want to analyze a complex problem or issue. The result may be a college paper on the Civil War, a company memo on improving quality control, a research report on solar heating, or a feature article on energy consumption. In all these cases the writer has something to say, the reader needs or wants to hear it, and the topic demands clear and logical discussion.

If expository, or analytical writing is so common, why is it often so difficult to do, or at least to do well? One reason is that a writer usually faces not one but three major tasks:

1. *Making meaning.* First he or she has to make sense out of complex situations, and do so in words. Intuitive understanding is not enough. A writer must use language to make meaning; that is, to name key issues, to describe their interrelationships, and turn that sense of the whole into concepts expressed in words.
2. *Communicating.* Second, a writer has to communicate that understanding so a reader will see what the writer meant. Simply expressing one's ideas is usually not enough. The writer must use language to anticipate and guide the reader.
3. *Persuading.* Finally, a writer often has to move another person not only to understand but to respond or take some action. The writer's goal is often persuasion as well as explanation.

In the rest of this chapter we are going to look at three real-world writing problems: a practical problem, a college assignment, and a personal reason to write. As you read them, notice how the writers' priorities differ—sometimes it is more important simply to describe a problem than to persuade a reader. But all three writers are seeking to make meaning, communicate it, and persuade their readers to respond.

A Practical Writing Problem

The following chain of events started in December when a staff writer for *City* magazine did a feature article on potholes (see Example 1). She wanted to analyze, from her perspective, why the local roads were in such bad repair despite rising road taxes. This article sparked a worried note from the City/County Commissioners' office to the Department of Roads saying: "What is the trouble? We must respond." So in response, a city transportation engineer was asked to look into the situation, define the problem more thoroughly, and write a report that explained why the local paving was falling apart (see Example 2). This report, in turn, led a research engineer with the local asphalt supplier to reply with

Example 1

THE POTHOLE 500

by May Britton

It starts slowly. Moisture seeps through the pavement to the soil below. A sudden drop in temperature and the ground heaves as it freezes. Later, when the ground thaws and contracts in the warm afternoon sun, the pavement doesn't. A few pockets you can still dodge begin to show up. Then comes the big freeze, the real snow, the salt trucks. The freeze, heave, and thaw cycle begins in earnest, and pretty soon salt water and traffic begin to gnaw and pound small holes into craters.

Potholes Are a Hole in Your Pocket

Last year the state spent $30 million to repair the potholes in its 45,000 miles of roadway—money you paid into the Motor Fund through license and registration fees and gas taxes. $30 million to repair, but what about the hidden costs of *disrepair?* Here's an armchair estimate of what your ticket to the Pothole 500 could cost you this year.

License	$10
Registration	25
Gasoline Tax	40
One bent rim (replace wheel)	20
Front end realigned	15
One pair shock absorbers	60
Broken springs	80
Ruptured tire	50
Lost hubcap	10
Dental filling replaced	40
Combat pay (driving to work)	self-assigned
This year's total:	$350+

Why Are We Paying This?
Two causes stand out: One is courtesy of Mother Nature, the other thanks to the County

Department of Transportation. Nature first. As any engineer will tell you, if a road doesn't have proper drainage, it has problems. Rainfall seeps in or subsurface springs "pump up" water through the surface, and the freeze cycle is set in motion. Add a marked increase in traffic on many roads, and craters are on the way.

Our terrain makes drainage as difficult as it is necessary, so the County has wisely devoted some of its maintenance funds to pothole prevention by installing new drainage systems on older roads.

The problem is that this foresight doesn't seem to extend throughout the Department's decision making. The Pine Road resurfacing done this spring laid down a 2-inch surface of asphalt. The New Jersey Turnpike lays down 12½ inches—and has had only minimal repairs in its 26 years of heavy use. Is this a case of penny-wise and pound-foolish?

A second case in point. The approved drill for patching potholes is clean the wound, apply the mix, and if the hole is small, compact it with a mechanical tamper. If a large area is resurfaced, use a 5-ton roller. Then, one wonders, why do we see road crews patting patches into place with thawks of a shovel, or rolling them down with the back wheels of a truck? Why is it the County is just now "looking into" equipment that will heat the mix laid in winter (cold patch) so that it will last as well as summer repairs?

The solution to the technical problems of good roads and dependable repairs lies with the City and County engineers. But all of us, since we're footing the bill in more ways than one, might well ask, "How good is the decision making that's coping with this problem?" Perhaps there should be an answer.

May Britton is a free-lance writer and member of the State Consumers Board.

Example 2

MCDR **MIDLAND COUNTY DEPARTMENT OF ROADS**
6230 Grafton, Midland 03416   Willard Harris, Director

January 20, 198—

The City/County Board of Commissioners
City/County Building
Midland 06102

Attention: Mr. Andrews, Transportation Supervisor

Subject: Special Briefing Report on Road Repair
                 Prepared for the February Open Hearing
                 of the Board of Commissioners

Attachments: Department of Roads Planning Paper No. 459-B

Gentlemen:

At your request we have prepared a special report on road
repair for the February Open Hearing. We hope it will allow
you not only to answer questions but to educate the public
about the real costs of good roads.

The Problem: Conditions and Costs
The underlying problem is that our area is a natural producer of potholes. Here, even the best-laid roads are subject
to the extremes of both natural and man-made conditions: a
hilly terrain, constant severe freeze and thaw conditions, un-
stable soil beneath the roadbed, heavy salting due to frequent
road ice, and increasing traffic density.
The stress placed on our roads is increasing, but the
funds to maintain the roads are not increasing at the same
rate. Our area is not alone in this: the national pothole
average is 49 holes per mile and we now maintain 45,000 miles
of road. This year there were 12,000 potholes reported and the
city made plans to resurface 100 miles of streets. On the
average that means buying 100 pounds of asphalt filler to patch
each pothole. Although our costs for crews and equipment are
subject to only normal inflation, the cost of asphalt is taking
sharp and unpredictable rises because it is a petroleum-based
product.

Example 2 (continued)

-2-

This combination of limited funds and severe pothole-producing conditions forces a series of trade-offs. Here is a typical problem. One way to keep asphalt from shrinking and cracking under winter conditions is to use a soft asphalt. But at high summer temperatures, cars running over soft asphalt will produce ruts, which create pools of rainwater and encourage hydroplaning and skidding. Using asphalt that is safe in summer can mean potholes in winter.

On top of that, the federal specifications on a number of recently "safety-updated roads" require a skid-resistant surface, which prevents an oily film from scumming the surface during a rain. In order to meet those specifications and qualify for federal monies from the Liquid Fuel Tax, we must switch to a large-particle aggregate. Yet this aggregate, unlike our local smaller stone, must be trucked in at considerably increased cost. Once again, there is often no perfect solution because of the natural conditions, but even when an optimal technical solution exists it is often prohibited by cost.

<u>Department Planning and Recommendations</u>

In the face of this the Department has two current plans: one a short-term plan for reallocating repair money and the other a long-term plan for improving new road building. These are presented in detail in the Department's Planning Paper No. 459-B.

In addition we suggest that the City-County Commission attempt to publicize the problem through newspaper publications, such as the <u>AAA Motorist</u>, which will run in-depth features on local problems. Given the current traffic conditions in our county, we can only improve road maintenance if we increase the budget.

Yours,

Thomas Chen

Thomas Chen
Supervisor

TC/jv
Attach.

Example 3

McGinnis ASPHALT Engineering

464 Line Road, Midland 03408

```
TO:       Jean Birch, Director of Sales
FROM:     Michael Rourke, Research Engineer
SUBJECT:  Research Update on County Road Repair
DATE:     January 20, 198—
```

    In response to your request for an update, the major problem is still the county road commission itself. Our new sulphur-asphalt mix could probably increase road life in this area by 20%, but the commission has consistently failed to lay test paving. Specifically, this mix:

1. offers a soft mix that also resists rutting
2. resists seepage and prevents stripping
3. provides better bonding, which allows the use of cheap local stone
4. will become cheaper as the cost of petroleum-based competitors increases.

If you could get the county to overcome its inertia and fund initial testing, we could offer improved mixes and the strong possibility of lower costs in the next three years. See the attached report for details.

---

a more technical analysis of the road mix the department was buying and the alternatives it had ignored (see Example 3).

As you will see in the examples, each writer viewed the problem differently and produced a very different-looking piece of prose. But all shared the three goals of making meaning out of the facts, communicating it, and persuading the reader to do or see something differently.

Different Formats but Common Principles

These three pieces of writing all look quite different from one another. The feature writer starts with a good "lead," or short, catchy introduction to get the reader's attention; she uses pictures, "take-outs" (the headline in the text), and vivid metaphoric language to direct the reader and make a point. By contrast, the research engineer follows a standard memo format; his first sentence bluntly states the reason for writing, and he punches out the final points he expects the reader to remember in numbered order, using technical terms such as "stripping" that a general reader would not understand.

It is important to know the formal features that belong to different kinds of writing. In Example 1, without a good title and lead your article might go unread. If you saved your best points until last in a news article, the editor might chop them off in order to fit the story to the layout. Or, if you omit an informative subject heading (see Example 3), your memo might be misfiled and never seen again.

In spite of these differences, there are two important features that underlie all these examples. First, they are *designed with their readers in mind.* The feature writer tackled her topic from the point of view of her readers: What are they interested in, what do they need to know, and how can I adapt my research to their concerns? Likewise, her visual layout guides readers by setting up expectations and leading the readers along. Both of the report writers are working in an organization in which other people must *use* their writing: the City/County Commissioners will use the first report at next month's open hearing of the Commission; the McGinnis sales director will use Michael Rourke's memo to sell the county on a new idea. As you can see, the headings, references to other reports, and numbered points are designed to let readers find just what they need to know, and find it quickly. Although the features of format may differ, the logic behind each format is the logic of meeting the readers' needs.

A second feature these pieces of writing share is an underlying hierarchical organization. That is, they are organized around a top-level issue or idea that is then broken down in the paper into its parts. These parts may be subissues, supporting details, steps, causes, or key points—anything that helps the writer organize his or her ideas. It helps to visualize a hierarchical structure as an upside-down tree, as in Figure 1-1. A good example of such a hierarchy would be a university. The university as a whole is at the top of this hierarchy—not because it is more important than the programs or the people who make it up, but because it is more inclusive.

The best way to think of a hierarchy is as a large system with a number of working parts. For example, a system or organization such as a university has a number of rather independent subsystems, such as the English department or the sophomore class, within its hierarchy. In the same way, a piece of writing has a number of working parts, such as an introduction, a body, and a conclusion. Each paragraph within these sections is another subsystem—a functional, working part of the whole.

Figure 1-1   *The basic form of a hierarchy with a tree for a university partly filled in*

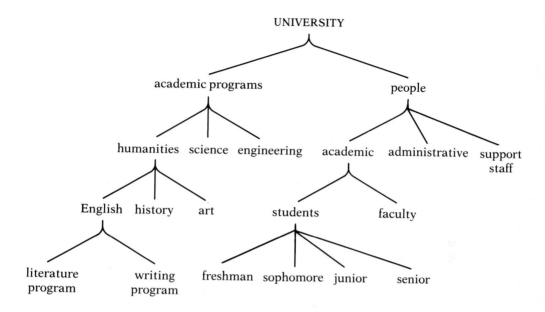

Some hierarchies are logical or highly conventional ones, such as the division of students into freshmen, sophomores, juniors, and seniors. However, the more interesting hierarchies are the ones people create themselves. Ask the next three people you see how they would categorize the different people at your college and you will see them creating their own hierarchical organizations of experience.

What happens when we apply this notion of hierarchical structures to writing? First, we notice that some kinds of writing have a very flat hierarchy, or none at all. For example, a narrative can use a simple chronological structure. "First this happened, then this happened, and then finally. . . ." Or imagine the pothole magazine article if it had been written as a rather rambling, stream-of-consciousness description of things the writer had observed. The paper would be organized like a grocery list, with each paragraph describing a new problem. This would produce a very flat tree and an unfocused paper (see Figure 1-2).

A list can give a lot of information, but it doesn't always reveal the logical relationship between ideas, such as the fact that bad drainage can *cause* water heaving. In order to turn this type of list into a tree and a well-organized report, the writer has to group the facts and create a set of organizing ideas with an underlying

Figure 1-2   ***A flat, undeveloped hierarchy***

ROAD PROBLEMS

bad drainage · water heaving · asphalt binder breaks down · no money for patching · cold patches don't hold · poor road mix

hierarchical organization. For example, the feature writer in Example 1 turned her information into a structure like the one shown in Figure 1-3a, whereas the county report writer (Example 2) set up the structure in Figure 1-3b. Each saw the problem differently, but each used a hierarchical organization to express ideas. And

Figure 1-3   ***Two different hierarchical organizations of information on the pothole problem***

(a) The feature writer's tree

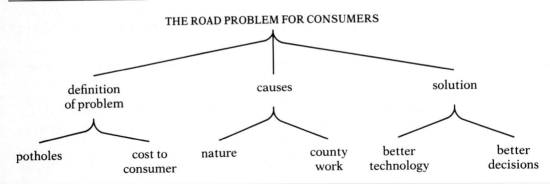

THE ROAD PROBLEM FOR CONSUMERS — definition of problem (potholes, cost to consumer), causes (nature, county work), solution (better technology, better decisions)

(b) The transportation department writer's tree

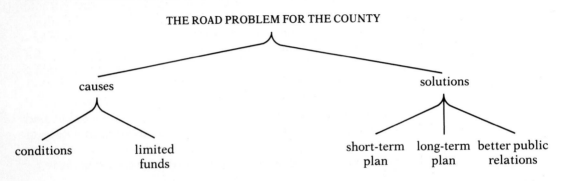

THE ROAD PROBLEM FOR THE COUNTY — causes (conditions, limited funds), solutions (short-term plan, long-term plan, better public relations)

each grouped his or her facts into logical categories such as problems/causes/solutions.

To sum up, then, although different kinds of analytical writing have different formal features, they share two things. They are designed with a reader in mind and they have an underlying hierarchical organization that gives the reader (1) a top-level organizing idea and (2) a logical presentation of the idea's subparts. A good piece of expository writing lets the reader see the tree (the underlying hierarchy of ideas) that lies behind the words.

A College Writing Problem

Now compare the professional writing problem we have just seen to a typical college assignment that asks the writer to understand and analyze some complex situation such as "Discuss the rise of the middle class" or "Analyze the probable effects of thermal pollution on a fresh-water pond." You will see that many of the writer's problems and goals are the same.

Sometimes college assignments are very explicit about the underlying goals of the task: they help the writer see a purpose behind the assignment and identify a real audience that needs to know. For example, it is easy to see the real-world goals within this assignment:

> Many students come to college thinking that textbooks all say the same thing and that all textbook writers agree on what should be taught and how to teach it. Do you think this is so? Find three different introductory textbooks on the same subject, whether it is psychology, statistics, composition, or history. Read the prefaces to learn more about the writers' assumptions and then compare the books. Look especially at what they include, what they consider important, and what they say on a few key topics. Then write an analysis of these textbooks and how they differ, with the goal of helping an entering freshman.

Sometimes, however, college assignments are not very explicit and it is harder to see their purpose, as in this one: "Analyze the impact of Darwin's theory of evolution on his time. Three pages." That means that you as a student must mentally rewrite the assignment as a real-world writing problem, filling in the unwritten assumptions the instructor makes but doesn't state. Here is how a student might think out the problem:

> *Everyone knows that Darwin's theory of evolution is important. But from the wording of this assignment—"impact on his time"—I'd better focus on the specific effects Darwin had on his contemporaries. This professor, in her role as an instructor, will naturally expect me to use*

the method of historical analysis she's been teaching in this class in answering the question. So I'll need to define Darwin's key ideas, then sift through the relevant information in the assigned books and articles.

The professor will also expect me to show I can do some other important things a historian does: make connections between my major points and generate some conclusions and ideas of my own. She'll expect me not only to offer my own interpretation of the facts but to convince her that it is a well-supported and reasonable way to view this historical event.

The following portion of a paper is a response to the assignment of comparing textbooks that was discussed above. In it, the student has combined a traditional analysis of three different texts

Analyzing Your Own Textbook

Are you in the introductory statistics course and in trouble? For many students those phrases mean the same thing. Do you sometimes feel the problem is that you just can't understand <u>statistics</u>? It may be that you just can't understand your statistics <u>textbook.</u> This paper is an analysis of three different first-year statistics textbooks, and as it will show, each book makes radically different assumptions about what you already know and why you want to learn statistics. So if you have trouble understanding the principles behind a chapter, you may find another textbook (and there are a number in the library) that will make the principles clear.

The most important difference among the textbook writers I studied is what they assume about their audience. My first text, by Dowland, assumes you not only know calculus but can understand it well enough to help make statistics clear. Dowland says he is writing for students in math and science, but do many science majors have the background he expects? In contrast, the textbook by Weinberg is called <u>Statistics: An Intuitive Approach</u> because the authors present each new chapter in terms of the basic, intuitive principle of the average or the balance point between two groups of data.

with a real-world purpose of communicating her discoveries and responses to students who will use the text. We will look at the first paragraph, in which the writer defines the problem, and the second paragraph, which sets out her first point of comparison.

Figure 1-4   *Tree of beginning two paragraphs*

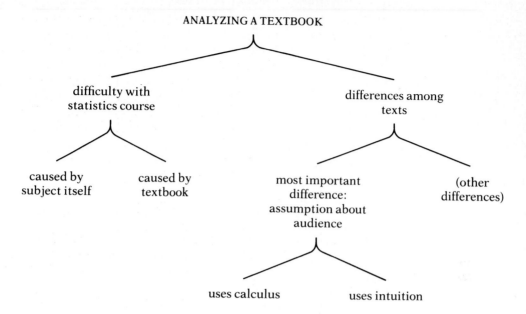

ANALYZING A TEXTBOOK

difficulty with statistics course

differences among texts

caused by subject itself

caused by textbook

most important difference: assumption about audience

(other differences)

uses calculus

uses intuition

As you can see from even this short excerpt, the writer has organized her paper around the question or problem raised in the assignment. Instead of merely describing the books, she has tried to use her analysis to answer the reader's question. Furthermore, she has given us a hierarchical structure in which her major, top-level ideas are clearly stated (see Figure 1-4).

A Personal Reason to Write

Probably the greatest personal reason for writing is to understand something for yourself, with no thought at all for a reader. Sometimes personal writing in the form of journals and diaries is a record or a private place for things you want to express yet keep to yourself. But for many people, personal writing is even more important as a way to think something through or to get down a new realization and make it more concrete. Although I don't keep a journal now, over the years I have left a trail of paper connected to the important ideas and decisions in my life. At those times I simply sat down and began to write, with no concern for sentences, paragraphs, or form—sometimes writing no more than personally loaded phrases and fragments. This writing was private—I didn't have to be right or even agree with myself. I was just trying to express what was on my mind in order to understand it. And time after time I have been surprised to see how this personal writing led me to say things I hadn't let myself say out loud before, but really felt. Or I was surprised to realize that I was telling myself things—right there on paper—that I really didn't feel or believe. Writing let me see and understand my own thoughts and feelings.

In addition to this private, expressive writing, many people use personal writing to record, explore, and analyze ideas and attitudes that they *do* want to express to someone else. They use writing to capture, mull over, try out, and understand a growing idea. Such writing may start with a journal entry or a letter, as in the example that follows. Some people, like me, are not systematic enough to keep a journal. But we carry around 3×5 cards or scraps of paper and a pencil wherever we go. You will see people who work this way going off into a corner at unlikely times because they want to write something to themselves. When an idea is on your mind, it pays to listen to your thoughts and write them down. The common thread in all such personal writing, whether it is in letters, journals, notes, or diaries, is simply the attempt to be articulate—to understand something better by capturing it in words.

Here are two examples of personal writing taken from a letter and a journal. The writer, Molly, is thinking through a problem she later writes about in a more formal essay, the beginning of which is printed here. In the journal entry, the letter, and the essay we can see Molly's series of attempts to understand something by writing about it. In part she is dealing with an important question in her field, the difference between a realistic style in art (which involves detailed rendering) and a more abstract or "gestural" style. In part, she appears to be dealing with a very personal issue as well. Do you see meaningful differences in the way she writes and thinks about this problem at different times?

Letter
October 10, 1983

Hi, Kevin, how are you? How is it going? Things with me are okay, except for drawing class. You know I'm not going to stop drawing representationally just because Laird doesn't like it. He picks at me—''a slave to detail'' he said last week. He thinks my style lacks imagination! I know you know this problem. You've had to deal with it, too. It's a constant battle correcting what is not right to your teachers' points of view so

chapter one / Writing to Make Things Happen

that it's correct to them, without losing your sense of
expressing yourself. I want to be noted for realism, in
the artistic sense and in an emotional sense. Without
doing the full rendering, realism is difficult or impossible for me to depict. If I would leave out the detail, I would leave out myself.

    Oh, well. I saw Joyce last week . . .

Journal Entry
October 15, 1983

    I'm going to write about drawing class because I
seem to be caught in a double bind there. If I do what
Laird wants, I'll have to stop doing what I want, and
what I want is important to me. I want to draw realis-
tically, showing all the details, the lights, the shadows. I think this is honest drawing—it feels honest to
me. I want to be straightforward and honest. I _am_ that
way, and I want to draw that way. But here I'm being
told that my work is unimaginative. What is imagination
for, if it isn't to understand things? How can I understand things if I don't look at them carefully and try
to represent what they _are_? When I came here, I thought
it would be neat to work with a famous guy like Laird.
Now I think he wants all his students to be just like
him—a lot of little clones.

Writing about a problem can change how you see it. It changes
your definition of the problem because it expands your sense of
what is at stake. Molly's letter describes her problem as a battle,
a struggle she and her friend share. But in her journal, she begins
to define the problem as a "double bind," a conflict that is in her
own mind as well as in the classroom. In the text below she approaches this problem a third time, as an essay writer. Once again
her audience and genre have changed. Will you be able to see a
change in her writing? Before you read on, make a prediction about
her purpose (what will she try to do in the essay?) and about her
definition of the problem (will she define it as a struggle, a double
bind, or in some more developed way?). Ask yourself what you as
an "essay reader" expect here.

The hardest decision I have to face right now involves being a student and an artist at the same time. I think of myself as extremely straightforward and honest, and I think that reflects the style of my art. It's hard for me to express myself when I draw gesturally (which is a problem in this school because many teachers feel that there is no imagination in realism). I feel that art is an act of expression, and it's very frustrating for me when I can't draw to reflect my personal qualities.

I want to represent myself accurately——as a person and as an artist. Objective accuracy is a way of portraying reality. I think the subject matter of the realists in the twentieth century is very objective. It's almost as if they don't want to offend anyone, so they paint everyday life. I can see where this may seem unimaginative for people that aren't looking deep enough. However, I feel it to be quite justified because I try to be an objective person. I try not to be judgmental. When I use the shading of light and dark to create tone and when I create lights and shadows, I am expressing myself to others. I feel that it is very deep and intense. Looking beyond the surface is something I believe in and represent. I want others to know that.

WRITERS, READERS, AND "GOOD WRITING"

Looking at the different sorts of writing reprinted in this chapter seems to leave us with a paradox. On the one hand, the problem-solving process that produces such texts is common to many kinds of writing: these writers had to *make meaning* out of a situation as they saw it; they had to find the best way to *communicate* that meaning to someone else; and they tried to *persuade* someone else to see or act in a particular way. We can see other general principles at work, too, such as the way these writers adjusted to an audience and created a hierarchical structure dictated by their individual reasons to write. But can general principles and problem-solving processes exist (ones which you can apply to many kinds of writing) when the texts themselves are so different? Why do some students feel that learning how to write a "good paper" for one course doesn't even transfer to writing for another college course? Are there any general principles of "good writing"? Consider the case of Harry.

Shortly after reading the pothole article, Harry and his new Italian 10-speed bike were forced off the road by traffic into a 6-inch pothole in concrete. The result was a pretzeled front wheel, crutches, and the end of spring training for tennis, a sport on which his hopes and a scholarship had been based. May Britton hadn't calculated some of the human costs.

On the other hand, it certainly gave him something to write about. Clever Harry decided he could write about the experience for both English class and *City* magazine. And then, with the permission of his instructor, he could use a part of that analysis to introduce his economics project, which was to apply economic theory to a real problem. He did some homework on the subject and wrote a paper which began:

```
    On March 3 I was riding down Shady Avenue on a new
10-speed bike.  The bike was a month's summer earnings
and my alternative to bus fares.  A commuter in a Dodge
who thought he was in the Grand Prix suddenly forced me
to the edge of the bike lane, and into the shoulder and
a 6-inch pothole.  It was too late to brake and the only
other choice was the curb.  The next thing I knew, my
new investment was undergoing rapid depreciation and I
was flying over the handlebars.  [The paragraph contin-
ues to review the facts, his knee injury, and so on.]
    May Britton states that a pothole costs $350.  But
there are other ways of seeing costs. The City planned
to repave the road, so fixing holes definitely didn't
seem cost effective to them.  But whose costs should you
consider?  The University, for instance, paid $4000 for
an athlete that can't play.  This is a year when our
team had a chance for the division title.  According to
the Coach, the title could make a difference in fund
raising.  Next year six seniors will be gone, so this
year is important for the title and for training a new
team that will be almost all sophomores.
    At the moment, this pothole has also cost Blue Cross
$2,500.  The premiums students pay are based on the num-
ber of claims.  [Harry's review of various financial and
personal costs continues.]
```

Do you predict that Harry's plan to write one text for three purposes worked or not? His composition instructor returned the draft with two comments on the first page:

I am not sure I can see the major purpose of your paper yet. Did you want to focus on this personal experience and its effect on you? Or were you out to challenge Britton's article? Or do you want to analyze the conflict between different ways of seeing "costs" (such as financial versus personal, the city's versus an individual's)?

As a reader, I expected to see your problem or topic defined very early in the paper, so that each paragraph could help carry out what was promised to me. Revise the beginning to preview your real purpose, and then we'll work on organization.

Harry's economics professor, however, responded to the first page of this draft differently:

What is the economic problem you are addressing? What economic model do you propose to apply? If you want to treat this as an example of "opportunity costs," make your analysis of implicit and explicit costs precise enough to avoid double counting. Recognize where the theory applies to this problem (and where it doesn't).

Use appropriate sources—don't cite a popular magazine. You need to establish a background for this analysis based on the readings we have done in the course—cut out the long description.

City magazine sent him its standard, preprinted rejection notice: "We are sorry that we are unable to use the manuscript you submitted." However, the editor had scribbled a note on the card which said:

This sounds like a paper for some class. But if you livened your story up with more vivid details, listed your costs, dropped the rest, and kept it to 150 words we might be able to print it in the *Letters* column.

Discourse Communities

What happened to Harry? Did he write a "bad" paper, despite all of his homework, or did he forget what his different readers were looking for? Harry's economics professor, for example, is not just a "common" reader. She belongs to what we can call a *discourse community*, that is, a community made up of people familiar with writing and talking about economics. They operate like a community because they share a set of expectations about what is sensible to say, about what will seem new or surprising or interesting to readers (or listeners), about how to use technical terms, and about how to organize and support an argument. In the discourse community in economics, for instance, one of the conventions for a college paper is to start with a review of the literature (in part, to show your credentials) and a statement about the ecomomic issue you want to discuss. You don't tell long personal narratives and you don't cite popular magazines as your authority. The discourse community in economics values precise analysis in which the figures are from reputable sources and the method of analysis, or the theory of economics one is applying is used in a clear and consistent way. Harry's paper didn't meet those expectations—*he didn't sound like a member of that community.*

Harry's English professor appeared to have a related, but less specific, set of expectations for how to talk within an academic community in general. She was prepared to read a personal reflection, an argument with another writer, or an analysis of an issue. But like the economics professor, she expected to see a purpose or an issue established at the outset. Members of the academic discourse community (in a variety of fields) expect to enter into a dialogue or analysis in which a writer thinks a problem through. Harry's draft didn't let readers enter into that dialogue. Although it offered information, it didn't function in the focused, reflective, and questioning way people expect academic writing to function.

But, you might say, Harry's draft didn't meet the expectations of the *City* editor either, even though Harry *does* belong to the discourse community that reads the magazine—and in fact so do his two professors, who also subscribe. But he didn't write to that community *as though he were a member.* When people pick up a magazine they expect a provocative "lead" that catches their interest, and they expect letters to the editor to state a personal position with some flair and few words.

All of us belong to many different discourse communities, and we must often pick which set of conventions we will use and which set of expectations we will anticipate. If you overheard Harry talking after tennis practice, for instance, you would see that he is a very adept member of the discourse community formed by tennis players. As he talks, he can switch from a technical analysis of someone's approach shots to in-jokes that only tennis players understand. When he describes an opponent's game, everyone listens to his analysis because Harry knows how to single out the key features of a player's strategy—just as people in the discourse community of economics can zero in on the key features of a financial game.

Entering the Conversation

The obvious answer to Harry's problem is for him to recognize that as a writer he is trying to participate in at least three different discourse communities—that of magazine writers (for a general interest magazine), economic analysts (in an introductory course), and academic writers more generally (in a composition class). He needs to write as though he were a member of each community, meeting its expectations and anticipating readers' responses. But Harry is a freshman. He has not done a lot of academic writing; this is his first course in economics; and even a letter to the editor turns out to have a number of special requirements. How do writers enter a new community?

It helps to think of this as much like the process of trying to enter a conversation. Kenneth Burke, a famous modern academic writer, describes discourse itself as an ongoing conversation:

> Imagine that you enter a parlor. You come late. When you arrive, others have long preceded you, and they are engaged in a heated discussion, too heated for them to pause and tell you exactly what it is about. In fact, the discussion had already begun long before any of them got there, so that no one present is qualified to retrace for you all the steps that have gone on before. You listen for a while, until you decide that you have caught the tenor of the argument; then you put in your oar. Someone answers; you answer him; another comes to your defense; another aligns himself against you, to either the embarrassment or gratification of your opponent, depending upon the quality of your ally's assistance. However, the discussion is interminable. The hour grows late; you must depart. And you do depart, with the discussion still vigorously in progress.

> *Source:* Kenneth Burke, *The Philosophy of Literary Form: Studies in Symbolic Action.* 3rd ed. (Berkeley: University of California Press, 1973), 110–11.

Put yourself in the position of the newcomer. What does it take to enter the conversation within a discipline or within a college class (not to dominate it, just join in)? Notice how the strategies which help you learn a new kind of discourse are similar to the ways people enter any new social group.

1. Listen carefully to the conversation already going on. What are the issues, what are the problems people care about, what are the questions they see as important?
2. Respond to those issues. Let people see how the new thing you have to add fits in the picture—even if you disagree with the picture.
3. Look for and use the conventions—the language, the organization, the kinds of evidence—that people in that discourse community expect and value. Try to understand the community in which you are writing and speak to readers in a language you and they can share.

Entering academic conversations within a given field, such as physics, literature, or anthropology, takes time as people become familiar with the topics, the questions, the language, and the discourse conventions of the field. But what about the immediate problem of writing an assigned paper? Does it even make sense to call this a "conversation" if the instructor assigns the task, already knows something about topic, and plans to grade the result? A written exam is clearly not a conversation. What is a college paper?

Let's look for a moment at the situation of writing for a class. Outside of school, writers often work with topics that are assigned by circumstances (for example, a pothole crisis) or by a supervisor, and people are frequently evaluated by their writing. The unusual thing about a college class is readers often play more than one role in this exchange. For instance, a classmate might read your paper as she would any contribution to a thoughtful conversation—looking for things to which she could relate, paying attention to anything that seemed interesting, surprising, or true, and losing interest as soon as a paragraph seemed boring or obvious. But if you asked her to read as an advisor or editor, she would look for and respond to different things.

Instructors play multiple roles, too. At one moment your instructor may respond as a teacher or coach—assigning, showing, testing, helping, and teaching. But at another point, he or she may respond as a regular member of the academic community, someone who expects you to add something interesting to the ongoing discourse. The academic conversation your paper has just entered might be on a general question, such as "career choice," on an educational problem, such as "what makes a good textbook," or on an issue in a given discipline, such as "the impact of Darwin." In a composition class, the topic of writing itself could become the focus of attention, as it is in this book. The peculiar thing about a college paper, then, is that sometimes readers/instructors *do* use writing to test your topic knowledge, and sometimes they *do* focus on writing problems and technique as a way to teach—those are roles they are supposed to assume. But at the same time, instructors and other students can also respond as participants in an academic conversation—people waiting to hear what you will have to say.

Finding Your Own Reason to Write

For many students the hardest problem in entering this conversation is the very first move—finding a topic or finding a problem that seems worth writing about (or listening to). Sometimes situations dictate a topic and purpose as they did for the pothole writers. But in the academic community people write not only to share information, to discuss, and to argue, but to explore new ideas and reflect on experience. The special value this community places on reflection and exploration asks writers to think deeply and ask questions they can't immediately answer. As a result, the first stage in such writing is often called *problem finding*. As the most important step in problem *solving*, it calls for both imagination and critical thinking.

The real problem writers face then is not finding a topic (the world is full of interesting topics), but finding a question or problem worth writing about—finding one's own reason to write. The advice often given to students on how to narrow a topic or build a thesis (see Chapters 5 and 8, for example) is not all that helpful unless writers already have a juicy question and a lot to say. Such advice can even be misleading if it pictures the process as a mechanical procedure, like picking a topic off the shelf. As you know, topics and good ideas often dry up when you are halfway into writing, whereas a problem that is meaningful to you can produce a continuing stream of things to say and a motivation to write.

The process of "finding" a good problem is often a matter of "defining" a problematic situation in a meaningful way, much as Molly did over the sequence of her letter, journal, and essay. Good topics often emerge as you work on them. However, if you look at examples of other students in this process of problem finding, you may notice some important principles that guide their search. (For examples, see pp. 33, 35–37, 53–55, 78–81, 135–138, 222–226, 259–272.)

One is that *they don't wait for inspiration;* they actively search their own experience and memories, they look for problems around them, they talk to people and test out ideas. A second principle is that *they test out topics and problems from a personal point of view.* They subject ideas to an acid test: Is this a meaningful problem for me? Will it be worth the time I spend thinking and writing about it? Yet at the same time *they look at possible topics from a reader's point of view:* Is this issue/problem/topic going to be meaningful or interesting to my reader? Will it let me join the conversation of my class and/or contribute something to a larger public conversation people care about? If your problem can pass both these tests you are ready to start.

At the end of this chapter, you will find a checklist with some more detailed ideas for finding a problem. But notice how this very practical task of choosing a topic pulls together the two main themes of this chapter. A good paper topic is not merely a good subject. It grows out of your response to a problem, an issue, or a question, and it reflects your own reason for writing. At the same time, it is your contribution to an ongoing conversation that

involves a reader. In the rest of this book we will loc̶
gies for doing both these things—carrying out your ow̶
as a writer and responding to the readers around you.

PROJECTS AND ASSIGNMENTS

1 Find an example of two people writing on the same topic, as in movie reviews, book reviews, or essays on a controversial subject. Discuss how two writers, looking at the same information, created different meanings and why.

2 Use writing to explore a personal decision you are making or will have to make. Start simply by writing about it in a journal to yourself, in a letter to a friend, or in a narrative about some incident connected to your decision. Then, looking back at the writing you did for yourself, try to write a one- to two-page description of this decision so another person can understand the decision and share your experience.

3 *Checklist: Finding a Problem to Write About.* Write a paper on a topic or problem of your own choice, using the following checklist to help you with the important process of problem *finding*.

☐a. *What are the problems, issues, questions, and experiences I have been thinking about lately?* Don't wait for inspiration; begin with an active search of your own knowledge and experience. Some writers start with what is called a *felt difficult;* they look for ideas that trouble them, or for conflicts in their own mind or in their everyday experience. They look for the issues or controversies that keep coming up in course-related reading or in lectures and class discussions. Some writers keep a journal of interesting observations, experiences they have puzzled over, or mini-inspirations that might be interesting to develop. A good way to begin a search is to spend 10 minutes jotting down a list of "topics I have been thinking about lately" or "topics on which I am a (relative) expert." The underlying principle is to listen to what is going on in your own mind and to actively review your own knowledge. Then ask these potential problems to pass a test or two.

☐b. *Is this problem worth analyzing—for me as the writer? Will writing this paper let me explore a question or conflict I see or think through an experience or issue I want to understand?* When writers ignore the goal of writing for themselves, they often start with enormous issues such as nuclear disarmament—problems on which they have limited inside information and an uncertain reason to write. They have a topic, but not a problem. Or they choose narrow practical problems they have already solved, such as, how can I budget my money over the next month? Practical problems can present an interesting puzzle, but who needs to resort to pondering, deep thinking, and/or writing to understand and solve them? Look for a problem that makes the time you put into writing personally worthwhile.

☐c. *Do I have more than just one "good idea?"* Unless you plan to do research, don't be seduced by a single "good idea." Do you have enough information or experience to explore the problem—as you have defined it? If not, could you define the issue to fit what you really do know about?

☐d. *Is my contribution to the conversation going to be meaningful to a real reader?* Remember, a "meaningful" contribution can be based on many things—on your personal experience, on having thought about a problem, or on having done some research. When writers ignore this test, they often write a clever, witty, "well-formed" essay, one that has a story line, or a gimmick, or which dutifully cranks out an introduction, three paragraphs, and a conclusion—but which simply fails to say anything interesting or significant that someone else might want to hear. This strategy also leads to papers on "significant topics" (more nuclear disarmament)—but in two pages what can you say on such topics that anyone would really want to read?

When writers forget the second half of this test (having a real reader in mind) they often sound as if they were writing to some imaginary reader/teacher who had a strange and perverse desire to read pompous, decorative essays built on grand generalizations and a staggering vocabulary. Forgetting that there is a real reader out there—a normally impatient and sensible person—can lead writers to produce a "well-crafted" but empty essay that no real reader would ever finish. The simple question, "Would I choose to read this to the end?" is a good test. If you wouldn't finish it, what are you assuming about the person who would?

④ You are a Rhetoric Detective. You have been assigned to figure out from the available evidence if the letter to Kevin and the essay written by Molly on pp. [16–18] are addressed to two different discourse communities. Did Molly's writing change when her reader changed from Kevin to her instructor and class? If so, how would you describe these two discourse communities—do the readers of letters and personal essays expect different things? Did she adapt enough to her different readers?

In writing your detective report, start with an overview of the case and your definition of the problem that you want to solve. In order to support your conclusion, draw on both your own intuition and the answers you get to the following *Discourse Community Checklist:*

☐a. What was the writer's motive or purpose(s) in each document? (Why write?)

☐b. What could the reader have expected to get by reading on? (Why read?)

□c. What discourse conventions did the writer use? (Why write it this way?) Does the text have any distinctive features that might reveal the conventions used in a given discourse community? These conventions can appear as global features, such as the sort of topic or organizing idea that appear to be suitable, or the kind of evidence and argument the writer uses, or the format and organization, or the voice and personal stance the writer takes, down to more local features of vocabulary, sentence style, and even punctuation.

□d. What was the context for each piece? (When, where, and why was it written; where was it sent, submitted, or published?)

5 Here is a more complicated Rhetoric Detective case. Take a controversial issue or problem (such as IQ testing, the effects of marijuana, or government loans to students) written up in a weekly news magazine. Then use the *New York Times Index* to locate a related news story in the *Times*. Finally, you can use the *Readers' Guide to Periodical Literature* or the *Social Sciences Index* to dig up your third piece of evidence—a more in-depth journal article on the same problem.

   Were these three articles written to different discourse communities or not? What can you figure out about the expectations and conventions of the community(ies) you investigated? (Use the *Discourse Community Checklist* in Project 4 above to help you build your case and be sure to give a full citation of your sources—and any other informants—in the report.)

6 The Rhetoric Detective turns to self-analysis. Find three examples of your own writing. (You may substitute a tape recording of oral discourse picked up by a hidden microphone for one of your texts.) Interview yourself and use the *Discourse Community Checklist* (in Project 4) to answer this question: Do you operate in different discourse communities; that is, does your writing or speaking change in meaningful ways when you enter different "conversations"?

7 *A Journal Entry.* As you work on your current assignment, take a close look at your process by jotting down notes as you are working and then developing your observations more fully in a journal. Pay special attention to how you carry out the separate activities of planning and getting ideas, drafting a text, and revising. Ask yourself, what was the most interesting feature of my own process?

IF YOU WOULD LIKE TO READ MORE

If you would like to know more about real-world writing—writing designed to meet the needs of the reader—see:

Boetinger, H. M. *Moving Mountains or the Art and Craft of Letting Others See Things Your Way.* New York: Macmillan, 1969. / This is a lively strategy book on "selling" your ideas in the practical world of business. See especially Chapter 2 on putting ideas in a persuasive context.

Britton, James, et al. *The Development of Writing Abilities (11–18)*. London: Macmillan, 1975. / If you would like to know more about how the real-world demands of the reader function in student writing, this is an excellent and imaginative study of writing in British schools.

Harmon, Margaret, ed. *Working with Words: Careers for Writers*. New York: Barnes and Noble Books, 1977. / If you like to write, this book describes a variety of careers that could use your skill, from financial writing and technical editing to writing scripts for television.

chapter two

Understanding
Your Own Writing Process

FOR SOME REASON, MANY COMMON expressions about writing make it sound like a pretty clean-cut, no-nonsense business. All you really have to do, they suggest, is "find a topic, decide what you want to say," and then, depending on which cliché you prefer, you "write it up, write it down, express yourself, say what you mean, put it in words, and/or polish your prose." Yet all of these common descriptions, which make writing seem fairly straightforward, fail to account for the sudden bursts of insight writing can bring, just as they fail to explain why sometimes the words don't come— even on a topic you know. Or why you may have to sit and mull over a paragraph for half an hour at a time.

Some people, when they find that words don't "flow," assume that they have a unique and personal problem: "they don't have a flair for writing, can't spell, don't have a big enough vocabulary, forget grammar." The problem, however, is really with their theory about the writing process. They are expecting the wrong things. The straightforward "put your thoughts into words" theory may capture what writing felt like on Monday, but it fails to mention that on Tuesday it can be a slow, perplexing journey as you try to follow out your ideas. Then on Wednesday it can be like getting to the top of a mountain and finally seeing the whole issue with a new understanding. Composing is like any kind of satisfying mental work: Some days it is hard, some days it is exhilarating, and some days it is simply fun. This means it is neither a dark mystery nor a task that should be simple. Writing is, itself, a thinking process. Choosing how you conduct this process is up to you.

Naturally, some of the writing people do is as simple as jotting down a note or writing in a diary. You don't need a book on writing to help you do that. The writing process I want to talk about is the process behind the significant and potentially difficult writing we all do when we are trying to explain, understand, or argue and we want the reader to see things the way we do.

There are two things to understand about this composing process. One is that it often takes time and energy, because writing is a way of thinking things through. People sometimes hate to admit it, but even experts on a subject find that putting their knowledge into words and sentences forces them to be more explicit. And once their ideas are down in black and white, even experts find that their ideas haven't always passed the acid test of prose—they need to think a little more in order to get it right. So when the words that come out on the page aren't what you intended, don't assume that the problem is with your "writing." Your writing is only showing that you are still working, still thinking things through.

The second thing to understand about your own composing process is that, like any other process, from being a tutor to doing long-distance running, you can learn to observe your own process, to recognize your strategies, to monitor how the process is going, and to change it when you need to. In the next two sections we will look at two aspects of composing: the process of thinking things through and the strategies you use to do it.

THINKING THINGS THROUGH IN WRITING

Thinking takes many forms such as daydreaming, exploring memory, asking questions, memorizing, and problem solving. People turn to problem solving when they have a problem or a goal and they want to figure out how to solve their problem or get to their goal. Problem solving, then, is a form of goal-directed thinking. It is also one of the major thinking processes that helps us get through the day, solving problems such as deciding what to accomplish today, how to get the cat in, whether to get married, and what's the point of this chapter on economic patterns?

A problem is a situation that occurs when you are at Point A and you want to be at Point B and you are not sure how to get there. To solve a problem you must figure out how to get from where you are to where you want to be—how to reach your goals. In Chapter 8 we will look in more detail at how to write a formal problem analysis that puts this process into writing. But for now there are two major things to realize about problems:

1. Problems are only problems for somebody. That is, a problem exists only when you feel a conflict between where you are

and where you want to be; that is, between your present state and your goals, or between your own goals. For example, choosing a college is a problem for you only if you feel you should decide on a sensible professional program but you really don't know which profession you would be good at and you feel much more at home at the low-key, but expensive, liberal arts college you visited. The conflicts among your own expectations, your limited knowledge about choices, your even more limited bank roll, and your goal of making an early decision are what make this a problem for you. The problem your parents, spouse, or banker perceive may be quite different. So remember, people define problems.

2. If you can define the problem, you may have solved it. The hardest part of solving many problems is trying to discover what the problem really is and define the conflict that makes it a problem. Writing is a powerful way to think problems through, because it helps you describe and name the conflicting parts of your own thinking. Consider, for example, the problem of trying to understand the point of your economics chapter. Like the college decision problem, your goal is to make sense out of a complicated body of information—in this case twenty pages of facts and figures. Your problem may be a practical difficulty—the chapter assumes a knowledgeable reader, but you don't know some of the major technical terms. Or it may simply be the common problem every reader faces: you must turn those twenty pages of text into a private mental summary of the key ideas and their connections. Or you may pinpoint a problem in your own understanding: You discover, for instance, that you know that two key points are indeed related—the rate of inflation "affects" interest rates—but you realize you don't know how.

Obviously, a clear sense of the particular problem this economics chapter creates for you would make you a better reader by focusing your attention on key issues. Writing is an extension of this defining and focusing process. If you were to write a paper on choosing a college or on economic patterns, the act of writing would, itself, be the act of taking a complex problem and thinking it through. Your writing would be an attempt to find the key issues and make sense out of what you know. In addition, it might clarify your thinking and help you solve the original problem.

WRITING AS A STRATEGIC PROCESS

If writing is a thinking process, what actually happens when you write? Sometimes this question is hard to answer. The writing process, like any other thinking process, has a way of going underground. We can struggle, ponder, write and rewrite for two hours running, then emerge with one page of text in hand and have almost no recollection of what we did all that time. And yet, during those two hours we were not passively waiting for words to come. Instead, we were actively carrying out a whole repertory of thinking processes such as planning, setting goals, generating new ideas, drawing inferences from old ideas, looking for relationships or patterns, creating trial text, evaluating our prose, detecting errors, and diagnosing problems and planning ways around them.

As transcripts of writers thinking aloud show us, much of this process is quite conscious at the time. Writers are constantly giving themselves instructions for how to write and what to do and then monitoring how well their current effort is going. Yet if writing is such a strategic process, why do people often remember so little of it? One reason is that, like all problem solvers, they are absorbed in reaching their goal—in this case in generating things to say. Once that goal is reached, people remember the result but not the process that got them there. Consider, for example, all the decisions you make when you are choosing what to order at a restaurant: how much will it cost, when did I last have squid, will it really be fresh in Omaha in December, and how will Aunt Cory react if I do? Yet this complex process of comparing, inferring, evaluating, and appetite testing quickly drops out of memory once the job is done. We could have expressed what we were doing at the time if anyone had cared to ask, but once the task is done, the efficient thing is to remember our order but wipe the details about our decision process off the slate of our working memory.

A second reason people are vague about their own writing process is that they notice the obvious outward events, such as starting to write at midnight, drinking a whole pot of coffee, and pacing the room, but they don't pay much attention to their own inner, mental actions. A writer who spends 15 mintues in a fruitless search for the "right" words is so preoccupied with her goal that she may be giving only a tiny portion of her attention to observing her own strategies and to noting how well they are (or aren't) working. However, being aware of your own composing process and the strategies you use can give you the enormous power of conscious choice—the power to guide, test, and alter your own problem-solving process.

The following transcript shows a writer thinking aloud as she works. Thoughts that are attempts to produce trial sentences are underlined. The rest of her thoughts are devoted to either planning or revising. In parentheses, I have noted some of her basic strategies as they occur. This junior in college is applying for a scholarship that would allow her to spend a month during the summer doing creative writing. Her general plan at this point (after about 10 minutes of work) is to convince the judges that "the way to learn is by doing."

TRANSCRIPT OF A WRITER THINKING ALOUD

. . . Um . . . and so maybe as a writer I don't need . . . to go to classes and have to hack out stuff that won't help me in my development as a writer. (Generating ideas) What I do need . . . I'm just thinking that that's the angle that's coming out (Monitoring and evaluating ideas), that um . . . it's the same old story about I am an artist so help me, feed me, pay me money so I can create and work. (laughs) (Drawing an inference and evaluating) I think. Umm . . . What I do need to say (Sets a goal) . . . I need to be allowed to develop on my own. (Writes text) and to go . . . For some reason, right when I started to write "develop on my own" I thought of Star Trek. The Star Trek Convention just popped into my head (Making associations) and um . . . that reminds me that one of the things I am interested in is . . . finding out exactly why stuff like that pops into your head. (Generating ideas) I'm thinking this is a good idea and I should get it down. (Monitoring process and setting a process goal) What are the cues that stimulate a person to remember something? (Generating ideas) How can I put this for those ladies in the pink hats? (Trying to set a goal) Ladies' Club women, want to give a scholarship . . . (Analyzing audience) O.K., the point is I want to learn as a writer how to go looking for those cues in the right place. (Writing trial text) How does that fit in? (Evaluating and trying to organize ideas) Let's see. Well, that's a kind of creativity and you sure have to learn that one on your own. (Drawing an inference; generating ideas) Maybe I should emphasize that instead. (Diagnosing and setting a goal) Like all writers I need to learn to find those cues on my own. (Revising text) O.K., now where am I . . .

As you can see, this writer is not merely turning out sentences; she is rapidly generating ideas, making associations, throwing up trial sentences, evaluating, diagnosing, and guiding her own process. Writing is a mental three-ring circus.

Common Problems

In the rest of this chapter we will look at some common problems writers have as they compose, and then at ways you can track and understand more about your own personal writing process. If your composing process runs into difficulty from time to time, you may be in good company. Here are some of the more common process problems people share:

1. I like to build on a draft, but I can never get started.
2. I can get started, but I just keep starting and throwing it away. I can't build on a draft.
3. The first part comes quickly, but then I dry up. I don't know what to do when that happens.
4. I can't write more than a two- or three-page paper. Once I've said it, I'm done.
5. I often think of good things to say but forget them by the time I sit down to write.
6. I often like my papers—they say what I want to say. But the teacher doesn't like them and I don't know why.
7. I feel that I can't judge whether what I have written is any good. I have actually worried myself into writer's block from the uncertainty.
8. In high school (a previous course, my last job) I got very good at doing one kind of writing (such as personal, expressive writing, five-paragraph themes, or even well-packaged hot air). Suddenly I find that what I know how to do doesn't work anymore and I don't really know how to do what is being asked for now (such as analyzing an issue, defending a thesis, or writing to an editor's specs).

A lot of these difficulties point to strategic problems—and to the need for a larger set of alternative strategies for reaching goals. Over the years, people sometimes build up a set of rituals—some magic patterns that "worked" in the past and then grow into rigid rules for how to write. When I was in high school I developed a ritual for writing book reports: I saved the final page of the book to read just before I was about to write. Then I sat down and wrote the whole thing in one flash of inspiration and understanding just before it was due. I guess I was lucky; my ritual made life exciting, and it often worked for high school book reports. But it didn't transfer very well to writing research papers. For one thing, it gave me no time to mull things over or to write a draft and revise. If inspiration didn't strike when I sat down "to write the paper," I was stuck. And even when it did, in its fashion, I was always surprised that the writing took longer than I had planned, and once again my paper was late. My ritual of one-draft inspirations had worked so well before that it took me quite a while to realize that it simply didn't transfer to this new, more demanding task. I needed thinking strategies, not magic rituals.

Of course sometimes rituals can be very effective—especially ones such as setting aside time and creating an atmosphere that says "I am going to concentrate." On the other hand, it often seems to me that some popular composing rituals, such as writing in bed, having the TV or stereo on, or writing on the bus at night, are either plainly counterproductive or are proof of the writer's extraordinary ability to write in spite of his or her own rituals. Rituals are often external props. The strategies we will look at now are internal, optional thinking techniques for getting to a goal.

We will now look at two practical problems: the problem of getting started and the problem of getting stopped, or temporary writer's block. If you have trouble getting started, if you depend heavily on inspiration or the threat of deadlines to motivate you, or if the idea of having to write makes you anxious and you try to avoid it, this discussion should be of some help to you.

GETTING STARTED

Nearly everybody has trouble getting started. Some people procrastinate as far from pen and paper as possible; others sit and stare at a blank page. Getting started is a common problem because it is not simply a question of ability (even good writers have difficulty getting started) or of knowledge about the subject (experts with a lot to say have trouble, too). Getting started is often a strategy problem directly related to how you tackle the task.

Let us look at the thinking process of a writer who is trying to begin a paper. What are some of the strategies and goals this writer seems to have? How well do they work?

TRANSCRIPT OF A WRITER THINKING ALOUD

My name is Jo Banta. I'm trying to write a paper on writer's block. In today's world . . . for today's student, writer's block is a matter **Trial and error** *of great concern . . . of universal concern. In today's high-pressure education, writer's block is a question that plagues many students. . . . In today's high-pressure education. . . . In the high-pressure education of today, writer's block is a problem of great, of universal concern that plagues. . . . In high-pressure education, writer's block is a matter of almost universal concern. . . . In high-pressure education of today, one problem that plagues many students is. . . .* **Perfect-draft** *This is a problem because. . . . Writer's block is a problem because.* **block** *. . . Due to the phenomenon of writer's block. . . . Because of its omnipresence, many writers fail to hand in assignments on time and thereby lose, . . . and they thereby receive, . . . they get lower grades. Because of the omnipresence, because of writer's block . . . oh what the hell do I know about writer's block. I think I'm having it! How can I write about writer's block when I'm in the middle of it!! What* *an awful assignment. Wonder what dinner will be tonight. Boy, that window's dirty.*

O.K., writer's block. . . .

Waiting for inspiration

Writer's block . . . maybe something will come. Just think about it a while. . . . Although many people fail to recognize it . . . Al-though. . . . Although what!? I don't know! Oh well. . . . Although

Words looking for an idea

many people don't know, don't recognize it, one of the most impor-tant determinants of students' grades is . . . is . . . what? O.K. Try again. . . . Not only is writer's block one of the most important, but

Brainstorming

. . . but . . . but. This is crazy. I'm getting nowhere writing sen-tences. . . . Let's see, what do I really know about writer's block? Sometimes I get it when I don't know what I'm talking about. Maybe because I don't have anything to say yet. But sometimes I get it when I do know a lot, when there's a lot of pressure, and I've got to turn a paper out, and I want it to be really good, and sound like I've got things covered. . . . All right, writer's block is a universal . . . universal problem for students when under conditions of pressure

WIRMI

. . . a universal situation in which students placed under pressures of today's university . . . oh, here I go again . . . what I really mean is . . . writer's block is a problem for students who have good ideas but can't express them because of . . . O.K., what are my choices . . . because of the

Notation

$$\left\{ \begin{array}{l} \textit{environment} \\ \textit{educational pressure} \\ \textit{pressure of time and grades} \\ \textit{limits of time and the pressure of grades} \end{array} \right.$$

Satisficing

That's not perfect, but I'll just bracket it as a problem and go on. It's always easier to make those decisions as an editor instead of when you're generating. O.K., now I haven't done much brainstorming yet,

Brainstorming

so let's see if I can map out what I do know and what I'll want to think about. It's time to brainstorm. What is a block?

Notation

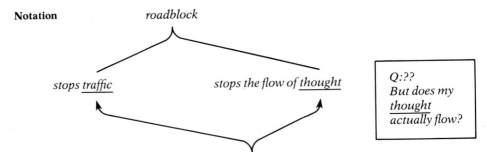

Does writer's block stop something *from coming out?*

That assumes that the "something" is already there.

Is it? That's a distinction I might play with. How about writer's blank?

Weak Strategies

The above transcription of a writer's thoughts demonstrates four composing strategies that often cause trouble for writers:

1. *A trial-and-error approach to producing sentences.* One of the first things we notice in this transcript is the almost random way the writer keeps trying to combine words and phrases in the hope that one version will finally sound acceptable. In working out her first major thought, she is trying out six alternative phrasings:

in today's world	*a matter of*
for today's student	*a question that*
in today's high-pressure education	*a problem of*

These trial-and-error stabs at producing sentences often produce only confusion, because in trying to juggle so many alternatives and keep them all in mind at once, the writer is likely to overload her short-term memory. The capacity of human short-term memory—what we might call our conscious attention span—is rather limited. That is why people often fail at tasks such as trying to listen to two conversations and think of something to say at the same time. Because we can consider only a few separate elements at one time (some say the limit is seven elements, plus or minus two), we are unable to simultaneously consider all the alternative versions of a sentence and make an efficient choice. So we keep reviewing the options. This writer's performance is also characteristic of trial and error in that she often loses track of her search and continues to reproduce previously rejected versions.

A trial-and-error strategy is not only confusing, it's slow. Say our writer had continued to hammer away at this one sentence alone, juggling its mere two sets of alternatives. There are at least 104 possible combinations and grammatical transformations—including passive, negative, declarative, interrogative, and so forth—that she might conceivably have had to try! Clearly, one of the first strategies a writer needs is a way to narrow this enormous field of options—of all the possible things one could say—down to a set of things one would want to say.

2. *A perfect-draft strategy.* Here the writer starts at the beginning and writes a perfected final draft in one slow, laborious pass-through. Looking at the first paragraph as a whole, we see that

instead of planning, jotting notes, or defining her goals, the writer has started out by trying to produce a perfect set of sentences. She is trying to generate her ideas and language in the flowing sequence of a finished text. The form of the final product is dictating the form of her mental process.

As inefficient as this strategy is, many people depend on it—spending hours trying to perfect their first paragraph or first page. Once they have sweated out that first paragraph, the rest of the paper does indeed come more easily. But why? It is because, in the act of writing those introductory sentences, they have also been planning the point and the organization of the entire paper. As if planning one's ideas wasn't hard enough, these writers are also trying to produce perfect sentences, create just the right tone, and make smooth connections between all their points. All of these things must eventually be done, but a perfect-draft strategy tries to do all of them at once. By jumping into producing finished prose before deciding what they want to say, such writers are unlikely to do either task well. They give themselves their own writer's block.

3. *Waiting for inspiration.* Some writers wait until they see the whole piece clearly in their mind or until words and sentences start "flowing" and they know just what they want to say. This is a chancy but well-known strategy that will be discussed in more detail later.

4. *Words looking for an idea.* The writer is still focusing her attention on producing sentences. In the second paragraph the expressions "Although . . . ," "is . . . ," and "Not only . . . , but . . ." sound promising, until the writer discovers she has no ideas to fill in the slots. She has let the momentum of language itself direct composition and lead her down the garden path.

Powerful Strategies

One of the advantages of this simulated transcript is that our writer can suddenly turn very obliging and clever. Once she realizes that the perfect-draft approach isn't working, she switches tactics and demonstrates a set of more powerful strategies that do work. Here are a few:

1. *Brainstorming.* Instead of producing perfect sentences, the writer concentrates on her ideas, jotting down thoughts in whatever order they come to her.

2. *Using WIRMI.* WIRMI is a strategy for getting yourself to make a clear and concise statement of your point whenever you find yourself bogged down in trying to perfect a sentence. Simply

say to yourself, *What I Really Mean Is* . . . and switch from writing prose to "talking to yourself." Just say what you think, then perfect the prose later.

3. *Using notation techniques.* In trying to write a sentence or get an idea clear, it often helps to get it down on paper so you can work with it visually, not just in your head. For example, it helps to write alternative phrasings under one another, or to use more exotic displays of relationships—flow charts, trees, brackets, boxes, arrows, and so forth. If you don't write down fragments and phrases as they come to you, you are likely either to lose them or to find yourself reproducing them over and over. But to take maximum advantage of your notations and visual displays, you must also leave room to rewrite and make changes on your draft. That means skipping lines and leaving generous margins. Your goal here is to ease the load on your limited short-term memory and let yourself write and edit rather than juggle alternatives in your head.

4. *Satisficing.* When you are writing a first draft it is often useful to accept an adequate, but imperfect, expression or idea in order to get on with more important problems. People have coined a rather odd but very useful word for this notion, which is "to satisfice." Problem-solvers satisfice, as it is called, when they take the first acceptable solution or alternative instead of searching for the very best one. People satisfice every day (to the relief of grocers) when they take the first acceptable peach at the fruit stall instead of rummaging through the entire bin for the very best one. And writers satisfice when they decide to write now and revise later. Things that are impossible to solve in the middle of composing often become simple when you are editing. So satisficing on a first draft can let you make the best use of your time.

GETTING STOPPED AND WRITING UNDER PRESSURE

Most of us write under pressure, whether it's the pressure of deadlines, grades, critical readers, or our own expectations. Some amount of pressure is a good source of motivation. But when worry or the desire to perform well is too great, it creates an additional task of coping with anxiety. When it comes to writing, some people are automatically so anxious that they can't get started, or they avoid the prospect at all costs by looking for courses and jobs that don't require writing.

These are the extreme cases. For most of us, getting stopped or having writer's block is a temporary condition. It comes at the end of a train of thought when we suddenly find ourselves unsure of what to do next, or when words refuse to fall into sentences and we are left stranded in midphrase.

The causes of writer's block vary. Although external forces such as a deadline often create pressure, it is internal forces that produce anxiety and writer's block. In other words, writer's block is an obstacle that writers throw in their own path. Two ways they commonly do this are by having an overly critical Internal Editor or by depending on an inefficient composing method.

People who write well or who wish they did are often their own worst enemy. Their success or failure in the past leads them to set extraordinarily high expectations: "This paper (which really means 'I,' the writer) must be brilliant, creative, original, or beyond criticism." High standards are a good idea (many writers could improve their performance substantially if they bothered or dared to reread and revise). But *unrealistic* expectations often produce nothing more than anxiety.

Here then is the problem. A writer who demands good results can demand them at the wrong time. He or she often sets up a highly critical Internal Editor who pounces on every scrap as it's written, rejecting the writer's half-formed thoughts because they are disorganized or don't sound like a polished piece of writing. Unfortunately, few papers, even good ones, emerge from the writer's mind in their full glory and polished form. Instead they come out in bits and pieces, in stray thoughts that later become important, and in tentative, disorganized sentences. When such unrealistic expectations set up a severe internal critic, this watchdog stops the thinking process before it starts, and the writer ends up with a series of false starts and crumpled, rejected drafts.

Why do writers do this to themselves? What leads them to expect their thoughts to flow out in polished, finished prose? The answer often lies in the assumptions they make about their composing process.

ALTERNATIVE COMPOSING METHODS

Let us look at the advantages and limitations of three major approaches to writing: the perfect-draft, inspiration, and problem-solving approaches.

The Perfect-Draft Approach

As noted earlier, this method, which attempts to produce a paper in one pass-through, can be efficient if it works. But if your ideas are not fully formed and you need to concentrate on purpose, content, or organization, it makes little sense to try to juggle the demands of polished prose at the same time.

The Inspiration Method

When we feel inspired, writing seems easy and exciting. The words seem to flow unbidden and the first draft is the final one. Unfortunately, muses are notoriously unreliable, and this makes inspiration a very poor choice as a standard composing method. Yet many people assume that it is the *only* method open to them if they want to produce a really good piece of writing. The perfect-draft approach and steady work can always turn out words on a page, but good writing comes when, and only when, the writer finally gets his or her "inspiration." Or so the myth goes.

One of the best descriptions of the myth of inspiration comes from poet Samuel Taylor Coleridge's account of how he came to compose his famous, mysterious poem *Kubla Khan*. You may think that the creative process of a major poet has little to do with normal expository writing, but, in fact, the exploits of heroes and artists are often the source of popular myths that tell us how the experience *should* be.

In his account Coleridge says that he had been reading a book called *Purchas's Pilgrimage*, a fabulous account of the marvels seen on seventeenth-century voyages of exploration. He had been taking opium, which he tells us was, of course, prescribed by his doctor. When he woke up, he began his poem with these words:

> In Xanadu did Kubla Khan
> A stately pleasure-dome decree:
> Where Alph, the sacred river, ran
> Through caverns measureless to man
> Down to a sunless sea.

Writing about this experience, and referring to himself in the third person, Coleridge says:

> . . . he fell asleep in his chair at the moment that he was reading the following sentence, or words of the same substance, in *Purchas's Pilgrimage:* "Here the Khan Kubla commanded a palace to be built and a stately garden thereunto. And thus ten miles of fertile ground were inclosed with a wall."

> 1. The Author continued for about three hours in a profound sleep, at least of the external senses, during which time he has the most vivid confidence, that he could not have composed less than from

2. two to three hundred lines: if that indeed can be called composition in which all the images rose up before him as things, with a

3. parallel production of the correspondent expressions, without any sensation or consciousness of effort. On awaking he appeared to himself to have a distinct recollection of the whole, and taking his pen, ink, and paper, instantly and eagerly wrote down the lines that are here preserved. At this moment he was unfortunately called out by a person on business from Porlock, and detained by him above an hour, and on his return to his room, found, to his no small surprise and mortification, that though he still retained some

4. vague and dim recollection of the general purport of the vision, yet with the exception of some eight or ten scattered lines and images, all the rest had passed away like the images on the surface of a stream into which a stone has been cast, but, alas! without the after restoration of the latter!

Coleridge's account of his experience contains four major elements of the myth of inspiration. This myth becomes a problem when people see it as a description of how the writing process *should* work. In the myth,

1. The vision comes to the writer in sleep. In other words, there is no conscious effort, no preparation or planning, no thinking.

2. The writer's inspiration or vision comes complete and fully assembled. He does not simply have an intuition or an idea that must then be developed; the state of inspiration reveals a "whole" product, in this case two or three hundred lines that we can assume will not have to be revised.

3. The act of composition itself is not the time-consuming task of testing and modifying alternatives. Instead, the author merely remembers and preserves the content of the dream or vision. This is appropriate because inspiration is often seen as a gift from the gods. Naturally you wouldn't expect such a gift to come only half-written. Moses received the Ten Commandments written on tablets of stone. Athena, the Greek goddess of wisdom, science, and the arts, and an appropriate emblem for creative thought, was said to have sprung fully armed from the head of Zeus. These elements of the myth of inspiration are old and well established.

4. The final element of this myth is the most critical one for us. Because the stuff of inspiration is, in a sense, a gift from the gods that appears without conscious effort, it cannot be duplicated or repeated. Once interrupted by a gentleman from Porlock, the vision will be lost forever. Like that proverbial "bolt from the blue," our ideas come from outside instead of from our own efforts to assemble our knowledge into new insights. These elements of the myth of inspiration suggest that writers are passive recipients of

visions and that the creative process is a mixture of waiting and luck. Fortunately that's just not true. Although the myth describes the way it often *feels* to create something, it isn't particularly accurate about what actually happens. The magic of inspiration is the magic of a mind hard at work. For example, literary sleuth John Livingston Lowes has shown how the images of *Kubla Khan* had their source in Coleridge's wide reading. Coleridge's combination and translation of these images were unique—a creative act—but the raw material of the creative process was the knowledge stored in his own mind.

If the myth of inspiration is neither a particularly accurate nor helpful model for the creative process, is there a better one that can also include the subjective experience of inspiration we've all felt? In *The Art of Thought* (1926), Graham Wallas showed that inspiration, or "illumination," is merely the third stage in a four-stage creative process:

1. *Preparation* is the first stage. "Chance," Pasteur said, "favors the prepared mind." This is a mind that has read, thought, and worked on the problem. Sometimes this stage can last for years.
2. *Incubation* is a second, little understood stage. No one knows quite what happens or why, but in periods of rest when the problem is not being actively considered, new combinations are formed, new ideas generated.
3. *Illumination*, the third stage, is simply the result of the previous two, but it is the stage that gets all the press. This may be a dramatic moment, or alternatively a quiet one, when preparation and thought pay off and you see your solution, an image of what you want to do. Unfortunately, most illuminations don't spring from the mind as fully armed Athenas or as completely written texts. What we usually "see" is only a plan or a sketch of what the solution might be. This leads to the next step.
4. *Verification* is the working out of the solution. For writers, this is often the complex and lengthy process of making language say exactly what they want it to say and making sure it says it to readers as well as to themselves. Any approach to composing, then, should recognize all four of these processes, not just the moment of illumination.

A Problem-Solving Approach to Composing

A problem-solving approach to writing differs from the perfect-draft and inspiration methods in two ways. It stresses a goal-directed kind of thinking, and it often draws on a variety of strategies (also known as *heuristics*) to achieve its end.

It may seem odd to think of writing as a "problem" with a "solution," since we often apply those terms to situations for which a precise solution *procedure* is already known, as it is in algebra. A problem, however, is simply any situation in which you are at point A and need to find some way to get to your goal, point B. Problem solving is the act of getting there, of achieving goals.

What sort of problem-solving approaches do you use when you write? Generally speaking, writers have three alternative ways to proceed. They can use (1) rules, (2) trial and error, or (3) heuristics:

1. *Using rules.* Rules tell you exactly what to do when. If you know the time and the rate, you can compute distance by using the rule T × R = D. In grade school many of us learned rules for writing: State your topic; make three main points about it; develop each point in three separate paragraphs, each of which has a topic sentence; then write a conclusion.

The virtue of rules is that they are explicit; anybody can follow them. Their weakness is that they are simple-minded and are inadequate for more complex problems such as solving our energy crisis, fixing a car that won't start, or writing a report on either of these.

2. *Using trial and error.* People like to use trial and error because it seems like a comfortable way to proceed. You don't have to plan or study the problem; you just start writing and see how it turns out. When the problem is small (for example, writing a note to leave on the refrigerator) or the problem solver is lucky, trial and error is efficient. But as we saw in the transcript on pages 35–36, this haphazard method can waste a lot of time if there are too many alternatives.

If your car wouldn't start and you began a systematic trial-and-error search of its 6,000 parts, you would, on the average, have twiddled 3,000 screws, plugs, and wires before you found the trouble. Proceeding without a plan can be easy, but expensive in terms of time.

3. *Using heuristics.* Heuristics—that is, efficient strategies or discovery procedures—are the heart of problem solving. Some of them are nothing more than small rules of thumb that say "try this first" and cut down the number of alternatives you must consider. They reduce the size of the problem. For example, in a typical chess game there are 10^{120} possible moves to make but only 10^{16} microseconds in a century in which to make them. So experts rely on a heuristic procedure such as "try to control the center with your pawn" instead of considering all the possible alternative moves.

Heuristics—or strategies, as I will be calling them—have another important feature. They are powerful; that is, they have a high probability of succeeding. For example, a good heuristic procedure for diagnosing a dead car is: first check the gas, then the battery, then the ignition. A powerful heuristic writers often use is "just try to jot down things without organizing them yet." The problem-solving strategies we will be looking at in this book are simply a set of heuristics or techniques that good writers rely on. Some of these strategies are as old as Aristotle's methods of forming comparisons. Some, such as brainstorming, come from the study of creative thinking done by scientists, inventors, and problem solvers in industry. And some come from recent studies of the thinking processes of writers themselves. In each of these cases, I have tried to translate a heuristic procedure that experts use into a practical strategy writers can learn.

Although heuristic procedures are powerful, they do not come with a guarantee. For example, many good tennis players rely on the following strategy: Try to make a hard, deep shot in order to get a soft return from your opponent, so you can then run up to the net and put the ball away. Unfortunately, as you are charging the net, your opponent might just hit a passing shot that goes right by you. Unlike a rule, which will always produce a "correct" answer if followed, a heuristic procedure is only a high-probability way to proceed, so a writer needs to know a variety of alternative techniques. However, for a complex problem such as writing, heuristics are the most dependable and most creative way to go.

One of the chief differences between good and poor writers, and good and poor problem solvers in general, is the repertory of strategies, or heuristics, on which they draw. Good writers not only have a large repertory of powerful strategies, but they have sufficient self-awareness of their own process to draw on these alternative techniques as they need them. In other words, they guide their own creative process. Although motivation, talent, or experience can strongly affect that process, it is a process writers *can* understand and change. The purpose of this book is to make the intuitive problem-solving process that good writers use more explicit and available to the rest of us.

Let us close this chapter, then, by applying a basic problem-solving principle to the problem of writing under pressure.

PRACTICAL SUGGESTIONS FOR COPING WITH PRESSURE

When you have trouble with getting started or with getting stopped, the cause may lie in the strategy you have chosen. If you can't eliminate external pressure you can cope with it by changing your own writing method. The key is a basic problem-solving principle: Break the large, complex problem of writing down into a set of smaller subproblems that you can concentrate on one at a time.

First, instead of sitting down to produce a paper in its entirety, give yourself a subgoal or separate task such as brainstorming or writing an individual page or paragraph on a topic you are already clear about. It often helps to separate these tasks in time: Tell yourself, "All I have to do this morning is jot down my ideas and make a rough plan for the paper. I don't have to do any writing unless I want to."

By concentrating on a manageable subtask, and only a subtask, you often do it better, and ironically, when the pressure is off, you may find that the writing is no longer so hard to do. By setting up a limited and achievable subgoal, you can seduce yourself into starting to write.

A second way to reduce pressure and create manageable subgoals is to use a "write and revise" method. Plan your writing so you can write a reasonably efficient first draft and satisfice on those places that would slow you down. If you don't know how to spell a word, don't give it a second thought. Just write it down and keep on going. Should you use a colon or semicolon here? If you aren't sure, figure it out later. Make this first draft as coherent and clear as you can; where you need to stop and think about your meaning, do so. But don't get sidetracked into perfecting your prose. Instead, count on revision to be a major second step in your writing process. Give yourself the freedom to just write a working draft.

There are good reasons for doing this. First of all, the fact that it is only a rough draft reduces the extra, internal pressure that causes anxiety and writer's block. Secondly, a two-step process of writing and revising is a smart way to use your time. Many local problems that seem insurmountable when you are in the midst of composing are problems because you are still deciding where you want to go next. If you keep the larger picture in mind while writing, minor problems will fall into place when you later edit and revise.

As a general rule, if you find your writing process becoming inefficient or unproductive, that is a signal that you need to switch tactics and tackle the problem in a new way. The following chapters on steps and strategies in writing will offer you some concrete, alternative ways to proceed.

PROJECTS AND ASSIGNMENTS

1 *A self-appraisal of your own writing process.* This self-analysis asks you to do three things: first, to look at your own writing process as

objectively as a musician, dancer, or athlete would look at his or her performance. What strategies do you typically rely on and how well do they usually work? Secondly, spend some time collecting data on yourself. What do you really do when trying to write? And finally, how does that compare to your image of what a good writer would do? Jot down your answers on a separate sheet.

A. What are the last four things you have written (excluding short notes), and who read them? We will refer to your writing here as a "paper," but it could have been a college composition, a letter, a memo, an announcement, a proposal, or a report. (In the questions that follow, whenever you find it difficult to decide what is typical for you, refer back to these four events as your norm.)

B. In general, how do you feel about writing?
   rather enjoy it   neutral   dislike it

C. Do you find it easy to write papers that say what you wanted them to say? In practical terms, is writing a relatively efficient process for you in which your time is in proportion to your intentions?

D. How many hours did you spend writing (drafting, writing, revising) the last three papers you did? Give number of hours and number of pages written (excluding appendixes). Is this normal?

E. Do you generally try to write a piece in one sitting from the beginning, or do you work on sections separately and at various times?

F. Do you generally end up having to do the actual writing of papers under pressure—that is, under a tight time constraint?

G. When you think of having to write a paper, what are the main things that come to mind for you?

H. Are any of these problems ones you frequently have?

   1. Getting started:
      Getting the whole paper ordered in your head before you write.
      Getting a beginning paragraph.
      Getting a first sentence.
      Sitting down to write.
      Turning on the flow of creative ideas.

   2. Organizing what you know into a paper:
      Finding a main idea or thesis that fits in all the things you have to say.
      Turning an outline or sketch into a fleshed-out, proper paper with sentences and paragraphs.
      Turning lots of good ideas into an outline.
      Writing a formal paper when you know you could explain it easily if you could just talk to the person.

3. Writing for an audience:

> Knowing what your reader really wants.
>
> Finding that readers miss the important things you thought were clearly stated.
>
> Finding that, upon rereading your writing, you don't understand it in the same way you did when you wrote it.

4. Controlling the circumstances under which you write:

> Trying to concentrate with noise and activity around you (the TV, stereo, friends, family).
>
> Writing when you feel tired or sleepy instead of during the most alert part of your day.
>
> Being inadequately prepared (you haven't had time to think the problem through before you start to compose).
>
> Having no time (or less than a day) to let the paper sit between writing and editing it.

I. Do you have any rituals that help you get in the mood to write? Many people depend on private rituals that help them to get started and maintain their concentration as they write. The rituals can vary from mere sharpened pencils to special rooms, desks, or times of day set aside for writing. Some people set subgoals and give themselves rewards when they achieve them. Do you have any private rituals that help you get in a frame of mind to write? If so, jot them down.

J. Once you have completed questions A–I, read over your responses. Try to define as perceptively as you can three major problems you have in writing. Make your definitions as specific as possible. Now develop a practical plan for dealing with each of your problems the next time it comes up.

2 *Thinking through a problem.* Everyone talks about the problems of the freshman year in college: living in a dorm, adjusting to a new environment, handling academic pressure, learning to budget time. Take one of these problems (or one like it) that you know well and use your writing to think the problem through. What is the real issue—what made/makes this a problem for you? (You may also want to use this paper as an opportunity to study your own writing process.)

3 *Experiment: Tracking your own composing process.* What happens when you compose? What strategies do you use? To run this experiment on your own writing process, start by making some predictions you would like to test, such as

A. How do I allocate my time? How much goes to planning, to producing a draft or final text, to revising, to avoiding writing?

B. Could I accurately express my main ideas or conclusions at the beginning of writing? What do I learn by writing?

C. What kinds of revisions do I make? Do I fix errors, change ideas, improve organization?

D. What strategies do I use most frequently?

Then, use one of the following tracking techniques to answer your questions. Notice that these different methods tap your process at different levels. Choose the one that will tell you what you want to know.

1. *Thinking aloud.*

   Use either a tape recorder or a partner to observe you as you think aloud on a fresh writing problem. (Start taping as soon as you read the assignment if you want to study your planning strategies.) The only rule is to keep talking out loud. Say whatever is going through your mind, even if it is silly or off the subject. Writing is not always a very rational process. This method will give you the most detailed record of your own thinking. Notice that it does not ask you to think and talk about your writing process itself as you write. Devote all of your attention to the task and just talk aloud to yourself as you work.

2. *An introspective report.*

   Observe yourself composing, and stop from time to time to take notes and make comments on your process. Look for surprising turns, difficult moments, or decision points. This method will tend to interfere more with your process, since you will be trying to pay attention to both the task and yourself performing the task. But it can also lead to some surprising on-the-spot insights.

3. *A process log.*

   At various key points in your composing process—when you begin, when you are in trouble, and when you take a break—make notes about your process. Keep a log with columns for dates, times, what you did, and problems or comments. (See Chapter 13 for an example.) Fill it in anytime you work on the paper, even if you were thinking about it while walking home or talking with a friend. This method will give you a good record of how you spend your time and information about some of the key events over the entire course of writing.

4. *A retrospective account.*

   Use a combination of any of these methods as your data, then look back over your composing process and construct a description of how it worked. Use as much factual data as you can, but try to make sense out of what happened and why. Write your account up as a thriller, an intellectual detective story, a sad moral tale, or a romance with a happy ending—whatever fits the data.

IF YOU WOULD LIKE TO READ MORE

If you want to know more about problem solving, creativity, and ways to explore your own writing process, see:

Elbow, Peter. *Writing Without Teachers.* London: Oxford, 1973. / This short and readable book has helped many people get over their worries about writing.

Hayes, John R. *Cognitive Psychology: Thinking and Creating.* Homewood, Ill.: Dorsey Press, 1978. / This highly readable book traces the history of modern psychology and how it has attempted to understand the mysterious processes of creative thinking. The book covers the major approaches, from introspection to computer simulation, and concludes with current research in cognitive psychology.

———. *The Complete Problem Solver.* Philadelphia: Franklin Institute Press, 1981. / This fascinating introduction to the art of problem solving puts theory and research to practical application. It discusses effective strategies for a wide range of intellectual and practical tasks, from planning to remembering information to decision making and creative thinking.

Koestler, Arthur. *The Act of Creation.* New York: Dell, 1967. / This classic combines a theory of creativity with hundreds of historical sketches and examples of both scientific and artistic creativity.

chapter three

Case Study: A Personal Profile

IN THE FOLLOWING CHAPTERS WE will be looking at nine steps in the composing process and at a variety of strategies for taking these steps.

PLANNING

    Step 1: Explore the Rhetorical Problem
    Step 2: Make a Plan

GENERATING IDEAS IN WORDS

    Step 3: Generate New Ideas
    Step 4: Organize Your Ideas

DESIGNING FOR A READER

    Step 5: Know the Needs of Your Reader
    Step 6: Transform Writer-Based Prose into Reader-Based Prose

REVISING FOR EFFECTIVENESS

    Step 7: Review Your Paper and Your Purpose
    Step 8: Test and Edit Your Writing
    Step 9: Edit for Connections and Coherence

Each of these nine steps represents a task that you as a writer will need to do. However, these steps are unusual: Unlike stair steps that march straight from A to B, each of these steps may need to be taken over and over in the process of writing. A simple-minded model of the composing process might pretend that writing was a neat, orderly, straightforward set of steps like those in Figure 3-1.

By contrast, the normal process of a writer is not a linear march forward; it is recursive. That is, writers constantly return to earlier steps such as planning in order to carry out later ones. For example, Figure 3-2 shows a more realistic graph of what a writer was doing over a 10-minute period. In the circled area the writer was editing a passage he had just written when he realized that

Figure 3-1   *A simple-minded model of the composing process*

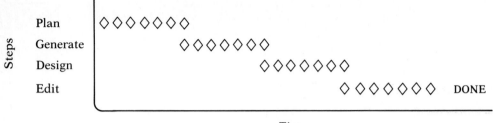

Time

there was a gap in his argument. So he stopped editing, popped back up to the planning step, generated some new ideas, organized them with the reader in mind, and then re-edited the whole passage and moved on, planning what he wanted to do next.

The following chapters, then, will describe nine major steps in the writing process, but the order in which you take the steps will depend on the stage you are in and how your writing develops. Presented along with each step will be a set of different strategies that will help you take those steps, such as strategies to help you plan more effectively, generate better ideas, or edit for certain specific effects. These strategies, based on the effective strategies good writers use, can help you increase your repertory of problem-solving skills for writing.

It is important to remember that these strategies are not rules or sure-fire formulas for writing. Instead they are simply an organized description of some of the things good writers normally do when they write. Many may be effective strategies you already use but didn't have a name for. Just to make this point more vivid, let us look at a case study of a real writer in action who uses many of the strategies we will discuss.

Figure 3-2   *Model of a normal composing process*

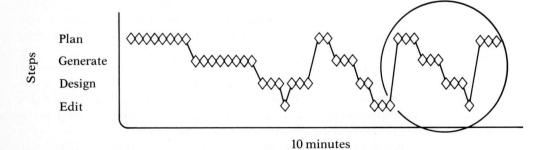

10 minutes

This short case study describes the experience of Joan, a real college student who has a writing problem: developing a personal essay for a scholarship application. The process of writing went on for nearly two weeks, from the time she started thinking about the essay until it was mailed. In this process she used a number of the writing strategies that will be discussed in the next few chapters. However, as you will see, she often used them without knowing that she was doing so, or in response to someone else's questions. This case study will let you see how individual techniques such as brainstorming or making analogies are often an instinctive part of the writing process. The only difference is that as a problem solver one has the power of conscious choice.

Joan is a junior in engineering at a large university. She is doing well in her courses, but her real career goal is medical engineering—she wants to combine research and working with people. A year in London would give her a firsthand experience of what medical research is really like before she has to specialize. But she can't afford to go to London on her own.

On day one her writing process starts with the decision to write her application. She has a strong desire to go to London and a good school record to back her up, but beyond that she doesn't know what to say. As a result, her writing process begins with a four-day wait for inspiration that doesn't come. On day five, with her deadline approaching, she sits down after dinner with the empty form, a pad of paper, and the TV, to write something anyway. By 12:30 A.M. there is nothing left to watch and she spends an hour and a half on the first draft.

In the hard light of the next morning the draft sounds alternately pompous ("I feel my achievements in scholastic and extracurricular activities will demonstrate my ability to take advantage of an educational opportunity of this sort. . . .") or it sounds young and naive ("The idea of spending a year at the University of London fulfills some of my oldest dreams. It is the kind of experience I most want. . . ."). The section on her courses and past activities was easier to write and sounded all right but was mostly a list and, she felt, rather dull. Whenever she thought of faculty members of a British university reading this humdrum essay, she felt depressed. There was no way of guessing what they were looking for.

At this point her writing plan had two main goals: to mention all the achievements she could think of and to make sure there were no errors in the essay. The first important change in her strategy came about on day six quite by chance when she stopped by to ask a professor to write a recommendation for her. Although

Professor Harris wanted to write a good letter, she knew nothing about medical engineering or the school. She read Joan's first draft and began pressing Joan for information. Joan later said, "It was like being grilled; she was asking me all these questions I couldn't answer. And yet I kept thinking: How can I be applying to this place if I can't answer them?" Here is how their conversation went. The notes in italics refer to strategies you will find discussed in later chapters.

HARRIS: A great idea. Wish I could be in London, too. But now tell me, why do you want to go to this particular place rather than some other city? *(Setting goals)*

JOAN: Well, it's a great opportunity. And I've never been to England, and I'd just like to get out on my own. . . . Well, I guess they wouldn't care about that. Well, . . . it's a very good place to study medical research. . . . I don't know, . . . if you ask me point blank. Anyone would want to go.

HARRIS: Well I sympathize, especially with being on your own, but that hardly seems like a compelling reason for them to put up $5000 for you to study in London. So there's no particular reason. . . .

JOAN: Oh, but wait a minute. You don't see, there is. . . . You see, I want to prepare myself for a rather new field. There aren't many medical engineers yet. And it's important for people with an engineering background to understand what the real problems in medicine are—to really be up to date in medical research and know where technology can help. What's more, this will help me figure out where to specialize after I graduate. Unlike American schools, British schools use a tutorial system that could be tailored to my special interests. And this is the perfect time in my career to do it. You see, I've taken all these courses in preparation. . . . *(Brainstorming)*

Maybe I should put some of this in the essay. I didn't know about the scholarship until a week ago, but I've been preparing myself in a sense for something like this for three years. People think my course schedule is crazy—physiology next to fluid mechanics. But you have to know those things to design an artificial heart.

O.K. now. I guess I do have some sort of answer. I want to go because it would be the best place—I could explain why—to prepare myself for a career in medical technology. This is also the time when I most need to make the bridge to medical research, before I decide where to specialize. *(Stating in a nutshell)*

HARRIS: Sounds good. But if you don't mind my asking, why would they want *you* specifically? *(Simulating a reader's response)* What I want to do in my letter is support, wherever I can, the arguments you are making in your application.

JOAN: This is awful. There will be hundreds of people applying—and lots of people have good grades. I'm not even in medicine. I don't know why anyone would want to give money away anyway, especially to me.

HARRIS: Well, how about looking at it as an investment rather than a gift? What kind of an investment would you be likely to make? *(Thinking by analogy)*

JOAN: Well, if you put it that way, I guess I might really pay off. For one thing, I'm really committed to this. I can show it, too, with my courses and my summer job in the Chicago lab, and I've just finished a first-aid course. I really do care about people; I'm good at engineering, and I've been preparing for this special career for a long time. I guess it also matters that I work hard, not just in classes but on independent projects, too. That would matter a lot for this particular year. *(Brainstorming)*

HARRIS: I'm getting convinced. Maybe if you could just say some of *this* in the application? Somehow all this is more persuasive than your first-draft generalizations, which I'm afraid made me feel, "Ho hum, I've heard this before."

JOAN: Yes, except. . . . Well, I just realized that the real problem here is to convince them that they want to give this scholarship to somebody in engineering instead of medicine. I've got to show them that it's good for undergraduates like me to spend a year in a medical research school. *(Setting goals and subgoals for writing)* That's the real thing. Maybe if your letter could somehow show that I really can bridge that gap between technology and human concerns. Maybe you could mention the project I did. *(Creating a more operational definition of a goal)*

If it's O.K., I'd like to do another draft of this and bring it in on Wednesday. *(Setting a subgoal)* That'll still give me a few more days to sit on it before the deadline. *(Incubation)*

When Joan set out to write the final version, her plan and priorities had changed significantly. First, she had a better idea of what she wanted the essay to accomplish for her. And in this draft, that's all she chose to worry about; polishing could come later. In other words, she broke the large problem of "write this essay" down into a set of more manageable tasks. *(Setting subgoals)* Since her father had asked a friend in the medical school to look over her draft, she tried writing it with him in mind, trying to anticipate his questions, such as "Do you know enough about medicine yet to benefit from a medical research program?" *(Talking to your reader)*

According to Joan, this is the first time she had thought this much about her reader, and she was surprised to find out how well the approach worked. In the next two chapters we will pick up the rest of Joan's writing process, using some of her notes to illustrate writing strategies. The final version of her application follows. Notice how she has tried to use the ideas we saw her generating.

NATIONAL INSTITUTE OF HEALTH

INTERNSHIP PROGRAM

PERSONAL ESSAY:

My Purpose in Applying

I am applying for the University of London Internship Program in biomedical research because it would give me firsthand
experience in medical research operations and the chance to
learn scientific, communication, and personal skills not rou-
tinely encountered during an undergraduate education. Furthermore, it is a unique opportunity to combine my interests in engineering and biological research and prepare me for a career
in medical engineering. The following is a brief description
of my education, experiences, and interests that contribute to
my ability to take full advantage of this internship.

Academic Studies

As a result of my strong interest in science and math, I
am presently completing a degree in engineering. However, I am
doing this as part of a self-designed interdisciplinary program
that combines engineering and medicine. This has enabled me to
pursue my interests in the biological sciences and to gain analytical and problem-solving skills. In addition to studying
chemistry, biology, physiology, and basic engineering sciences,
such as thermodynamics and mechanics, I have elected engineering courses related to the biological sciences. For example, I
am presently studying the electrical biophysics of muscle,
nerve, and synapse and am taking a chemical engineering course
in the dynamics of biological systems. This knowledge of both
biology and engineering would aid me in understanding the scientific theories and techniques employed in biomedical engineering research.

Goals and Practical Experience

As a biomedical researcher, I would fulfill my goal of a
career that will help other people while at the same time be
challenging scientifically. I had exposure to research while
doing a biochemical assay for a neuropsychopharmocologist at
----- Clinic in Chicago. Besides learning the scientific procedures and techniques that are used, I learned how to deal
with some of the practical and organizational problems encountered in research. I saw how the lack of equipment and funds
often calls for real cooperation between departments and care-

ful planning of one's own project. The experience also helped me develop more of the patience research requires and recognize the enormous amounts of time, paperwork, and careful steps required for testing a hypothesis that is only one very small but necessary part of the overall project.

But besides knowing some of the frustrations, I also know that many medical advancements, such as the cardiac pacemaker, artificial limbs, and cures for diseases, exist and benefit many people because of the efforts of researchers. Therefore I would like to pursue my interest in research by participating in the NIH Internship Program. The exposure to many diverse projects, designed to better understand and improve the body's functioning, would help me to decide which areas of biomedical engineering to pursue. For example, I would be interested in projects emphasizing chemical, electrical, or mechanical knowledge; work performed on a cellular or macroscopic level; and work concerned with the design of machines and products or the discovery of new processes within the body.

Qualities and Skills

Although my academic program has been of central importance, it has not been of single importance. I feel I have learned many nonacademic skills and qualities necessary for research by participation outside of the classroom. My skills in organization and communication have been enhanced by planning programs, keeping records, writing letters, and working with people as an officer of Tau Beta Pi, the National Engineering Honor Society. I have gained leadership skills as a supervisor of a swim club, learned how to handle staff problems and emergency situations, and learned the importance of maintaining accurate and current financial records. I had to analyze problem situations, search for alternatives, make the best decision possible, and then accept and defend it until it was necessary to change. I feel I have learned self-discipline, motivation, and the value of goal-setting by participating for ten years on competitive swimming and basketball teams.

Summary

A scholarship to the NIH Internship Program would give me both new scientific knowledge and practical insight into biomedical research. In addition it would give me the opportunity, at the best time in my academic program, to wisely plan a career in medical technology. I feel that with this scholarship I could help engineering make a significant contribution to the field of medical research.

PROJECTS AND ASSIGNMENTS

1 You have decided to apply for a job, summer internship, or scholarship in your field of interest. As part of your application you have been asked to write a one- to two-page statement of your background *as it is related to* your career objectives, your interests, and your abilities. Since the reader will also have a copy of your résumé with the dates and facts, this statement, or personal profile, is to be your analysis of the meaning of those facts. Select a specific audience for this essay and write a profile that shows how your abilities fit the audience's needs.

You may wish to work on this assignment (and the following one) as you read the next three chapters. Therefore, for help in *planning* your paper, see Chapter 5; for help in *generating ideas*, see Chapter 6; and for help in *organizing ideas*, see Chapter 7.

2 *Checklist: Personal Profile.* The following checklist will help you judge how well you have met three important expectations readers bring to reading résumés and personal statements.

☐a. *The goal statement.* This statement at the beginning of your profile should include a career or personal goal that is both true about you and relevant to your reader's goals. This statement and/or goal should also preview or tie together the abilities and qualities you later present in the profile.

☐b. *Use of concepts.* Your task as a writer is to turn a set of facts (which might be listed in a résumé) into a set of qualities and abilities. This means that the profile should present a set of concepts supported by facts. In most cases this means that the topic sentence of each paragraph should contain a concept that ties together the information in the paragraph.

☐c. *Structure of ideas.* The overall structure of the profile should be a hierarchy. At the top level should be a statement that combines your goals and your reader's concerns. The rest of the profile should support this organizing idea. Each paragraph should present a clear point you wish to make. Avoid writing merely an expanded, elaborated list of the things you have done.

3 Take one of your own abilities or strengths that you find important but difficult to explain. Set aside 15 minutes and begin writing. Free association, partial sentences, odd statements are fine—but keep writing. Get down everything that comes to mind about that ability. Then at the end of 15 minutes (you can go longer but not less), read your raw material. Try to sum up what you know about that ability now in one or two paragraphs. If you haven't said it all, try another 15-minute exploration.

4 If the place to which you are applying doesn't invite a personal statement, write a letter of application to accompany your résumé and adapt the checklist above to this shorter format. In addition to the standard features of a business letter (see your handbook), place a version of your goal statement in the first paragraph. Use the middle paragraphs to present a miniature profile or set of relevant concepts about yourself—help the reader interpret the facts of your résumé in the way you would, if asked. Use the final paragraph to politely request action and aid the reader in contacting you.

chapter four

Planning and Learning

WHAT DOES IT MEAN WHEN a person says, "I know what I mean, but I can't say it in words"? What do you really "know" that you can't express? One answer is that you don't really "know" anything yet—all you have are vague intuitions or feelings, not actual ideas. Another equally extreme answer is that such intuitions and non-verbal knowing may be an even better, more profound kind of knowing than knowledge expressed in words. I want to offer you a third answer—one that is less evaluative, more descriptive. This answer says that "knowing" is an action, the act of representing information to yourself. And people's mental representation of information can take some dramatically different forms. For instance, some are verbal and some, such as knowing the feel of a good tennis swing, are not.

We often use metaphors to talk about this experience of having different kinds of knowing. For example, we say that people tap different "pockets" of knowledge or that they have notions in the "back of their mind." The underlying fact is that people *create internal, mental representations* of new information in order to remember it and think with it, and these inner representations can be both *verbal and nonverbal*. When it comes to writing, some of these mental images are easily translated into a verbal representation, but some are not.

A writer then is a little like a film director trying to create a scene. The director has built in his mind's eye a representation of that scene in the various languages of film. He can imagine the scene in terms of music, the script, the unstated theme or idea, and the film conventions it uses, as well as the physical and emotional presence of the actors, the sound of their voices, and the visual image created by lighting, staging, and cropping. The writer may find that she has an equal range of mental images in her mind's eye. Her job as a writer is to translate all these different ways of representing knowledge into prose. Her job becomes difficult when her initial representation is not as explicit or detailed as it needs to be to write prose.

Consider the nature of knowledge in this situation: You are walking through an open pine woods in Wyoming when above and behind you, you hear a faint, high scream that turns into a dark shape with spread wings diving through the trees in your direction. As the hawk pulls up, you see a nest in a tall lodgepole pine and a second hawk coming toward you from the right with a similar wonderful but ominous cry. You decide it would be wise to move on.

What do you know from this experience? How much of it is verbal? Back at home, with the help of your field guide, you find a name for this apparition, so you can now talk about seeing a red-tailed hawk, and you infer that there was a pair guarding a nest and that they were, indeed, speaking to you. But until you began to talk about this to yourself or to write it down, much of your knowledge was decidedly nonverbal: the shape of the bird and its wingspan, the arc and sound of its flight, the cry you described as a scream, the feeling of tension in your muscles, the shock running down your back, and that mixture of fear and elation you felt, even as you made sense of the event.

Looking back at your field guide you can see that the authors, Robbins, Bruun, and Zim, have had to struggle with the same problem of translating various kinds of knowing—visual, verbal, and emotional—into formal prose. Furthermore, assuming that one of them "knew hawks," he would have had to select (from all he knew) those features that his reader, wanting to identify birds, would need. A closer look at *Birds of North America* shows us how these writers tried to solve the problem of turning various kinds of verbal and nonverbal knowledge into the kind of written and pictorial representation you could print in a book.[1]

What does a hawk look like in the field? In Figure 4-1, these authors try to represent such information in three ways: One is verbal (a description of distinctive features), and the other two are visual (a series of paintings and a silhouette of the hawk among other birds). What does each representation accomplish for these writers?

What does a hawk look like? Notice how the authors give us two different kinds of visual information. The paintings are good for showing details of color, pattern, and age and sex differences. The silhouettes, however, are much better at expressing the

[1]Chandler S. Robbins, Bertel Bruun, and Herbert S. Zim, *Birds of North America* (Racine, Wisc.: Western Publishing, 1966) pp. 70–71.

Figure 4-1   *Different ways of knowing and representing hawks*

(a) Verbal Description: A well-known and common buteo [note the author's use of the Latin genus name for hawk]; nests in woodlands and feeds in open country. The uniformly colored tail of the adult—reddish above, light pink beneath—and the dark belly band are the best field marks. . . . Body is heavier than other buteos', plumage extremely variable. Flying head-on, light wrist area gives impression of a pair of "headlights." Often perches on poles or treetops, rarely hovers.

(b) Visual Representation: Painting

(c) Visual Representation: Silhouette

(d) Verbal Description of Sound: "Call is a high scream, often imitated by jays."

(e) Visual Representation of Sound: Sonagram of red-tailed hawk

(f) Visual Representation of Range: Map

hawk's relative size, shape, and posture. (Did the needs of the reader/user of this book influence these representations?)

How do you translate your knowledge of a sound into words? Robbins et al. try two ways: They give us a verbal description ("Call is a high scream . . .") and a visual one in the form of a sonagram—little squiggles on a graph showing changes in pitch and timbre over a 3-second period. Why? Finally, consider how you would present the years of data the U.S. Fish and Wildlife Service has collected on the location of these birds. Remember that this knowledge starts out as lists of individual sightings and counts at specific spots across North America. Robbins et al. solve this problem by translating that information into a map using colors, shading, and lines to show summer, winter, and migratory ranges.

A book like this field guide shows us how writers must often struggle to represent their full knowledge in words. And in some cases, nonverbal representations such as silhouettes are more effective than words. But these writers have come nowhere near representing the full experience of seeing hawks. Compare the representation Robbins et al. created to this one from Henry David Thoreau's journal/essay on living at Walden Pond (*Walden*, 1854). Would you say that one is more precise than the other, or are they trying to capture different aspects of experience?

> Looking up I observed a very slight and graceful hawk, like a nighthawk. . . . It was the most ethereal flight I had ever witnessed. It did not simply flutter like a butterfly, nor soar like the larger hawks, but it sported with proud reliance in the fields of air; mounting again and again with its strange chuckle, it repeated its free and beautiful fall, turning over and over like a kite, and then recovering from its lofty tumbling, as if it had never set its foot on *terra firma*. It appeared to have no companion in the universe—sporting there alone—and to need none but the morning and the ether with which it played. It was not lonely, but made all the earth lonely beneath it.

Thoreau uses prose to describe his nighthawk. In the following poem, written a few years later, Tennyson uses rhyme, a regular meter, and alliteration to "describe" an eagle. Do you think these writers used different verbal forms in order to create different meanings, different representations of experience? How would the poetic devices Tennyson used work for him?

The Eagle
He clasps the crag with crooked hands;
Close to the sun in lonely lands,
Ring'd with the azure world, he stands.

The wrinkled sea beneath him crawls;
He watches from his mountain walls,
And like a thunderbolt he falls.

Alfred, Lord Tennyson (1851)

The point of this set of examples is simple. When you sit down to write, your knowledge may be, like a hawk-seer's, rich and complex but also rather vague and unspecific. In building a prose representation you have the luxury of many alternative ways to do the job. But keep in mind that you are also building new knowledge when you give yourself, and your reader, this new, more elaborate representation of what it means to "see a hawk."

PLANNING IN WRITING

Planning in writing is the act of calling up mental representations such as these for the purpose of thinking about what you know and what you want to say. Planning for a paper doesn't start when you sit down to write. It may start as you are walking down the hall and begin to tap some of these different pockets of knowledge. The knowledge you find in your own memory may be, in part, visual images, sounds and rhythms, or feelings. Even your verbal knowledge, when you begin to plan, may be rather general. For example, you know that the bird "swooped toward you," but should you think of it or express it as an attack, a threat, or merely anxiety behavior? At this point you may also know that certain ideas are connected, but you may not yet be able to say how. Writing, as a way of thinking things through, is often a process of re-representation—making your knowledge as verbal and as explicit as you can.

Notice that we have answered the question "What do you really know that you can't express?" The answer is that you may know a lot, but writing is a special and particularly demanding way of thinking about what you know. By making things explicit, writing not only lets you remember and communicate your ideas, but it lets you test them. When you write an idea down it is easier to stand back and ask, "Does that version of my knowledge do justice to what I really know?"

Although this analogy isn't always true, I find it helps to think of writing as both a journey and a process in which you are exploring and then restructuring your knowledge into a new representation that someone else can understand. You often start out happily wandering around in ways of knowing that are a long way from finished text, or maybe even from words: images, feelings, memories of events, loosely related ideas, or at best, unconnected fragments of coherent discourse that don't yet add up to a whole. At the other end of this journey you want to end up with polished prose, which is a very powerful, but also a very specialized way of expressing your knowledge. Look, for instance, at some of the features polished prose must have: It must be in words, show logical connections (your private associations are no longer enough), fit some standard format, follow the rules of grammar, use standard spelling, and more. Notice that in planning and writing drafts, you often choose, quite sensibly, to ignore some of these special features of prose. Features such as spelling, word choice, and sentence style are necessary parts of the final "prose" representation, but they aren't crucial early in the journey, or even in some draft stages. In the following example, compare the amount of information contained in these four different verbal representations of my knowledge. In one I have listed only topics, in the second, key words and abstract relations, and in the last two I have tried to express my meaning in prose. What have I been able to communicate by taking on the extra demands of finished prose?

TOPICS
  HEAT   WATER   POLLUTION   ALGAE   FISH

KEY WORDS AND RELATIONS
  Heat + Water = Pollution (= thermal pollution)
  Pollution ⇒ Dead fish
  Cause of dead fish = uncontrolled algae growth

PROSE: With a Focus on the Process
  The heated water from local industries (a form of thermal pollution) kills many species of fish by triggering the uncontrolled growth of oxygen-stealing algae.

PROSE: With a Focus on Definition
  Thermal pollution—a side effect of industrial waste disposal—occurs when industrial wastes heat a river or lake, stimulating the uncontrolled growth of algae, which eventually suffocates the fish. (What would happen if I added just one word and said "unavoidable" side effect, or change it to "unregulated" side effect?

The Purpose of Planning: Setting Goals and Getting a Gist

In describing writing as a journey that restructures knowledge, we all have a good image of the final result—polished text—and of the stage before that—a working draft. But what are you trying to achieve as you plan? This question seems hard to answer because planning is work that goes on in the head more often than on paper. It is done when you are walking down the street, going to sleep, or just sitting, thinking, and writing notes. Some people produce outlines, but others don't. So if you can't equate planning with anything that is written, such as a draft, what should you try to produce as you plan?

There is probably no single answer to this question, but experienced writers often concentrate on two main things as they plan. First, they create a sense of their major goals and subgoals. Second, they form a sense of their gist and the general structure of their ideas. These are common-sense notions, but I will define them briefly here, and then use the next section to illustrate some of the different forms these goals and gists can take.

Your **goals** for a paper say how you want to link and present ideas (for example, are you aiming for a forceful argument or a personal reflection), and they might include the effect you want to have on a reader (paragraph by paragraph). Your goals will also be the standards and criteria you want to keep in mind (that is, stick to your point). A genre will always dictate certain conventional goals (for example, news stories have to have a "lead"), but in the planning stage you are also setting your unique goals for this paper.

A **gist** is a summary statement of the essential things you want to say. In order to have such a top-level statement of the main points or the big idea, you have to have explored your own knowledge and/or done some reading and have figured out what is important. The gist is the guiding idea. It also includes a tentative sense of structure: knowing how your important ideas are related to each other. The first goal of planning, then, is to be able to walk up to someone and say (in fifty words or less), "I'm writing a paper that basically says: (gist), because what I want to do is (goals)." A detailed outline of the paper itself is only an optional end result of planning.

Here are some maxims that sum up some of the critical features of planning:

1. Plans are made to be broken.
2. Any plan is better than no plan. (Minsky's Maxim)
3. Plans are instructions you give yourself, so give yourself good ones. (Note: The form doesn't matter. You can talk to yourself in doodles, outlines, or full-color images; if it works, it is good.)
4. Good plans are detailed enough to argue with and cheap enough to throw away.
5. Bad plans are plans you can't use (even if they look great on paper).

Can Writing Change Knowledge?

In order to make our discussion of planning more concrete, I would like to show you some snapshots from the planning process of Joan, the writer discussed in Chapter 3. We will look at the planning that led to her third paragraph, the one on her goals and experience. This paragraph is interesting because it involves so many different kinds of knowledge, from images to narrative memories to goals and gists, before it becomes polished prose.

Joan's planning for this section really began when Professor Harris asked her, "Do you have any experience in this area?" and she tried to answer by telling the story of her summer job at the Chicago Clinic. Notice how her knowledge starts with a strong visual image and is structured around a memory for people, events, and her own feelings. These memories will be the raw material for her later planning.

CONVERSATION: Well I tried to get some experience in my summer job. I can still see that lab book. I lived with it—all those little boxes you filled in, every detail about the experiment: times, dates, measurements. You wouldn't believe the detail. And you couldn't guess or fill it in later like you do in high school. (Note the visual image. How would you translate this memory into a statement about her "work experience"? What does this knowledge "mean" given her writing task?)

And the Clinic itself was a zoo. This guy Ranjar ran the adjacent lab. When I came he was really nice to me and always asked me how things were going in my lab. He looked like your father—this silver hair—but, I don't know, you had to watch out. He was a fox. One time we were working on a test that had to be done at 12-hour intervals, and there was never enough money and equipment for each lab to have its own machines. I came in early one Wednesday to run the fourth test and the equipment was gone. I finally tracked it down to Ranjar. Apparently he needed it, and he was all sorry, friendly, and slick. Promised to get it back. Well, he didn't. I had to run the whole series over. Some of the people there were really building empires. But you just had to cooperate to get things done. The competition hurt everyone. (Note the narrative memory of people and events. What does Joan "know" about her "work experience"?)

In Figure 4-2 you will see another way we can represent some of the knowledge in Joan's memory. This memory network is a schematic diagram of some of the concepts in her memory, such as Ranjar and fox. The lines that link these concepts are named: **is** indicates a definition (Ranjar is not good); **isa** indicates that something belongs to a larger class of things (having insufficient equipment is an example of a realistic situation); and **has** indicates a property or feature (having a fatherly look is a property

Figure 4-2   ***A piece of a memory network***

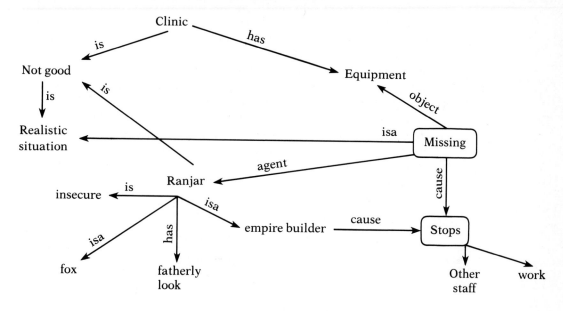

of Ranjar). In this system for representing knowledge in memory, episodes and events are named with a verb, such as "missing," and put in an oval circle. Actions are linked to agents (which cause things to happen) and to objects (which receive the effect of an action).

What does this representation show us that a narrative doesn't? Notice first that major ideas in this network are ones that have a lot of links—all roads lead to Rome. Ideas with many links in memory are easy to get to; you are likely to remember them. Ideas that have few links may be things that you "know" but have trouble remembering. They may be knowledge you have but don't use because you don't call it up when you need it. Finally, this network shows how people like Joan can hold concepts that may actually conflict with one another—how can Ranjar be both a "fox"and a "father"? Thinking or writing about this knowledge may make this conflict more apparent and lead Joan, as it does in her narrative, to try to make a new link. In this case we can imagine a revised network in which both "fox" and "fatherly look" are connected by a new idea such as "looks are deceptive."

This network tells us one more thing about knowledge: Much of what people know is probably stored in an abstract form, much like these memory networks. That means that most of the information in our memory is not stored in sentences or even in words and phrases. Instead it is stored as complex "concepts" that may not even have a name. For example, imagine all of the nonverbal feelings attached in Joan's memory to the concept we have labeled "not good." In addition, we may have a strong sense that two ideas like "fox" and "father" are connected, but we may not be able to say in words just what that connection is. Writing is a process of trying to think about those connections and make them explicit. In trying to write, you actually learn new information by forging new links between the concepts you already have.

In order to write, Joan has to translate these memories, images, and abstract connections into more explicit ones that are relevant to her purpose: to show that she has useful experience. We can see this happening by looking at how she plans the text itself. Notice how her plans and her notes are in fact a new and different image of knowledge: they re-represent what she knows in a new form.

> PLANNING THOUGHTS: I've got to show what I got out of all this. What can I show for this. . . . It's experience, but it has to be something I've learned. I sure learned how to keep records. So what, I'm not applying for bookkeeper. But, . . . yeah. Scientific, being scientific. That careful . . . all those steps you have to go through. And then mention records and testing. OK.

Notes

$$Records = \left(\text{Scientific}\right)$$

- *steps*
- *records*
- *testing*

If we look closely we can see that even the scribbled notes themselves are full of information. The equals sign and the large circle are graphic, or nonverbal, ways of saying that the meaning of "records" is not the records themselves but the idea they support: the notion that she learned to be "scientific." The line tells us that she is going to elaborate that idea and the dots are a graphic way of saying "cover these ideas in this order."

These notes with their combination of key words and structural information capture the *gist* of what Joan wants to say. Notice what happens to this gist when she elaborates it into a complete text (pages 56–57). Then consider another piece of her planning.

> PLANNING THOUGHTS: Ranjar, oh boy. Well, actually I learned how to work around him. Maybe it is important to let them know I'm not naive or inept here. I know that there are people problems even in

Figure 4-3   *Joan's goals*

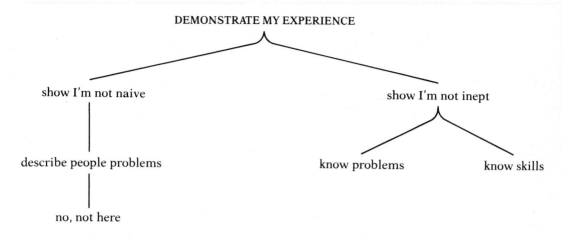

pure research. Some people are a real headache and you have to . . . you have to get results anyway. Guess I don't really want to say that here, maybe in the interview or something. My point is, what? I got to see the problems of working in an organization. Money, records, all those are practical problems, but you also learn to cooperate, share equipment—or die—and to plan. OK, organizational problems.

Joan's planning also creates a number of goals. In the above excerpt, for instance, she decides to achieve her major goal—demonstrating her experience—with a pair of subgoals to show she is neither naive nor inept. Her initial plan is to tackle the "naive" subgoal by talking about people problems, but then she decides that "people problems" is a better topic for an interview. So her main subgoal then becomes to show what she can do by discussing both the practical problems and the skills of research. Notice how her goals also form a tree structure that has the most inclusive goals at the top supported by subgoals beneath (see Figure 4-3).

To sum up, Joan's planning shows a writer working with many different ways of representing her knowledge. She starts with visual images, a memory of a personal experience, and some partially connected concepts. She creates notes that contain both visual and verbal information. As she plans, she translates her knowledge into a set of goals and a gist adapted to her purpose in writing.

PROJECTS AND ASSIGNMENTS

1 In this chapter we looked at the way the writers of *Birds of North America* dealt with the problem of representing some very different kinds of knowledge about hawks. As writers in the popular Golden Guide series of field guides, they also had the problem of adapting their knowledge to the needs of the reader. Think about some alternative ways of writing about a bird and examine the choices these writers made. Did the needs of the reader have any effect on the information they selected and the way they presented it?

2 This exercise is a journal entry you might do to help you with a paper you are currently working on. Start planning as Joan did by jotting down notes about visual images, remembered experiences, or conversations. Use your writing to recall your knowledge, however it may be represented in your own mind. Try pictures, notes, dialogues, stream of consciousness—whatever taps your best knowledge. Then given your purpose in writing, try to express your knowledge as a **gist**—say what it means. Secondly, show how this meaning fits your **goals**—say why you want to use that information and what you want it to do for you.

3 Have you ever had an experience that was hard to capture in words? Consider, for instance: being at a concert, a sports event, or a tense social situation; appreciating the style of someone's performance in any of those; making music, or doing something athletic, physical, or social yourself. Create a small portfolio of perspectives on this experience. Feel free to use or create photos, drawings, audio tapes, *and* a variety of verbal representations (such as, a blow-by-blow account, a dramatization that highlights key features, a speculative reflection on the meaning of the experience, versions of the story that you would give to different people).

Look at some of the interesting ways the representations in your portfolio differ from one another. As you write a commentary on those differences, speculate about an answer to this question: Are some ways of representing your knowledge especially adapted to (or good at) capturing certain aspects of experience?

4 Do you think historians, writers, and media people give us qualitatively different representations of common public events or just additional facts? Consider an event (large or small) that has made the news (historically or yesterday). Create a portfolio of representations (see Assignment 3 for ideas). Consider not only TV, radio, and newspapers, but historical accounts, reviews, commentaries, and interviews. For example, if your event were a scene from a local play, you could use the performance, the text, program notes, current and historical reviews, scholarly criticism, and a talk with an actor. These accounts will naturally contain different facts and conclusions, but do they also represent different aspects of experience, including emotion, values, implications, personal meaning, logical connections, or causation? Write a paper in which you think about this question: Do some of these representations seem to offer a distinctive way of knowing that event that the others can't (or don't) provide? If some people only saw one of two of these accounts, would these differences have any implications?

5 This writer is trying to describe the unique discourse community created in her drawing class by the weekly "crit" or critique in which student work is analyzed by the instructor and the group. But how do you talk about a visual experience, especially when you are still learning to see things in a special way?

To analyze how this writer did it, apply four of the concepts from this chapter to the paragraph. Is it possible to see (or infer) any **goal(s)** she had for this paragraph (beyond giving a description)? Can you state the **gist**? (What features of the text were your "tip-offs" to her goals and gist?) Finally, sketch a quick version of what her **memory network** for a "strong" and "weak" drawing appears to include. (How many connections do you see?) Now look at the particular ways she *chose* with each sentence to **represent** those perceptions and relations in prose. Could you have done it differently?

The crit goes on as we begin to pick the drawings we want to discuss. Drawings are discussed by speaking about their strong and weak points. A strong drawing means that its composition or the way its parts are put together to make up its whole work well, or it is visually pleasing. An example of a drawing that is not visually pleasing or which doesn't work well could be a drawing done with some very dark shades of grey and some very light grey tones but no middle tones. Drawings like this tend to be spotty. If middle shades of grey are added to the drawing, it helps it to flow together and connect its parts making it into a whole. Another example of a weak drawing could be one whose negative space, the space or air around a subject, is too large for the subject. Let's say the subject is a drawing of a frog. If the space around the frog is too big, then the teacher may suggest that the drawing be cropped. Cropping a drawing means to cut off some of the negative space. Things like these are discussed throughout the critique, teaching the students how to see and how to change their own drawings.

IF YOU WOULD LIKE TO READ MORE

If you would like to know more about how people build mental representations, see:

Anderson, John R. *Cognitive Psychology and Its Implications.* San Francisco: W. H. Freeman, 1980. / This book describes the controversy over how people think with images.

Flower, Linda, and John R. Hayes. "Images, Plans, and Prose: The Representation of Meaning in Writing." *Written Communication* 1 (January 1984), 120–160. / This paper looks at how writers must often translate from one representation to another.

Lindsay, Peter, and Donald Norman. *Human Information Processing: An Introduction to Psychology.* New York: Academic Press, 1972. / These authors provide an entertaining but rigorous introduction to the theory of memory networks, which they in fact helped develop.

chapter five

Making Plans

STEP 1   EXPLORE the rhetorical problem

Decide how you are going to represent this rhetorical problem to yourself.

Strategy 1   EXPLORE YOUR IMAGE OF THE PROBLEM

Strategy 2   EXPLAIN THE ASSIGNMENT TO YOURSELF

STEP 2   MAKE a plan

Sketch out an initial plan to guide your thinking. As you compose, return to this plan, changing and developing it as you go along.

Strategy 1   MAKE A PLAN TO DO AND A PLAN TO SAY

Strategy 2   MAKE YOUR GOALS MORE OPERATIONAL

Strategy 3   LISTEN TO INTUITION AND CHANGE YOUR PLAN

Strategy 4   REVEAL YOUR PLAN TO THE READER

If good writers and problem solvers have a secret power, it is planning. Trial and error can often generate useful results, but if you rely solely on this method you are taking blind luck as your guide. Problem solvers rely on plans. The twenty minutes you spend planning can save you hours in writing. And good planning, as you shall see, can also have a dramatic effect on the quality of your paper. In this chapter we will look at two steps in planning: exploring the rhetorical problem and planning your response.

STEP 1   EXPLORE the Rhetorical Problem

A rhetorical situation or rhetorical problem is like a rather large, uncharted territory that contains you, your reader, your ideas, and all the things you possibly could do. As you make a mental tour of this territory selecting the goals that matter and the strategies you will use, you are building your own image or representation of the task. For example, consider the way two car owners I know see the task of "washing the car." In owner A's image, you need to wash the car when the dirt is so thick you can't see the color and somebody has written "wash me" on the back window. His goals: save the body, save face, remove the top layer of dirt. This job is saved for weddings and funerals. His strategies: wait for a warm day, give it a hose, and sponge once over—a 12-minute task. In owner B's image of "washing the car," this task is called for when a salt spray, an afternoon shower, or a dusty road sullies his cream puff. His goal: to see his reflection. His strategies: go to the high-priced car wash for hot soap and a blow dry, vacuum the carpets, do the windows, dust the ashtray, hose the underbody, wax the chrome wheels, and touch up with Poly-Guard. If two representations of a simple task like "washing the car" can differ so much, what happens when people have to represent a more complex rhetorical problem to themselves?

For instance, when you are given a writing assignment in a college class, how do you represent the task to yourself? The answer may seem obvious: "I just read the assignment and do what it says." But, in fact, it is more accurate to say that writers *create* their own image or representation of every task they do. That is, they decide which goals (of all they could set) are most important, which ideas (out of many) are relevant, and which text conventions seem most appropriate. It turns out that this "creative" process matters because different writers, reading the same assignment, can have strikingly different images of what is appropriate.

Strategy 1   EXPLORE YOUR IMAGE OF THE PROBLEM

Although we have looked at various kinds of writing, from feature articles to memos and applications, most of the writing you will do in college could be defined as "academic discourse." But do you always know when you have met the expectations of that community? What is your image of this task called "academic writing"?

What is "Academic Discourse"?

Here are some "mystery texts" that come from different discourse communities, including academic discourse published in journals and student writing for courses as well as popular journalism and professional writing. Read each mystery text and decide: is it an example of "academic discourse" or not? Was it written by a professor, a graduate student, an undergraduate, or a non-academic writer? Make a note of at least *three features* in each text that you saw as "tip-offs."

Mystery Text 1. Looking at a finished paper, a reader has no feel for what went on before. But for a writer, first drafts and throwaways are all a part of the final work. Revision for many writers can be a way to reevaluate their thinking.

Mystery Text 2. Recent research about the way experienced writers approach the revision process reveals some surprisingly consistent findings. It suggests that experienced writers tend to pay more attention to preliminary planning, to setting goals, to suiting subject matter to these goals, and to writing several drafts in which they make major changes that affect the meaning of the discourse, not just the style.

Mystery Text 3. Revision, the establishment asserts, is a powerful, generative process. Many students, however, seem to operate with a different definition. . . . If teachers and professionals are right about the nature and power of revision, why are students slow to take advantage of such a good thing?

Mystery Text 4. The method I used is not perfect; no research method is. . . . My purpose and my method reflect a logic of exploration and discovery, which is necessary in order to increase our understanding of a very complex human activity.

Mystery Text 5. I like to compare my method with that of painters centuries ago, proceeding, as it were, from layer to layer. The first draft is quite crude, far from being perfect, by no means finished; although even then, even at that point, it has its final structure, the form is visible.

Mystery Text 6. The schools are not always hospitable environments, however. Some teachers actually penalize critical thinking, says Richard Paul, director of California's Sonoma State University Center for Critical Thinking and Moral Critique: because the system tends to value the answer more than the process, a student who ably defends a socially unacceptable belief often gets a lower grade than one with an unreflective but safe view.

Have you made your decisions and jotted down your reasons? To get the most out of this mystery, discuss it with other members of your class. I will reveal the "answers" later because the real purpose of this mystery is to let you take a look at your own assumptions about your images of "academic writing." For instance, look at the three reasons you jotted down. Which features did you look for to evaluate these texts?

Formal Features. Are you looking for the formal features of the text, such as sentence length, word choice, style? Are you focusing on conventional rules?

Content. Are you basing your decision on the content: on what is said, on the position the writer takes?

Rhetorical Features. Are you using the rhetorical features of the text to make your decision: looking at the writer's purpose, the apparent context for the text, and the writer's relationship with the reader?

These mystery texts let you uncover some of your own assumptions about academic writing and how to evaluate it. If you look at your own private mental image of an "academic" text, what is in the foreground; in other words, what is the focus of your image: words, rules, and local stylistic features or rhetorical ones? When you switch from evaluating a text to writing one, you will find that focusing on rhetorical featues may be more useful to you. Do these mystery texts let you speculate on different ways people in this particular discourse community—academic discourse—seem to use writing?

How Do You Represent a Reading-to-Write Task?

Let's now look at an actual college assignment that asks you to read-in-order-to-write-a-paper. Read the assignment and the excerpt from the source materials and ask yourself, how do I represent this task to myself?

Assignment: Here are some notes, including research results and observations on time management. Please read and interpret these data in order to make a brief (1–2 page) comprehensive statement about this subject. Your statement should interpret and synthesize all the relevant findings in the text.

Excerpt from the Reading Notes:
The key to success, according to efficiency expert Alan Lakein in his recent book *How to Get Control of Your Time and Your*

Life, lies in pacing and planning. The average worker has two kinds of "prime time" to plan: external time and internal time. External time is the best time to attend to other people. Internal prime time is the period in which one works best.

Noted philosopher and psychologist William James found that most people do not use their mental energies in sufficient depth. He advocated continued concentration in the face of apparent mental fatigue: "The fatigue gets worse up to a certain critical point, when gradually or suddenly it passes away, and we are fresher than before. We have evidently tapped a new level of energy."

In his guide to intellectual life, Jean Guitton stresses the importance of preparation for peak performance, asserting that it is vital to rest at the least sign of fatigue and to go to work with a relaxed attitude. Find a place that is at once calm and stimulating. Tolerate nothing that is not useful or beautiful.

In a recent survey, students reported some of the following as their standard strategies for getting through assignments and minimizing some of the debilitating effects of long-range pressures.

Do what's due; postpone big projects.
Create a crisis.
Allow the minimal estimate of time it will take to get a project completed.
Read the material once; don't try to remember it until it's needed.

Now write your statement about time management based on your interpretation of these data.

What do you think this read-to-write assignment calls for? And do you think everyone would see it as you do? A group of teachers and researchers at the Center for the Study of Writing asked 72 freshman students to do the expanded version of this assignment and report back on their representation of the task. Below is a checklist of the major options people considered. Mark your choices and your predictions for what the freshmen chose. For instance, under Source of Information, some people said, "the text," while others said, "what I already knew." Under Text Format and Features, some students thought this sort of assignment just called for a short summary with an opinion paragraph added on at the end; whereas others assumed the "appropriate" format was standard school theme with an introduction, a few paragraphs, and a conclusion. And still others had the conventions of a more formal, publishable essay in mind. Perhaps the most important decision people made was a decision about the Organizing Plan, since it lead some students to write a careful summary, while for others the sources became a springboard for a personal reflection on the topic. Some writers created a synthesis, organized around a concept they defined, such as, "advice for students" or "alternative theories of time management." And still others used the sources for a purpose of their own, such as raising the question of whether time management is teachable at all, given all this contradictory advice. Are all of these decisions a reasonable response to the task?

Some Options for a Read-to-Write Assignment

MAJOR SOURCE OF INFORMATION	TEXT FORMAT AND FEATURES
☐ Text	☐ Notes/Summary Paragraph
☐ Text + My Comments	☐ Summary + Opinion Paragraph
☐ What I Already Knew	☐ Standard School Theme
☐ Other Texts	☐ Persuasive Essay

ORGANIZING PLAN FOR WRITING
☐ Summarize the Readings
☐ Free Response to the Topic
☐ Organize around a Synthesizing Concept
☐ Interpret for a Purpose of My Own

The teacher and students who conducted this study found that people didn't agree on what this "typical college assignment" called for. Each student built his or her own representation of the task—assuming it was the "right" or "obvious" representation—but the person in class beside him or her was assuming something quite different. Here are some results: Under *Source*, 32% said "text" and 52% said text plus comments; under *Format*, 50% picked the "standard theme" (which leaves 50% with other ideas); under *Organizing Plan*, 43% chose to do a "summary," 25% a "synthesis," and only 11% an "interpretation with a purpose."

Can you spot the different organizing plans from some introductory sentences?

"Basically, time management is broken into two parts, planning and pacing. Also an important factor is efficiency."

"I found that this research was relevant to my endeavors. I do plan ahead, but procrastination always occurs when an assignment is due. I find myself writing late at night when I am tired and concentration just isn't there because the only thing I'm thinking about is sleep."

"There are several theories as to the most efficient theories of time management. Some say. . . . But others say. . . ."

"The basic problem of time management for college students involves changing schedules and finding a good working environment. As Lakein says. . . ."

"Based on the research and self-help books, I feel the solution to the problem of time management will have to be a compromise among the opinions of these professionals, many of whom disagree with each other. In fact, many of their "helpful hints" based on business workers are really obstacles to many students."

Now, you may be asking, is there a "right" answer to this assignment? We can respond to this question in two ways.

1. When you receive a "typical" assignment, do you know what your instructor expects? For instance, many instructors want you to summarize the readings to show you understand them. But other instructors "assume" that a good paper will synthesize information, that is, that you, the writer, will create a new concept to which all the key ideas in *your* essay are linked. Those instructors want you to make sense of your reading, organize your observations, and maybe even come up with a new controlling idea. And still other instructors may expect a good paper to go one step further and apply the reading to some topic or problem being discussed in the course.

In academic writing all of these organizing plans are valuable—there are times you need to summarize, times to synthesize, times to interpret and apply. But each plan produces a very different sort of paper. If you and your instructor represent the task differently without realizing it, you could turn in a "good summary" but a "poor synthesis"—a paper that failed to show what you really can do. One always wishes that teachers, supervisors, and clients who ask for writing would be more explicit about what they want, but as a writer it is your job to explore the rhetorical situation before you plunge in.

2. On the other hand, what if the "best" representation is not dictated by the situation; what if it is up to you? This study showed us that the most important thing is to realize that *you* are making the choice—that you are building your own representation. Many students in the study did not realize how many different options there were. It may help to look at your choices in terms of the costs and benefits to you.

Making Your Own Choices

For instance, a *summary* helps you remember the reading and if you had lots of practice doing summaries in high school, it may be easier to write a good summary than a good synthesis. However, there are hidden costs in deciding to summarize: you aren't developing any ideas of your own and readers in the academic discourse community often expect to learn something new from a text—they are likely to be bored by a mere summary.

Think about some of the costs and benefits of using *synthesis* as an organizing plan. It lets you introduce your own ideas and experience and come up with a new way to look at your sources. But what if the sources are like Lakein, James, Guitton, and the students and don't provide a ready-made synthesizing concept? One cost of this plan is that you will have to create your own concept. You will have to look for links and try to define an interesting connection (or organizing concept). Finding a good concept that does justice to all of your key points and says something worthwhile can require thought. For instance, the teachers who read the time management essays decided that a topic sentence such as "There are many ideas about time management" didn't really qualify as a new synthesizing concept. Although it was a tidy way to link all the paragraphs, it seemed too obvious and uninteresting to these academic readers to qualify as a new concept.

Interpreting the sources for *your own purpose* gives you much more independence and opportunity to think about something you care about. (The examples on pages 95–97 are all organized by a purpose the writers themselves set.) However, as we know, defining one's purpose and using it to organize a whole text often takes thought and revision—it has a cost. For me as a writer, adapting outside sources to my own purposes is almost always worth the effort, but there are times when it is not. When somebody asks me to write a short report on a project, I have the choice simply to cut and paste material from an old report (lowest cost), to summarize off the top of my head or synthesize around some obvious concepts (moderate costs; more benefits), or to write a special report adapted to what my readers need or to what I especially want them to hear (highest cost and highest potential benefit). Although academic writing places a premium on new knowledge and using knowledge to address an issue or problem, the most important fact for you as a writer to know is that *you create your own goals.* Exploring the rhetorical situation will let you make the most sensible decision for yourself.

⬅ Strategy 2   EXPLAIN THE ASSIGNMENT TO YOURSELF

Assignments are a special kind of rhetorical problem in which certain parts of the problem are already specified. But even in an assignment, many parts of the problem are implied—the professor assumes you will fill in the unstated pieces of the puzzle.

Knowing how to explain an assignment to yourself by elaborating its assumptions, key terms, and unstated criteria is a critical skill in writing. It can mean the difference between writing a successful paper and writing one that doesn't succeed, because it solves the wrong problem.

Let's suppose that you are enrolled in a History of Western Civilization course and your teacher has just asked you to write a short paper on the question: "Why was Erasmus considered to be the Prince of Humanists?" How would you develop the paper?

When an assignment asks a direct question, there is a temptation to do a **memory dump**—that is, simply to write everything you can remember about Erasmus. But that is not what the question asks for, and such an answer will often earn a low grade.

One step up from the memory dump is the **definition + example** type of answer: after defining Humanism, one then explains what Erasmus did that made him a famous humanist. This strategy addresses the two parts of the question and it fits Erasmus into the Humanist tradition. But it does not *answer* the question.

To answer the question, you need a **definition + comparison + context answer.** That is, after you define Humanism, you must think about why Erasmus was more of a humanist than anyone else. Consider what a **comparison plus context** might entail: Was he more humane, more kind, more virtuous? Is being the Prince of Humanists a matter of *quantity*—did he write more letters and books, learn more languages, know more theology, have more friends than any other humanist? Is it a matter of *quality*—did he write better books, have more interesting friends, and so on? Is it a matter of *primacy*—was Erasmus the first humanist, or did he influence more people than any other humanist? Or is it a matter of *notoriety*—did he get into more trouble or make more enemies than any other humanist? Or is the answer a combination of these? Or something else? (And who gave Erasmus this title, anyway?)

The point is, to answer this question, one must do three things. First, one must define Humanism. Then, one must analyze the meaning of "prince," which suggests "best" or "most," and consider what that comparison means. Finally, one must create a basis for that comparison. To explain why Erasmus was the "Prince of Humanists," one must know something about the people who were lesser humanists. The question really asks you to place Erasmus and the Humanist movement in a *context*. Your teacher will not believe that you understand this material unless you can talk about not only the aims and ideals of Humanism but what it came out of, what it was a reaction to, and perhaps what opposition the people who belonged to it faced. If you know these things, you can explain why Erasmus embodied the ideals of the movement more than anyone else did.

It is possible to say most or all of these things in a "memory dump" answer. Yet such a response will usually receive a lower evaluation than will a definition + contrast + context answer, because in the second kind of answer the information is focused. After all, when instructors ask questions such as this one, what do they want to know? Beyond factual information, they want to know whether you can *use* the facts—that is, think about them and connect them for yourself. Instructors know that rote memory knowledge, the kind displayed in the "memory dump" answer, is shallow and transient. Deep knowledge, of the kind meant by the word "education," is usable knowledge. That is why assignments ask you to reorganize ideas around a question, and why instructors use words such as *define, analyze,* and *compare.*

One way to read an assignment is to predict that it will probably ask you (in one way or another) to do three major mental actions: to define something, to make a comparison, and to connect something to its context. So when you read an assignment, look for the terms or clues that say what you should define, what you should compare, and what context you should discuss. You can do this even for short questions. One reason they are short is that they have left the task of explaining or interpreting the assignment up to you. For example, you can rewrite the assignment "What was enlightened about the Enlightenment?" to say,

Define "enlightened."
Compare it to its opposite or to other ways of conducting society.
Show what effect its context, the period called the Enlighten-
  ment, had on the idea of being "enlightened."

Understanding an assignment, then, is often a process of rewriting and expanding a question into a set of **actions** you could take. Many key words in assignments suggest actions:

compare   List or discuss similarities in order of importance (usually most to least).
contrast   List or discuss differences in order of importance.
evaluate   Judge the worth of something by measuring (comparing and contrasting) its key features against a standard; the standard may be either what is *normal* or what is *ideal.*
how   "By what means does it happen that . . ." asks for cause/effect (*not* narrative!).
justify/support   Corroborate with reasons, explain the rationale for each reason, and support the rationales with facts.
significance   "Give/tell/show the significance of . . ." means describe the important consequences or implications (the cause/effect relationships).

summarize Restate the main facts or points concisely, using your own words.

superlatives "Prince," for example, asks for comparison or contrast.

why "For what reasons . . ." asks for cause/effect.

Sometimes questions will ask you to do even more "rewriting" and to supply the key terms and actions yourself. For example, how would you answer the question "Imagine that Plato is reading Thomas Paine's pamphlet *Common Sense*. What would he say about it?"

If you decided that this question asks you to compare and contrast the ideas of Plato and Paine and to express these comparisons in terms of Plato's response to Paine, you are right. If you know anything about the ideas of these two philosophers, you probably also realize that a good answer would involve definitions of key terms (*citizen*, for example) and that your comments about Plato would probably be based on his book *Republic*. The question also implicitly asks you to distinguish important concepts from less important ones and to evaluate Plato's probable response to Paine's book. Your knowledge of the times and circumstances in which Paine and Plato wrote—the context of fourth-century Greece and eighteenth-century America—will help you evaluate this response and explain why these philosophers agree and disagree.

People often define the same question in quite different ways. Consider this assignment: "Analyze some aspect of the relation between politics and culture in the twentieth century." Compare your interpretation with the problem/purpose statement of the writer in Example 1 at the end of this chapter.

STEP 2   MAKE a Plan

Goals state where you want to end up. Plans say how you are going to get there. One of the virtues of a plan is that it is cheaper to build than the real solution would be. Therefore, architects start with blueprints rather than concrete, and writers plan a twenty-page paper before they write. As an inexpensive representation of your solution, a plan lets you test and discard ideas as you work. So a good plan needs to be detailed enough to test, but *cheap enough to throw away.*

Minsky's Maxim may be right—any plan is better than no plan. But some plans are also a lot better than others. For instance, compare these two plans:

Topic-Based Plan	*Goal-Based Plan*
I'm going to write a paper on the psychological effects of noise.	I'm going to show my readers (college students and professors) how noise can affect their mood and productivity. Then I'll use the research I've found to suggest strategies people can use to cope with noise.
One effect is. . . . Another effect is. . . . Effect #101 is. . . .	That means I'll want to start with a vivid demonstration of how noise actually affects us, then survey the history of the study of noise. . . .

One of the chief virtues of setting goals is that it lets you cut enormous problems down to size. So instead of covering the topic of noise, you choose the information you need in order to meet your goals. Traditional outlines are often merely topic-based plans, or arrangements of information, unrelated to the writer's goals. Figuring out your goals is obviously more difficult than just naming or outlining a topic (for example, "I'm writing about noise"). But of the two procedures, it's the one that will actually help you write. Outlines, especially premature ones, are often dominated by the structure of the available information (all the things that could be said about noise), whereas a goal-based plan is governed by the writer (what *you* want or need to say to explain a new idea, stimulate your reader, or perhaps change his or her mind). Frequently, an outline is a list of the topics you might want to cover in your paper, whereas a goal-based plan is an expression of what you want to do by writing.

Look at planning as a goal-directed attempt to make two kinds of plans fit together: plans for what you want **to do** and plans for what you want **to say.**

✏ Strategy 1   MAKE A PLAN **TO DO** AND A PLAN **TO SAY**

In the case study of Joan in Chapter 3, we imagined her group of goals. A practical planning technique is to actually sketch your own plan for what you want **to do**—an outline of your goals and your plan for achieving them. The special feature of this kind of outline is that instead of focusing on your topic, it focuses on what you want to do with the information you have.

Figure 5-1   *Goal-based plan for a letter of application*

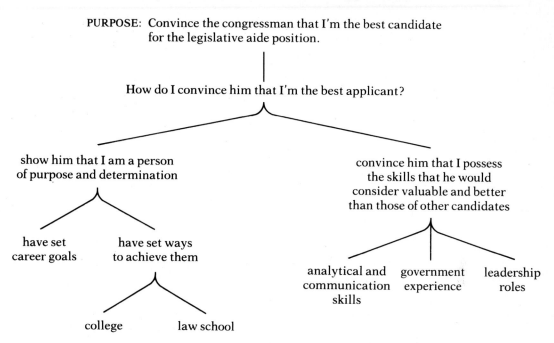

PURPOSE: Convince the congressman that I'm the best candidate for the legislative aide position.

How do I convince him that I'm the best applicant?

show him that I am a person of purpose and determination

convince him that I possess the skills that he would consider valuable and better than those of other candidates

have set career goals

have set ways to achieve them

analytical and communication skills

government experience

leadership roles

college

law school

Start by writing down one of your top-level goals: What do you expect this piece of writing to do for you? Think of the text as a stand-in actor that will go to the reader in your place. What exactly do you want the reader to see, to think, or to do?

Figure 5-1 shows a plan sketched out by a college student who wanted to get a summer job as a legislative aide. Instead of merely listing his courses and extracurricular activities ("I want to describe things I've done"), he established a goal ("I want to convince the congressman I'm the best candidate"). He then made the goal operational by exploring *how* he could convince the congressman. Notice how he used the facts about himself to create the effect he wanted to have. In his final letter of application, he began by showing how his desire to be a legislative aide was part of a larger career plan and how he had chosen his college and his courses in light of that career.

In making your own goal-based plan, ask yourself, "How am I going to accomplish my goals? What will I have to do?" The writer in the example spent some time figuring out how he could convince his congressman. In the process, he threw away a number of alternative plans, including one to describe his own student senate campaign and the crazy, successful stunts they pulled. It

Figure 5-2   *Preliminary sketch for a magazine article*

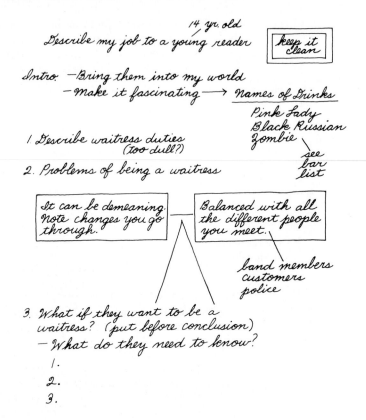

sounded, he decided, like a great plan for a story but a bad plan for convincing a congressman.

Once you have formed even a tentative plan for what you want **to do,** it is easier to start a plan for what you will need **to say.** Let the two kinds of planning feed on each other. A plan to do something lets you do a more goal-directed search of your own memory and other resources as you go after the information you will need. At other times, knowing something you wish **to say**—whether it is a key word, a good phrase, or a whole argument and set of facts—can help you see a potential new goal. Figure 5-2 is a nice example of how plans are a way of playing around with your ideas and considering things you might do. Sometimes, when you are trying to juggle many options and ideas in your head, it helps to express them visually on paper, whether you use flow charts, diagrams, trees (as in Figure 5-1), or just doodles and connecting lines. Figure 5-2 shows a plan sketched out by a writer as she began an article for *Seventeen* magazine on her job as a cocktail waitress. Notice how her plan combines both goals and content and how it visually indicates the structure of her ideas, revealing main points, supporting details, and a balance between the pros and cons of the job. Although the plan is very rough, you can see how the writer uses it to adapt her knowledge about the job to the needs and interests of her reader. This sketch is not just a simple printout or outline of the *information* she has stored about this job. It is the beginning of a plan for what to do with that information as a writer. A good plan contains both content and goals for using that content.

Plans take many forms, from mental notes to informal sketches done on the backs of old envelopes to well-developed written plans such as outlines and proposals. The most useful plans are ones that combine topic information (what you want **to say**) with goals and plans for using that information (what you want **to do**).

❧ Strategy 2   MAKE YOUR GOALS MORE OPERATIONAL

Let's suppose you have set up a goal: "I'm going to write a letter of application requesting a summer job." You realize that merely stating your request probably isn't enough. But what else can you do to meet your goal? To write that letter you need to make your goals more specific, or more operational. An operational statement is one that specifies actions—it tells you how to operate, what to do. For example, a more operational goal would be: "I'll try to arouse the reader's interest enough so that he or she will read my résumé, will remember at least two things about me, and will then ask me for an interview." Note that once you have established this set of subgoals or steps in accomplishing your overall goal, every paragraph in the letter you write will have a function. You will expect it to affect your reader in some specific ways, not just list the facts about you.

Goals that aren't operational are often highly abstract, such as: "I want to discuss team sports," "I'd like to impress my reader," "My aim is to do well in this course." They don't give you a clue about *how* to do it. Operational goals are more concrete and specify a set of separate subgoals you can achieve along the way. For example, compare these two goal statements, one abstract, the other with a set of operational subgoals.

1. I intend to become rich and famous.
2. I intend to study probability and statistics so I can get rich quickly in Las Vegas, then study writing and become famous by writing a best seller on how I did it.

We can apply this same process to writing. Let us suppose you were going to write a paper on the role of nonverbal communication in classrooms. In general, your goal is to be persuasive: "to convince the reader to see things my way." You might then define this more operationally as "I'll try to forcefully argue both sides of this controversy in order to show the reader that I have pinpointed the crucial issues and also to pave the way for my own ideas." For this particular paper you might then set up a number of subgoals such as:

1. Define nonverbal communication.
2. Use examples to show how it works in the classroom (perhaps putting this section at the beginning for dramatic effect).
3. Review the conflicting studies on whether or not a teacher's nonverbal communication can affect students' IQ or achievement scores.
4. Argue for your position, supporting it with your own observations of the specific ways children respond to nonverbal communication in the classroom (describe Head Start experiences).

When do you need to use this strategy and make your plan more "operational"? Maybe never. An operational plan, like a good road map, lets you decide where to turn next. But sometimes you don't need a map. You may want to start out with a good intuition or a rather vague goal and wait to see what comes out when you write. Plunging in can open the door to discovery. But it can also get you lost. This strategy of *trying to be operational*—of trying to figure how you might reach your goals—is particularly valuable under three circumstances. One is, of course, at the beginning when you want to make a good plan as useable as possible. The second is when you feel momentarily stuck or uncertain. That feeling is a signal to look at your plan (not at the word or sentence you may be stuck on) and try to spell out how such a plan could operate, what you might do next. A third time to get operational is when you want to think over your own options for a given assignment, as in the situation below.

The students who wrote the papers on time management discussed earlier had a number of practical strategies for doing this assignment. Let me describe in an operational way four strategies which I observed writers using in this read-to-write assignment and ask you to compare the costs and benefits of these plans for yourself.

Some students used a familiar "gist and list" strategy. To do this you go through the readings to find key words and figure out the "gist" or main idea of each passage. Once you have notes that summarize each authority, you use this list of "gists" to write your paper, maybe adding comments of your own as you go along or at the end of the paper. In class, we began to call this the "efficiency" strategy. Do you see some costs and benefits? Will this strategy help you learn the material? Yet what role does this "operational" plan give to your own ideas? What would a reader who liked a "gist and list" paper have to want?

Other students used a strategy we named the "TIA" strategy, for the words True, Important, and I Agree. To use this method, you go through the readings looking, not for the gist, but for ideas that seem True, Important, or ones with which you Agree. You pick out ideas you find interesting or relevant, even if they are not related to each other or to the author's main idea. From this pool of TIA ideas you write your paper, commenting on what you found interesting. Taken alone the TIA won't let you write a synthesis, but it can build a foundation.

One problem with the TIA way of planning a paper is that it can lead a writer simply *to select familiar ideas* without thinking over contradictions to those ideas, evidence for or against them, or what the authors in the source are trying to say. So some students we observed added a "dialogue" strategy in which they would argue with the text in their own thoughts. They would think about their own experience, pull in other information, and talk to the author. And then they would let the author talk back, as they tried to imagine another point of view. For instance, a student might "dialogue" with William James by thinking, "Yeah, that is true, it's like getting a second wind when I'm running. But it doesn't always work—if it's 3:00 A.M., you don't remember what you read even if you do push on because you aren't alert. But maybe if he means mental fatigue, not lack of sleep, then this would make sense." Notice how the dialogue lets you include your own ideas and still come up with a more balanced and qualified response. (Notice the little words such as "true," "but," "if," "maybe," "sometimes, but not always," "then," and "because." These are signals that you are building a more conditional, qualified, balanced idea of what is "true." Look for them in your own thinking and in your prose.)

Finally, a few students added a "constructive" strategy to their planning. In addition to selecting ideas they wanted to use, they spent some time actually thinking about their goals for the paper and what might be a good way to get to those goals. As one writer said to himself part way through: "Unless I just restate a lot of this stuff, talk about the fact that, you know, it is important. . . . But that's not what they want. They want me to assimilate this, to come up with some conclusions—and I guess they should be related to something. So . . . Yeah, I'm gonna deal with the problem, yeah, the problem of how to attack time management. This is good."

When you spend time like this writer thinking about your options, about how to construct a paper, and how to guide your own process, you have just made your goals more operational. Does the benefit of planning seem worth the cost?

⤎ Strategy 3   LISTEN TO INTUITION AND CHANGE YOUR PLAN

Do the examples of planning you have seen so far look more rational and neat than your plans look (even given the fact that a textbook must be as clear as possible)? Or have you found that even when you had a well-developed plan, like those in Strategy 1, that you still hit a roadblock part way into writing? If so, your experience is perfectly normal. In fact, experienced writers who use private mental dialogues and see their writing as part of the ongoing conversation Burke described in Chapter 1 expect changes, just as you expect a live conversation to affect your thinking. There are many paths to a good paper. Here are three common ones:

1. *Plan and write.* This path lets you start with the big picture, build a plan that takes your own goals and your reader into account, and carry out that good plan in writing. A good plan may only exist in your head and it may be messy and vague at spots, but it is a map that charts your journey.

2. *Plan, abandon, and replan.* However, if your rhetorical problem is complex or you have high standards for this paper, you are likely to take a different path. Although you started with a good plan and may have written part of the text, your intuition tells you it isn't going to work as you intended. Or perhaps you have discovered a new organizing idea or you realize your own purpose and goals have changed as the result of planning and writing. This is the point to abandon your plans, follow your intuition, and build a new and better plan to guide your writing. That new plan may even save some of the text you wrote or it may send you back to the drawing board. Plans are made to be abandoned when a better plan comes along.

3. *Write and then plan.* Sometimes the best course of action is simply to start writing. If the topic is new, if it seems perplexing, or if you are feeling blocked for one reason or another, use writing itself to discover what you might have to say about a topic. Techniques such as freewriting and brainstorming, discussed in Chapter 6, let you ignore matters such as spelling, complete sentences and even organization in order just to get your thoughts down in writing. Then, when you can look back at what you are thinking, build a plan based on your best ideas.

As you probably already know, the hardest part of pl
not getting plans or writing text, but being willing to
of them up when you discover things, as writers no
through writing.

⮜ Strategy 4   REVEAL YOUR PLAN TO THE READER

Having a good plan makes a paper easier to write. It also makes
it easier for a reader to read, particularly if you indicate your
plan early on. Revealing your plan is like showing the reader a
road map; it helps him or her follow the discussion, see your point,
and grasp the importance of what you are saying.

One of the best ways to do this is to open your paper with a
problem/purpose statement. Such a statement is a concise, informative introduction that does two things. First, it sets up the
problem, issue, or thesis on which you will focus. Second, it states
the purpose of your particular paper—that is, it tells the reader
what you are going to do with your topic and what he can expect
to get out of reading further. A good problem/purpose statement
not only informs but motivates. It convinces the reader that there
is a reason for what you have written—and a reason for him to
read it. As you can see, a problem/purpose statement simply combines the introductory problem definition, which was discussed
in Chapter 1, with a statement of your rhetorical purpose.

A problem/purpose statement is often simple and direct, as in
the examples below. It could be a paragraph or a page long; it
could be labeled "Introduction" or "Background," or it could just
come at the beginning. It might be embedded within a dramatic
example or an interesting lead-in to your discussion. The particular form your problem/purpose statement takes is not important. Just be sure the information is there, because your reader
will be looking for it.

Here are some sample beginnings of papers. The purpose statements are underscored. Notice that in Examples 2 and 3 the beginning sentences define a problem that the reader is also
concerned about. And Example 3 includes a preview of how the
paper is organized, giving the reader a helpful plan for reading.

A finished problem/purpose statement looks simple and
straightforward but is sometimes hard to write, for this reason:
In order to adapt your statement for the reader, you must switch
roles, from being a researcher to being a writer. For example, a
psychology student who has been researching the theories of Carl
Jung may discover, when formulating her purpose statement, that
her implicit purpose has been to "show all the things I know about
Jung." Yet she realizes that the intended reader, her professor,

will be less interested in the quantity of details she has accumulated than in whether she fully understands Jung's theories. A more realistic purpose for her paper would be "to show I have a clear grasp of Jung's concepts and can contrast them with several other important theories," and her revised statement should reflect this plan.

Problem/purpose statements help not only the reader but the writer. Working on a purpose statement can bring a writer back to the questions of "What is my goal?" and "Who is my reader?"—questions that should always govern the writing process. The importance of designing for a reader and writing reader-based prose will be discussed further in Chapters 9 and 10.

Writers use various conventions or text patterns to express their plan. Although the names for these text conventions often have more than one meaning, here are the standard terms:

The word **theme** is sometimes used to refer simply to the **topic** of the paper (for example, the theme of Chapter 9 in *Word Play* is naming). Other times the term theme refers to the **main point** or **gist.** It describes what you might want a reader to think or remember if they summed up your paper. This second, more complex definition of theme, which involves the writer's point of view or conclusion about the topic, is more useful.

The term **topic sentence** is used in the same two ways as "theme" when talking about paragraphs. Sometimes a topic sentence simply announces the topic (such as, "Dictionaries work in many ways"). At other times it states the gist or point the writer wanted to make *about* the topic (as in, "Despite what most people believe, dictionaries do not give 'meanings' of words, but present 'meaning' by offering a selection of synonymous words and phrases").

The term **purpose** can refer to a conventional purpose—such as describe, argue, define, and so on—or it can refer to the unique rhetorical purpose behind a given text or even a given paragraph (for example, "I want to show why a dictionary definition fails to capture a word's 'meaning in use' ").

In general, readers want to know the topic, the theme or point of the text, and the writer's purpose as soon as possible. If this information isn't actually stated, they will infer it, even though they may guess wrong. If your prose is clear and under control, your reader should be able to state both the gist of what you have to say and your thesis or major claim. To make sure that readers get these things right, writers depend on three standard text conventions.

One is the familiar **topic sentence** that gives the gist of the paragraph. The second is the **thesis statement** that not only states the writer's claim or thesis, but signals the reader that this claim is the major one. Some of the most common signals include putting the thesis statement in the form of an assertion, putting it at the end of an introductory paragraph, or putting it at the end of a "Some people think, but, in fact . . ." argument. (We will discuss the process of building a thesis in more detail in Chapter 8.)

The third convention, shown in these examples, is the problem/purpose statement. A **problem/purpose statement** is a specific sentence (or group of sentences) in the text which lays out the problem or issue under discussion and reveals what the writer proposes to do in this paper. As with the thesis statement and topic sentence, writers use various conventions of placement and wording to help the reader recognize the problem/purpose statement. (We will look at problem definitions in more detail in Chapter 8.)

Do these three text conventions ever appear in the same sentence? A writer could simply assert a thesis without defining a problem or indicating the purpose of the paper. In that case, there would be no overlap. But if the writer's main purpose were to explore, evaluate, or argue for a given thesis (as in Example 1 below), then the problem/purpose statement might contain a statement of that thesis within it. Notice how the underlined statement in Example 1 presents the problem or conflict that sparked this whole discussion, a thesis about German art and politics, and an indication of the purpose which will organize the essay (to understand why people followed Hitler) and a purpose which might motivate us to read (to have a more complete history). But also notice how the first and second paragraphs begin with their own, more local topic sentences about political movements and the role of artistic images. Each of these could have been the thesis for an entire essay—but they weren't. Could you as a reader have picked out the problem, purpose, and thesis if it hadn't been underlined?

Example 1   *Essay for a Course in Western Civilization*

```
           Wagnerian Opera in Hitler's Germany


      Political movements often seem abstract to the peo-
ple who live during them.  For that reason, people will
often view the movement in terms of some specific image,
often an image of a group of people.  For example, peo-
ple who lived in the northern United States during the
1850s and 1860s tended to see the problems of the time
```

in terms of slavery, as described in Uncle Tom's Cabin, rather than in terms of economics. In the same way, Germans during the 1920s and 1930s found it easier to think of Germany's economic problems as being caused by an international conspiracy headed by Jews rather than as being caused by a world-wide depression.

The images people use to understand the times they live in are often provided by artists and musicians. Sometimes the artists create these images spontaneously and deliberately, as Wagner did in his operas during the mid-1800s. At other times, a government may choose an image that it likes, as Hitler chose Wagner's mythic images of the German people—fifty years after Wagner's death. Either way, the artists and the images they create give people specific symbols to which they can attach their feelings about social problems, and which they can use in deciding how to act. In this way, artists help people to participate in the events of their time. The pictures of heroic-looking soldiers and vicious Jews created by Hitler's artists increased anti-Semitic feeling in Germany. At the same time, Hitler's personal friendship with the revered Wagner family linked him and his growing war machine with musical images of Aryan supremacy. Thus, Hitler's patronage of Wagner's operas encouraged the German people to see themselves as direct descendants of the gods and heroes in those operas. <u>Although it may seem incongruous to discuss a political movement such as the Third Reich in terms of the art it encouraged, no history of the Reich can be complete without such a discussion, because without it we cannot fully understand why the German people followed Hitler into World War II.</u>

Example 2   *Report to the College Placement Director*

Many students perform poorly in job interviews even though they are skilled in their subject area and well qualified for the job. The most frequent problem in such interviews is that students are unnerved by certain kinds of questions. Although they can answer any technical questions concerning their field of study, they have difficulty answering questions about personal motives, weaknesses, and strengths. In addition, they

lack experience in interviewing situations. The purpose
of this paper is <u>to propose a program for giving stu-</u>
<u>dents an introductory experience in interviewing and an-</u>
<u>swering the personal questions interviewers regularly</u>
<u>ask.</u>

Example 3   ***Guide to Dealing with Rent Hikes***

Recent inflation has created an increased conflict
between realtors and tenants in our area. Landlords
need higher rents to pay for rising costs and to make a
profit from their business. Tenants are also faced with
increasing prices and want to keep rents as low as possible. When landlords raise rents sharply, tenants are
faced with the problem of deciding how to react, since
no action is itself a response.

The tenants' reaction to a rent hike consists of two
steps: (1) making the right choice among the alternative
actions available, and (2) given that choice, executing
it in the best possible way. This report <u>explores the</u>
<u>tenants' options, the factors to consider in choosing an</u>
<u>option, and the procedures tenants should follow for</u>
<u>each kind of response.</u>

PROJECTS AND ASSIGNMENTS

In doing the writing assignments below, use this chapter to help you
begin your plan, but as you work, you may also wish to read the chapters
on generating and organizing ideas which follow.

1 In responding to the "mystery texts" on pp. 77–78, some students
found that they assumed that "academic writing" was, by nature,
"stuffy, boring, bland, limited, strictly factual, impersonal, and not
creative." If you have to do academic writing, this is a pretty discouraging image of the task. Do you think this image is *necessarily*
true? Do some of the features of academic discourse, for instance,
work quite well for "insiders" but not for new readers?

If you could imagine an "ideal academic essay," that could be written by a student and also meet the needs of the academic discourse
community, what would it be like? Use a text (from an academic
journal, a textbook, or a student paper) to help you describe your
ideal by supplying examples of features you would keep or change.
See if you can convince other students and your instructor that your
ideal version is the one worth writing.

[Here, by the way, are the sources of the mystery texts: (1.) An undergraduate student's paper based on readings on revision. (2.) A graduate student's paper on the same readings. (3.) A report from a collaborative research project on revision by Linda Flower, John R. Hayes, Linda Carey, Karen Schriver, and James Stratman (all teachers and researchers) published as "Detection, Diagnosis and the Strategies of Revision" in *College Composition and Communication* 37 (Feb. 1986), p. 16. (4.) A paper titled "Pre-Text and Composing" also published in *CCC* [38 (Dec. 1987), p. 397] by Stephen Witte (who is a researcher, teacher and also the editor of another scholarly journal, *Written Communication*). (5.) From an interview with the novelist Alberto Moravia in *Writers at Work: The Paris Review Interviews*, ed. Malcolm Cowley (NY: Viking Press, 1957), p. 220. (6.) From the Education section of *Newsweek* (Jan. 27, 1986) in an article titled "Why Johnny Can't Reason," signed by William D. Marabach with Connie Leslie in New York and bureau reports.]

2 Rewrite one of the mystery texts on pp. 77–78 (or a short piece of your own) to belong to a different kind of discourse: adapt the format, the voice, the purpose, and conventions you use for a different group of readers. Test your old and new mystery texts on real readers: Can they guess the type of writing from your samples; can they spot the original? Keep notes on the decisions you made in order to revise and on the clues your readers used to predict who was who. Discuss what you now see as the key features of "academic writing."

3 Look back at a paper you have written for another class. Use the Read-to-Write list of options on p. 80 to analyze what you did. Did you make some choices consciously on that paper and just assume others; what were the costs and benefits of your decision?

4 Give yourself the task of interpreting a text by using it for your own purpose. Read your source text, and instead of summarizing or synthesizing what the author(s) said, try to apply whatever seems relevant in the sources to understanding a problem you bring or to carrying out a purpose of your own. Try to signal your purpose to the reader in your problem/purpose statement and stick to that purpose by making each paragraph contribute to your plan. (To create a realistic academic conversation, your instructor may suggest an issue or sources that could be shared with your class. But the purpose of this paper is up to you.)

5 Explain the following assignments by translating them into actions you might take as a writer.

Name an economic liberal and explain why and how his ideas place him in the category of liberals.

Analyze the meaning of the raft in *Huckleberry Finn*.

In what ways did the Romantic movement affect nineteenth- and early twentieth-century society?

"Although history is often seen in terms of great individuals, looking at it in that way can give a seriously distorted understanding of the time and events in which that individual participated." Discuss this statement as it applies to Napoleon Bonaparte.

6   *Checklist: A Problem/Purpose Statement.* Write a problem/purpose statement and ask someone else to role-play the part of your intended reader. Have him (or her) respond by telling you what he would want from such a paper and what your statement has led him to expect. Or evaluate your statement using the checklist below.

□a. Have you defined a problem, a critical issue, or a thesis on which your paper will focus?

□b. Have you told the reader the purpose of your paper?

□c. Have you given the reader any preview of how your paper is organized, any road map for reading?

7   Good ideas and better plans have a habit of developing while you are writing a draft. Can you help this writer out? Here is her initial problem/purpose statement.

> In a discussion of "linguistic chauvinism," Peter Farb asserts that "English is a sexist language" and many of his examples show sexual bias in the university (p. 142). He also shows how other linguists dispute whether this bias exists or if it is a serious problem. However, student writers have to evaluate the implications of these different viewpoints. If they hope to reach an audience that includes a significant number of women (including professors and other students) they need to learn ways to express their thoughts that do not "make women invisible."

This seems like a good beginning, however, because this writer made a planning tape (as described in Chapter 2), we can see how her plan developed.

> I'm ready to take a break and I find I'm having a lot of trouble getting my paper to hold together. As I've been writing I've gradually decided that what I'm trying to say here is that I agree with Farb's basic argument, but I think he stops short. Let's see, when was this written . . . oh, 1974. Oh, . . . he just seems to throw up his hands at some point and say language can't change the system. It's like the system has to change first. There's nothing you can do. And I think that ignores some . . . some good alternatives for avoiding sexist language. And that seems to be what I have ended up writing about most, all the alternatives. Yeah, that's the point. I guess my focus has just changed. Now what?

Can you help this writer take advantage of her expanded sense of the problem? Rewrite or expand her initial paragraph and problem/purpose statement to include this new view of the problem and to make it preview both sets of ideas.

8 In his book *Word Play* (New York: Knopf, 1974, p. 6) Peter Farb says that "The language game shares certain characteristics with all other true games." He names five characteristics of a language game: (1.) It has a minimum of two players. (2.) Social pressure may force even bystanders to play. (3.) Something must be at stake for both players. (4.) Players are usually distinguished by their particular style and by their ability to shift styles if needed (as in shifting from formal to folksy speech). (5.) Finally, like all games it is structured by rules people learn unconsciously as part of a discourse community (such as who speaks when, what not to say, how to make your point, and expressions or attitudes that show you are an insider).

How well does this theory fit your experience of language in action? Write a paper in which you interpret and apply Farb's ideas to this question. Think of a language game in which you are relatively expert (such as, talking like an insider about music and musicians, about football, feminism, or computers) or take an everyday game such as counseling friends or negotiating with parents, roommates, teachers, or dates. Play the game to get a fresh observation and some notes, then use Farb's five rules to help you analyze the language game you just played. Keep at least two purposes in mind as you write your paper: try to explain your own language game to an outsider and try to test Farb's theory. Address your paper to other people in this academic conversation who have also read Farb and wondered about his theory.

(As a journal entry, you might wish to keep notes on how your task representation of this assignment develops as you work. These notes will help you on assignments in Chapter 8.)

IF YOU WOULD LIKE TO READ MORE

If you would like to know more about the nature of plans and exploring your rhetorical problem, see:

Flower, Linda, and John R. Hayes. "The Cognition of Discovery: Defining a Rhetorical Problem." *College Composition and Communication* 31 (February 1980) 21–32. / This study compares the ways in which experienced and novice writers define their own rhetorical problems.

Miller, George, Eugene Galanter, and Karl Pribram. *Plans and the Structure of Behavior.* New York: Holt, 1960. / This stimulating book shows the manner in which planning works as a moment-to-moment feature of everyday thinking.

chapter six

Generating Ideas

STEP 3   GENERATE new ideas

Use the strategies of creative thinking to explore your own knowledge. Your goal is to discover useful ideas stored in your memory and to create new ideas by forging connections among the old.

Strategy 1   TURN OFF THE EDITOR AND BRAINSTORM

Strategy 2   TALK TO YOUR READER

Strategy 3   SYSTEMATICALLY EXPLORE YOUR TOPIC

Strategy 4   REST AND INCUBATE

Generating and organizing ideas are like two sides of a coin. They represent two different kinds of thinking every writer needs to do. In this chapter we will take up creative thinking, which is a form of mental *play:* It asks you to plunge into the problem and seek out ideas without trying to edit or tidy them up. This sort of energetic intellectual play lets you be a more creative and productive thinker. Compared to the method of grinding a paper out, creative play can do three things. First, it helps a writer break his or her mental "set" and get out of those well-worn thought patterns that often stifle new ideas. Second, it captures those elusive intuitions that are often censored and lost when a writer only pays attention to fully formed ideas. Finally, it helps a writer to draw inferences and discover new, surprising connections among his or her own ideas.

If creative thinking is a form of *play*, organizing ideas (which we will discuss in the next chapter) is a way to *push* your ideas for all they are worth. Organizing is equally powerful because it lets you work in a systematic, logical way to test out ideas, determine their implications, and fit them into a meaningful whole.

And planning, as we have discussed, lets you create the goals that direct both the generation and organization of your ideas. Taken together, planning, generating, and organizing form a creative trio. Good writers constantly shift back and forth from one mode of thought to another as they work on a problem. In the heat of writing you can remind yourself to switch strategies by remembering this three-step formula: plan, play, push.

STEP 3   GENERATE New Ideas

The four strategies discussed in this chapter cover a wide range of creative techniques. They range from the goal-directed–anything-goes process of brainstorming to the venerable rhetorical method of Aristotle's "topics" and the modern systematic art of tagmemics, to end finally in the only too pleasurable strategy of "rest and incubate." The point of this chapter is simple: There are many ways to get good ideas, and the more alternative strategies you know and can use, the better.

⏎ *Strategy 1*   TURN OFF THE EDITOR AND BRAINSTORM

Once you have a sense of your goal and the problem before you, brainstorming is a good way to jump in. Brainstorming is a form of creative, goal-directed play. Your brainstorming can take any form you wish, whether it is jotting down notes such as we saw in the planning chapter, or writing out fragments or even whole passages, as long as your goal is to energetically generate ideas.

My writing inevitably starts with brainstorming. I sit down with clean paper—a fair pile of it—good pencils, and some time officially set aside for just brainstorming. I have no obligation to produce prose, not even a draft. I'm just trying to think up a storm and get down all the things that seem relevant to my problem. Sometimes I just produce notes and a plan, sometimes I write out whole sections of the discussion as I follow a train of thought. For some reason, knowing that all you have to do is brainstorm for the next half hour or so makes it easier to get started even when you have small blocks of time. And I often find that I have written some important pieces of the paper when I am done. At the very least, I have a better image of the territory I want to cover.

The purpose of brainstorming is to stimulate creative thought, so as a procedure it has three rules that try to protect those half-formed suggestive ideas we often censor. The first rule then is: Don't censor any possibilities—just write them down. When you come up with an idea or a phrase that isn't quite right, resist the temptation to throw it out and start again. Just write it down. You may come back later and see what it really meant.

The second rule is: Don't try to write "polished prose" when you are brainstorming. Don't stop to perfect spelling, grammar, or even phrasing. Keep working at the level of ideas whether you are jotting notes, drawing sketches, or writing out a monologue as you talk to yourself.

Finally, try to keep your eye on the question or the problem you have set for yourself. Brainstorming is not free association; it is a goal-directed effort to discover ideas relevant to your problem. So when your flow of thought begins to slow down or dry up, don't worry about having lost your "flow" or inspiration. Associative flows always dry up eventually. Just ask yourself, "What else do I want to consider here; what else do I know?" Then return to the problem at hand.

Brainstorming is a goal-directed search for ideas. This is what makes it different from either freewriting or writing a first draft. In writing a draft, you are always under pressure from your draft to start from the most recent paragraph and extend the current text, even if you have hit a dead end. The text locks you into its own pattern very early. Freewriting, as its name says, is a freely associative technique rather than a goal-directed one. It depends on the rich associative power of words to unlock new connections.

If you are writing an essay, especially one that explores your own thoughts and feelings, freewriting can be another excellent way to get started. In freewriting, you try to write out whatever comes to mind just as though you were taking dictation from your imagination. But keep in mind that freewriting is not the same as writing a draft. It is a technique for generating ideas that has its own rules: Start with the topic that is on your mind and begin to write. Don't worry about correctness, but do keep writing. In fact, if you go blank, just keeping writing "I feel a blank" until something comes. Let the words tumble out and let associations come as you use your own words to elicit other words and ideas. Then—and this is the crucial step—go back to that rambling text and try to discover your key ideas and build a new gist out of your own writing.

Freewriting is especially valuable when you feel blocked or when you feel insecure about your writing or your ability to say anything sensible on the topic. At such times, simply tell yourself to sit down and write for 10 minutes by the clock, writing whatever comes. By letting your thoughts wander in the storehouse of your memory, calling on the enormous associative power of words, freewriting often offers amazing proof of what you do have to say and gets the process started again. Bear in mind that it is often hard to edit associative freewriting into a paper. So use it as the basis for writing a new, more focused draft and as a smart technique to get yourself going, even when you are feeling stumped.

➤ Strategy 2 TALK TO YOUR READER

People often come up with their best ideas and most powerful arguments when they are engaged in a face-to-face discussion. You can give yourself this same advantage by acting out such a discussion in your own mind, especially if you play all the parts. Everyone has a natural ability to play various roles, such as the role of the "mature and responsible person" we try to project at a job interview. And with a little thought, we can play the role of our interviewer as well. That is, we can switch parts, take on a hard-nosed, "show me" attitude, and carry on our own simulated discussion.

You can use role-playing to help you get better ideas and *to get them down in words.* Instead of staring at blank paper, imagine yourself walking into your reader's office: You have three minutes to tell this person what you have to say, and you want to make him or her listen. So talk it out and write it down. Or, imagine yourself giving a lecture to fifteen high school students who can't wait to talk back. As you go along, simulate the responses of your various readers and listeners: Make them ask you questions (basic and difficult ones), raise objections, or make their own interpretations. For example, what would your reader's first response probably be, and what would you say back to him? To get extra power out of this technique, give yourself different audiences with distinct expectations: a professor or supervisor listening carefully to your logic, a prospective employer looking to see what you can offer her, an enthusiastic audience of beginners sitting in on your lecture, or a friend listening to you over a cup of coffee.

This technique works for two reasons. First, by putting you in a realistic situation with a "live audience" it helps you choose the things you *need* to say out of all the things you *could* say. Secondly, it lets you switch to a "talk" strategy, muttering to yourself as you walk around the room, instead of trying to write finished prose. Whenever you do this, you may have to edit the result a little later. But you are reducing some of the constraints on yourself, and the words and ideas should flow more easily.

SYSTEMATICALLY EXPLORE YOUR TOPIC

Ever since Aristotle, people have been devising ways to think systematically about complex topics. In classical rhetoric this was called the art of invention. Conducting a systematic exploration of your topic has two important advantages. First, it leads you to see your topic from various points of view, many of which would never have occurred to you. That is, it leads you to see new connections and invent new ideas. Secondly, a powerful systematic procedure not only directs your attention by asking questions but it asks the right questions. For example, the familiar "Who? What? Where? When? Why? How?" formula of journalism leads you to the heart of an event by asking you to consider its most important features.

We are going to look briefly at three systematic approaches to the art of invention: Aristotelian topics, modern tagmemics, and the use of analogy. Like any serious systematic procedure, these methods work best when you understand and know them well. In-depth coverage of the methods is outside the scope of this book; my purpose is simply to introduce each approach and the kinds of questions it asks, then indicate where you could learn more.

Imagine the following situation. You are working on a paper about reading strategies and have already done a good deal of research and thinking about reading itself. You've decided to focus on the notion of the "active reader" and want to systematically explore everything you know about the subject. Let us see how each of our three methods of exploration could be used in approaching your problem.

First, consider Aristotelian "topics." *The Rhetoric* of Aristotle was designed to instruct public speakers of fourth-century Greece in what Aristotle called the "available means of persuasion." Taken together, these patterns of argument are called the "topics." Each "topic" represents a way of organizing ideas, or arguing for a position that most listeners will find logical or persuasive. As you will see from even this short list, Aristotle's "topics" cover some of the basic ways people think about a subject and organize their ideas. Here is how a writer might use the "topics" to explore the subject of the "active reader."

Aristotle's "Topics"	Ideas
Definition	Active reading is a constructive process in which a person seeks information and builds a coherent meaning from a text.
Comparison and contrast	It is unlike passive reading, in which the reader works on the

	principle of the sponge, trying to absorb each word or sentence in the hope that it will all make sense in the end.
Cause and effect	Active reading leads to greater comprehension because the reader is actively hooking each new idea to things he or she already knows.
Support from evidence	A number of studies show that even brief training in active reading increases both speed and comprehension of complex prose.

A modern method for systematic thinking is called *tagmemics*. It is a powerful tool for analysis because it is both simple and comprehensive. This method is built on the premise that one of the best ways to understand the true nature of a thing is to see it from various perspectives. In particular, it helps to look at your problem or subject as a *particle* (a thing in itself), as a *wave* (something that changes over time), and as part of a *field* (an element within a larger context). Although simple on the surface, tagmemics is a rich and complex approach to generating ideas and well worth learning. With regard to our subject it could lead us to observations such as these:

The Three Perspectives of Tagmemics	*Ideas*
See your topic as a particle (as a thing in itself)	Active reading is made up of a number of processes, including previewing the text to set up expectations and questions that reading will fulfill; searching for key information as one reads; summarizing the gist of the passage to oneself; and making connections as one reads.
See your topic as a wave (a thing changing over time)	The method of active reading changes with the difficulty of the text and individual passages. Skimming often works for newspapers, but with textbooks, active readers switch from fast previewing and brisk reading of introductions and examples, to slow, careful reading and summarizing of difficult passages.

See your topic as part of a field (as a thing in its context)	Active reading is part of the larger process of comprehension, which includes not only recording new information but integrating it into the elaborate patterns of knowledge the reader already possesses. Active reading makes these intellectual processes more accurate and efficient.

The third technique we will look at depends on the generative power of analogies. It has a simple basic premise that much research on the psychology of creativity supports: namely, one of the best ways to understand a new problem is to see an analogy between it and things you already know. One systematic method that uses analogies, called *synectics*, was developed by a think-tank group of inventors, artists, and psychologists who were trying to find creative new solutions to practical problems. Using synectics, a group or individual tries to generate four kinds of analogies to the problem at hand: personal analogies, direct analogies, symbolic analogies, and fantasy analogies. By its very nature, the approach leads you to come up with offbeat, impossible ideas in the hope of finding one startling new insight.

The Four Analogies of Synectics	*Ideas*
Personal analogy (imagine you are the topic or the solution to a problem)	As an active reader I see myself trying to make each idea my own personal possession. Or it is as if I were trying to explain the text to a child who kept asking questions.
Direct analogy (compare it to something concrete)	It's like using an erector set to build a structure (of meaning). The author gave me the materials and a blueprint, but I built the final structure.
Symbolic analogy (compare it to an abstract principle)	Active reading works on the principle that for every action (the author's), there is a separate and equal reaction (the reader's).
Fantasy analogy (anything goes)	It's like walking right inside the writer's head and getting him or her to answer your questions (even if the author helped draft the questions you want to ask).

Another mode of thinking-by-analogy is simply to change your vocabulary: Use the language and concepts from one area you know to understand another. Say your problem is to analyze what your college has to offer, but the college catalog vocabulary of "intellectual community" and "integrated programs" doesn't let you say what you want. If you are familiar with systems engineering, you might assess your college in terms of its work flow and productivity. Or you might switch to the outlook and special language of marketing, asking such questions as "What 'commodities' do colleges typically promise to deliver?" and "How could one test the college's 'advertising claims'?" Often a change in your vocabulary will bring about a change in your "idea set," or way of viewing the problem. By changing terms you tap different pockets of your own knowledge.

⤝ Strategy 4   REST AND INCUBATE

Sometimes this can be the most productive strategy of all, but only if you do it correctly. That is, before you stop work, make sure you have formulated the next unsolved problem you want to be thinking about. There needs to be something in the "incubator" if it's going to hatch.

People agree that incubation works; nobody understands quite why. The folklore is that your unconscious mind goes to work and solves the problem while you sleep. A more recent explanation of the process says that before people explore a problem in detail, they often create a rather limited or ineffective plan for solving it. Working on the problem, they learn a great deal that doesn't fit into their original plan. What happens in incubation is that people simply *forget* or abandon their old, inadequate plan and are then able to take advantage of all they've learned. For example, after working on the problem and doing a first draft, they come back to their writing with a new, more powerful plan that can work.

Incubation, then, is a strategy you can actively use. Sometimes even half an hour can make a difference. So starting a paper early is a practical decision; otherwise you simply lose the benefit of one of the easiest strategies available, and you will probably spend more actual time on the paper. When you use incubation, keep two points in mind: Return to your unfinished business from time to time so as to keep it *actively* simmering in the back of your mind; then, when a new idea or connection comes to you, *write it down.* Most experienced writers carry around note cards of some sort for just this purpose. Don't expect inspiration to knock twice.

PROJECTS AND ASSIGNMENTS

1 Hold an in-class workshop to try out the idea-generating strategies described in Step 3. Working in a group or with a friend, try out each of the strategies on some common problem. For example, you might take this as your problem: "Writing is a lot like talking, yet many people who can tell you something have trouble writing it. Why? In particular, why is it that even students who know the material thoroughly have trouble writing papers in college?"

☐a. *Brainstorming.* You are the member of a think-tank or professional problem-solving group. Use brainstorming and try to come up with fifteen good ideas on the problem within the next 5 minutes. Don't just jot down code words, but try to explain briefly what each idea means.

☐b. *Talking to the reader.* Break up into two groups to generate ideas for a reader. For example, if your problem were "Why Writing Is Difficult," you could tell the group that they have a late paper and must prepare a statement for a professor explaining why writing is difficult. Let the other group decide what they would say about the same problem to a friend. Then compare your two sets of ideas. Are they different? How?

☐c. *Systematic exploration.* Break into three groups and analyze a common topic from the three different perspectives of Aristotle's "topics," tagmemics, and analogy. Use each of these systematic methods to create new ideas and develop insight into your subject. Then compare your results. What would you say are the special strengths of each method?

2 Use the creative thinking strategies of Step 3 to write a paper that explores both sides of an issue. Choose an issue about which you yourself have conflicting feelings: for example, the value of grades versus a pass-fail system, the decision to ask a friend out on a date, or the choice of a profession. In one form or another, use all four strategies discussed in this chapter to generate ideas and argue both sides of your question.

3 After you have done Assignment 2, compare your notes from each strategy to your final text. Write a brief commentary on which strategies did the most (or the least) for you and why.

IF YOU WOULD LIKE TO READ MORE

If you would like to know more about creativity and other strategies for generating ideas, see:

Aristotle, *The Rhetoric*. Trans. Lane Cooper. New York: Appleton-Century-Crofts, 1932. / This is the work that established the study of systematic idea generation called, in classical rhetoric, the art of invention. Aristotle's "topics" are still powerful.

Gordon, William. *Synectics: The Development of Creative Capacity*. New York: Harper & Row, 1961. / This book describes how the system of synectics was developed and has proved its worth in industry, both as a way of producing new inventions and as a method for creative problem solving.

Young, Richard, Alton Becker, and Kenneth Pike. *Rhetoric: Discovery and Change*. New York: Harcourt Brace Jovanovich, 1970. / A groundbreaking work in the field of rhetoric, this book presents the tagmemic method for exploring complex problems.

chapter seven

Organizing Ideas

STEP 4 ORGANIZE your ideas

Use these strategies to develop and focus your ideas. Your goal is to turn good intuitions into precise, well-developed ideas that you can express in clear, logical relationships to one another.

Strategy 1 EXPAND YOUR OWN CODE WORDS

Strategy 2 NUTSHELL YOUR IDEAS AND TEACH THEM

Strategy 3 BUILD AN ISSUE TREE

Getting good ideas is half the battle. The other half is making sense out of what you know. The techniques we discussed in Chapter 6 will help you generate a wealth of ideas, but sometimes those ideas will seem more like intuitions than clearly stated arguments. Or they will be in the form of key words or brief notes to yourself that you will have to flesh out in detail for a reader to understand. And sometimes you will end up with a rich but unfocused body of ideas whose only organization is the order in which they occurred to you. This chapter will help you turn such intuitions into clearly stated ideas and then organize and develop those ideas into a logical, well-supported argument.

STEP 4 **ORGANIZE Your Ideas**

Each strategy in this chapter suggests ways you can use your own plans, notes, or drafts to develop and organize your ideas. Strategy 1 helps you expand your own loaded expressions into a more meaningful discussion, while Strategy 2 helps you pull key points or concepts out of such a discussion. Strategy 3 gives ideas for organizing all these elements in a clear, logical way. And, as you will notice, these strategies help you start taking your reader into account, even as you explore and organize what you know.

← Strategy 1   EXPAND YOUR OWN CODE WORDS

Many times writers find that their important, key words in a passage are really "code words." That is, these words carry a great deal of meaning for the writer that they would not carry for the average reader.

For example, what does the expression "problem solving" mean to you? To some people it means nothing more than the process of doing an algebra problem. But for me, "problem solving" is not only a basic thinking procedure that gets people through everyday life but a process that leads to bursts of creative thinking and new insight. And it is also a branch of psychology.

Thus, for me the term evokes a large, complex network of ideas. But just because "problem solving" is a loaded expression for me— a code word I think with—I cannot simply use it and expect most of my readers to fully understand me, to make the same connections I make. When I use such code words, I must explain and develop the meaning I really have in mind.

A writer's code words can be jargon, special terms such as "problem solving," or simply complex concepts such as "persona" that some readers wouldn't understand. But often they are merely abstractions, as in the remark "He has a very interesting job." Here "interesting" is a kind of mental shorthand that stands for a body of related ideas—ideas that may be evident to the writer but are unlikely to be perceived by the reader. In fact, such words may sound like nothing more than vague generalizations or hot air.

Your own code words, then, can sometimes create a problem because they mean much more than they actually express. However, they can also open the door to a very effective strategy for developing and focusing your ideas. Only you, the writer, can tell empty abstractions from solid concepts. For example, ask yourself "What did I really mean by 'interesting'?" One of the best ways to develop your writing ideas and fill in the gaps for the reader is to show or explain what you mean by your own code words. This strategy is especially useful when you feel you need to develop an argument or reinforce a point but aren't sure what else to say.

Example 1   *The Buried Meaning in Code Words*

The theory of continental drift was a major breakthrough in geology.

It drew on enormous amounts of information from different fields, including paleontology and physics as well as geology.

It contradicted major assumptions everyone had made about the rigid nature of continents.

It led to new kinds of studies, such as ones that described and dated the life cycles of continents. It changed the way people studied geology.

It gave us a whole new image of the earth's surface as plastic and dynamic.

All in all, it changed both the study of geology and popular notions about the earth. (Note: Use this idea to organize the paragraph.)

The strategy is simple. First go through your notes or a draft of your paper and locate some of the key words or phrases (ones that you intend to carry much meaning in your paper). Look both for abstractions and for key words and complex concepts that you depend on. Then see if they might also be working as code words, ones that may not convey all your intentions to the reader. Look for words that stand at the center of a whole network of ideas and experience that are *unique to you*. Then ask, "What do I mean by this code word or term?" Try to push that complex meaning into words, using it as a springboard for developing your own ideas. Then transfer this new understanding to your paper.

Example 1 above shows just how many interesting and important ideas can be buried beneath a code word or phrase. In her first draft of a geology paper, the writer had asserted that Alfred Wegener's 1912 theory of continental drift was a "major breakthrough" in the field of geology. She knew this was a strong point she needed to support and develop. After fruitlessly searching for quotes that would support it, she realized that it would be far more effective simply to explain in her own words what she meant. So she used her intuition and her code words as starting points for exploring what she really meant by saying that the theory was a "breakthrough."

Above are some of the ideas she jotted down and eventually worked into her paper. They show how much information she already had on the topic when she began seriously to probe her own network of ideas.

Think back for a moment to the writer's original assertion. Would you as a reader have been able to fill in all of the ideas behind "breakthrough" that the writer knew but didn't tell you? As a geology instructor, would you have assumed that the student knew all the supporting facts she didn't express? Code words are like intuitions. They offer a starting point for thinking about the reader and for developing your own ideas.

Example 2 demonstrates how this strategy can lead you back through the entire process of planning, generating, and organizing your ideas. The passage below comes from a draft of the scholarship application that Joan was writing in Chapter 3. She has underscored a few of the key terms that are loaded with information for her but are in danger of just seeming abstract to a reader. Play the role of a reader on the scholarship committee wondering if this applicant really understands research well enough to benefit from the scholarship. How would you interpret the terms that are underscored?

The response of a friend to whom Joan showed the draft wasn't very encouraging. According to the friend, "It sounds OK—it's organized and everything—but I felt as if I'd read it before. It's saying things that 'couldn't be wrong,' but I don't have a sense of what you think or what you have actually done. What is a 'relevant area' for you? I don't know, and this draft gives me the feeling you may not know either."

Now look at the notes Joan jotted down (see Example 3) as she thought about one of the phrases underscored in her draft. Then review her revised draft (Example 4), with new material underscored. You will notice two interesting things. First, the revision contains the kind of additional, specific details that make Joan's key words meaningful and convincing. In addition, the very process of developing her own code words has led Joan to express a new idea about the benefits of research that was an important but unstated part of her own personal network of ideas. Her code words provided a leaping-off point for generating new ideas.

Example 2   **Finding Code Words in Text**

```
I want a career that will help other people and at the
same time be challenging scientifically.  I had the op-
portunity to do a biochemical assay for a neuropsycho-
pharmacologist at ----- Clinic in Chicago.  Besides
learning the scientific procedures and techniques that
are used, I learned how to deal with some of the prob-
lems encountered in research.  This internship pro-
gram would let me pursue further my interest in
```

research, while currently exposing me to relevant and diverse areas.

Example 3   *Excerpts from the Writer's Notes as She Worked on One of the Underscored Phrases*

problems encountered in research

practical

{ Hard to see how research at the Sleep Center tied in with overall program of the Clinic. But you needed to see the big picture to make decisions.

No definite guidelines given to the biochem people on how to run the assay. }

Lots of paperwork for even a small study.

organizational

{ Difficulty getting equipment
1. Politics between administrators Photometer at the University even though the Clinic had bought it.
2. Ordering time; insufficient inventory; had to hunt through boxes for chemicals.
3. Had to use personal contacts to borrow equipment. Needed to schedule and plan ahead to do so. }

But breakthroughs do occur--pacemaker, artificial limbs, and so on.

Example 4   *Revised Draft with Additions Underscored*

Besides learning the scientific procedures and techniques that are used, I learned how to deal with some of the practical and organizational problems encountered in research. I saw how the lack of equipment and funds often calls for real cooperation between departments and careful planning of one's own project. The experience

also helped me develop more of the patience research requires and recognize the enormous amounts of time, paperwork, and careful steps required for testing a
hypothesis that is only one very small but necessary
part of the overall project.

But besides knowing some of the frustrations, I also
know that many medical advancements, such as the cardiac
pacemaker, artificial limbs, and cures for diseases, exist and benefit many people because of the efforts of
researchers. Therefore I would like to pursue my interest in research by participating in the NIH Internship
Program. The exposure to many diverse projects, designed to better understand and improve the body's functioning, would help me to decide which areas of
biomedical engineering to pursue.

Strategy 2 NUTSHELL YOUR IDEAS AND TEACH THEM

?Find someone, a fellow student or a long-suffering friend, who is willing to listen as you explain the essence of your argument. Then, in a few sentences—in a nutshell—try to lay out the whole substance of your paper. Stating a gist practically forces you to distinguish major ideas from minor ones and to decide how these major ideas are related to one another. Expressing your argument in a nutshell helps you put "noisy," supporting information in its place and focus on the essentials of what you have to say. For example, the outline at the beginning of this chapter conveys in a nutshell what the main ideas of this chapter will be.

Besides helping people to separate main points from interesting but merely supporting ones, nutshelling has another benefit. In trying to condense their thoughts, people often synthesize or combine ideas and create a new concept that expresses or encompasses all they have in mind. For instance, Joan did this in Example 3, when she looked at her notes and decided that a number of points could be grouped and labeled an "organizational" problem. This process of conceptualizing is probably the writer's most difficult yet also most creative action. Stating the gist of your argument helps you do it.

The second part of this strategy, teaching, takes the process one step further. Once you can express your idea in a nutshell to yourself, think about how you would *teach* those ideas to someone else. How would you have to introduce or organize your brief discussion so someone else would understand and remember it? Like nutshelling, trying to teach your ideas helps you form concepts so that your listener gets *the point*, not just a list of facts. Further-more, as a teacher you have to think about which concepts will be most meaningful to your reader. In explaining the dangers of germs to a five-year-old, for example, you would probably find "dangerous things" a more effective organizing concept than "public health problems." Nothing helps you stand back, evalu-ate, and reorganize your ideas more quickly than trying to teach them to someone else who doesn't understand.

Even if you don't have a live audience to talk to, there is an easy and practical way to use this strategy of nutshelling and teaching when you write. Simply imagine your intended reader sitting before you, think about what you want that person to learn or do when you're through, and then try to teach your ideas in writing so that you get results.

≈ *Strategy 3*   BUILD AN ISSUE TREE

Most of the idea-generating strategies described so far ask you to think and write without the straightjacket of an extensive outline. However, one of your goals is to produce a paper with a tight, logical structure. Experienced writers resolve this dilemma in the following way: they try to *pull* an outline *out* of the ideas they generate, rather than write to *fill* an outline *in*. Building an issue tree is a technique for organizing the ideas you generate.

WHAT IS AN ISSUE TREE AND WHY USE ONE?

As noted in Chapter 1, an issue tree is a sketch like an upside-down tree that puts your ideas in a hierarchical order. As you know, in a hierarchy, the top-level idea is the most inclusive. All the other ideas are a response to it or a part of it, like subsystems in a larger system. This does not mean that they are less impor-tant (a subsystem of the body, such as the brain, can be crucial), but they are less inclusive.

Issue trees have two main things to offer writers. First, they let you sketch or test out ideas and relationships as you write. At the same time they let you visualize the whole argument and see how all the parts might fit together. Issue trees can also help you gen-erate new ideas. A traditional outline, written before you start the paper, only arranges the facts and ideas you already know. An issue tree highlights missing links in your argument and helps you draw inferences and create new concepts.

In the sections that follow we will look at ways of using an issue tree to organize your brainstorming, to develop a paper, and to test the organization of your first draft.

Using an Issue Tree to Organize Your Brainstorming

To show how useful an issue tree can be in organizing ideas, we will watch a writer in action using a tree to organize his ideas and write an essay. Here is the assigned topic:

> In England there is a saying that every Englishman is branded on his tongue. Is this true in the United States? Do a person's speech traits—from pronunciation, to pitch, to choice of words—mean anything in the American social system?

Figure 7-1 shows the first three steps a writer might take in answering this question.

1. Generate some ideas on the problem. At this point the writer's goal is simply to answer the question "Do speech traits communicate anything to me?" and generate some ideas. These are jotted down like a list.
2. Find a key word or phrase for each idea.
3. Put the key words in a hierarchically organized tree.

Figure 7-1   ***Organizing brainstorming into a tree***

Brainstorming	*Key Words*
As with the British, Americans' traits differ according to upper, middle, and lower class	class
They are like social markers or tags that identify people	social markers
Affected by education	education
Biggest source must be the region one grows up in	region

Tree

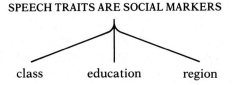

SPEECH TRAITS ARE SOCIAL MARKERS

class   education   region

In Figure 7-1, the line connecting "speech traits are social markers" and "education" simply tells us that there is a general relationship between the two. It will be up to the writer to eventually make that relationship more explicit (for example, is education a cause or an effect of speech traits?). As we will see, an issue tree can help you create concepts that give order and meaning to your own ideas.

Sometimes the best organization of one's ideas is self-evident, as it was for the ideas in Figure 7-1. But when it isn't, when things seem confusing, an issue tree can help you spot the missing links in your thinking and generate new concepts that will organize your ideas. For example, Figure 7-2 shows a set of ideas our writer generated after reading a number of studies on people's responses to voice. These ideas didn't neatly fit onto the tree. "Breathiness," "throatiness," and "pitch" are clearly related to the top-level idea of speech traits as social markers, but they certainly do not belong on the same level with "class," "education," and "region." Nor are they subordinate to (a part of) those larger categories. Taken as group, however, they add up to another kind of social marker that would be comparable to a regional or class trait. The question is, what should the writer call it?

The writer's task is to generate a new concept that sums up these facts. In other words, he must examine the material and propose a new unifying idea. In this case the unifying idea he arrived at was that speech traits also suggest or reflect a person's sex role (see Figure 7-3).

Creating a unifying idea or concept from facts is something we do all the time. The problem is that in the heat of writing, when ideas just don't seem to jell, people often continue to flounder rather than stop, think, and *create* new organizing ideas. At such times the writer needs to turn from searching his or her memory for the "right" word (because it isn't there) and start looking for relationships and developing new ideas. An issue tree helps do this.

Using an Issue Tree to Develop a Paper

You can also use an issue tree to help develop or flesh out a paper. As you think and write, your issue tree will keep changing, reflecting your developing set of ideas. For example, our essay writer eventually decided not to treat the issue of education and decided that he had two major ideas to discuss on the subject of speech traits. Here are his notes for the beginning of the essay:

Figure 7-2   *Using an issue tree to spot missing concepts*

Brainstorming

Breathiness is considered a "sexy" trait in women.

Throatiness (i.e., a husky, quite deep voice) is considered "unfeminine" in women but mature in men.

A wide pitch range is heard as "effeminate" in men and as "flighty" or "frivolous" in women.

Key Words

breathiness

throatiness

pitch

Trees

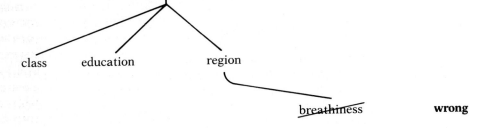

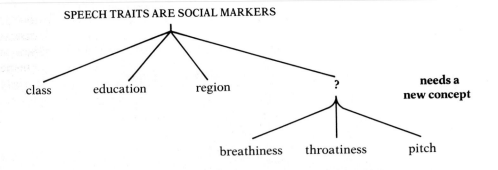

Figure 7-3   *Grouping ideas under a unifying concept*

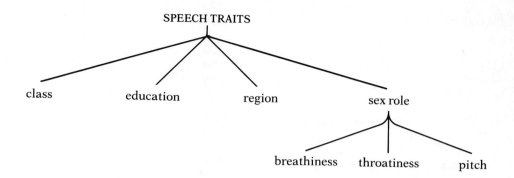

Speech traits are an important means of communication in
the United States. First of all, <u>listeners</u> use them to
determine someone's social identity, especially in the
areas of class, regional background, and sex role. In
addition, <u>speakers</u> use them, either deliberately or unconsciously, to communicate certain things as well.

       (what things? to project a self-image maybe?
       or fit in with a group?)

As Figure 7-4 shows, the writer's working tree reflects this two-part reorganization of his ideas. And it shows exactly where he needs to support those ideas with more evidence and examples. So again he turns to brainstorming, now with the goal of refining and supporting his major points. Notice how his thinking is working in two directions, from the bottom up and from the top down. Sometimes he starts with an inclusive idea such as "listeners interpret regional speech traits" and tries to work from the top down to support that idea with more facts and examples. Sometimes he starts with facts and examples, such as the facts about New Yorkers, and works from the bottom of the tree up, finding relationships and creating a new idea.

The revised tree shows how much of the writer's final argument was created in the process of organizing and developing his ideas, that is, in the process of building a tree. An issue tree, then, offers a writer three important things:

1. It is a flexible tool for thinking that develops as your ideas develop.

Figure 7-4   **Developing a paper**

<u>Working issue tree</u>

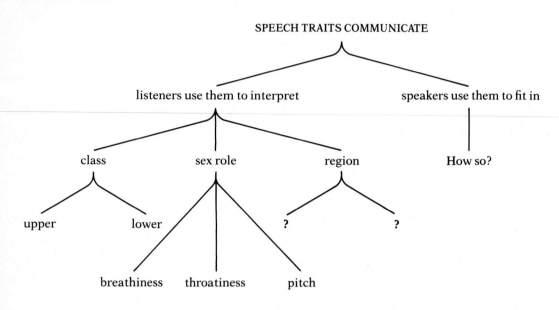

SPEECH TRAITS COMMUNICATE

listeners use them to interpret   speakers use them to fit in

class   sex role   region   How so?

upper   lower   ?   ?

breathiness   throatiness   pitch

<u>Brainstorming</u>

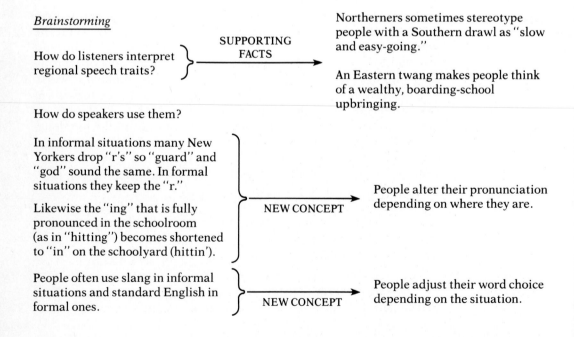

How do listeners interpret regional speech traits? } → SUPPORTING FACTS →

Northerners sometimes stereotype people with a Southern drawl as "slow and easy-going."

An Eastern twang makes people think of a wealthy, boarding-school upbringing.

How do speakers use them?

In informal situations many New Yorkers drop "r's" so "guard" and "god" sound the same. In formal situations they keep the "r."

Likewise the "ing" that is fully pronounced in the schoolroom (as in "hitting") becomes shortened to "in" on the schoolyard (hittin'). } → NEW CONCEPT →

People alter their pronunciation depending on where they are.

People often use slang in informal situations and standard English in formal ones. } → NEW CONCEPT →

People adjust their word choice depending on the situation.

Figure 7–4 (continued)

Revised issue tree

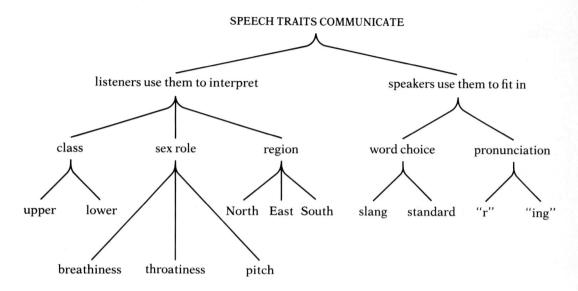

2. It helps you visualize, organize, and support the ideas you have.

3. It signals when you must stop to look for relationships and create new unifying ideas.

By this point in the writing process, the issue tree has done its job and the writer is well into writing paragraphs, but knowing as he writes how each part fits logically into the whole.

Using an Issue Tree to Test Your First Draft

One of the best ways to compare your *thought* with what you actually *wrote* is to do a tree of your own first draft or, if you can, ask a reader to do this for you. The procedure is simple: From your draft, pull out all the main ideas (use a brief phrase such as "statistics show decline"). You might jot these down in the margin of your paper. Make sure you don't include any ideas that are in your head but not on the paper. Although you can expect readers to see connections and fill in *some* organizing ideas as they read, you can't expect them always to arrive at the same interpretation you did. By building an issue tree, you can find out what your paper is actually saying. The tree will reveal the focus and underlying structure of your prose.

Example 5   *Draft with an Uncertain Focus*

<u>The Writing Problem</u>

America has a writing problem. Like the Constitution, American education is based on democratic principles, which means it is committed to teaching reading, writing, and arithmetic to everyone as a basic right, like the right to vote. The history of American education is the history of an attempt to turn these principles into practice for everyone. In 1975, <u>Newsweek</u> magazine, in a famous exposé article entitled ''Why Johnny Can't Write,'' started a crusade against poor writing. The vivid, even shocking examples in this article came from colleges all over the country. Other disturbing findings on writing skills have come from various sources, including the National Assessment of Educational Progress, the College English Education Board, and the Department of Health, Education, and Welfare. However, many people have been most appalled by the statistics on basic literacy itself. These statistics are especially revealing. The majority of Americans use only the simplest sentence structures and the most elementary vocabulary.

Many things have led to this decline—the schools themselves, television, and our changing social values. In an attempt to create relevant, attractive courses, many schools have understressed the old-fashioned basics of reading and writing. The long-term impact of television has lulled people into a more simplistic speaking style. Writing, on the other hand, is essentially book talk, which goes as far back as the invention of movable type. But today students spend time watching television that they might have spent reading 20 years ago. Studies have shown that many students watch more than 8 hours of TV per day. TV has in fact replaced books, newspapers, and even movies as our primary source of entertainment and information. Instead of actively participating in learning, people prefer the more passive

experience of watching ''the tube.'' According to Mar-
shall McLuhan, ''literary culture is through.'' It belonged to the world of the printing press. And who
wants to watch a printing press?

In the next example, a tree diagram is used to look at the underlying structure of individual paragraphs. When you apply this
technique to a whole paper, you might want to work in larger
units and let each point on your tree summarize the point of an
entire paragraph. The two paragraphs in Example 5, taken from
the beginning of a student's paper, demonstrate two of the most
common problems a tree will uncover: a top-heavy or unfocused
organization (seen in the first paragraph) and a runaway branch
(seen in the second). Read the first paragraph and then look at
Figure 7-5 (page 126), which shows the structure of the discussion
as a reader saw it.

Consider the first paragraph of this draft. It is hard to see the
paragraph's focus. Is the main idea the democratic ideal and the
failure of education, is it the decline of writing skills, or is it the
drama of the *Newsweek* crusade? According to the writer, he really
had intended to focus on how American education was failing to
teach writing. Figure 7-5 compares the tree the reader saw with
the tree the writer really wanted to produce. Notice that all
the reader saw was a list of facts, whereas the writer really had
intended to use those facts to support the idea that skills
had declined.

In sketching his intended tree, the writer uncovered another
problem. Although he felt his comments about democratic ideals
were relevant, he really didn't want to discuss that issue in this
paragraph. He realized it would make more sense to discuss it in
a later section about how the writing problem is also a failure to
meet the historical goals of American education. Sketching out a
tree of the paragraph helped the writer take a bird's eye view of
his organization and compare his private mental tree (or the one
he would like to have) with the idea structure his prose actually
presented to the reader. Example 6 is a revision of the first
paragraph in which the writer tries to keep a clear focus and show
the reader how each sentence and point are connected to his
main point.

A second problem that a tree will reveal is the presence of a
long, trailing branch. In the second paragraph of Example 4, the
author began discussing causes of this decline, and one idea led
to another, to another, and yet another. Each idea was a response
to the one before, but they got further and further from the writer's top-level idea. The branch simply ran away with the writer
and produced an unbalanced paragraph in which very little time

Figure 7-5   *The opening paragraph: the tree the reader saw versus the tree the writer intended*

The reader's tree

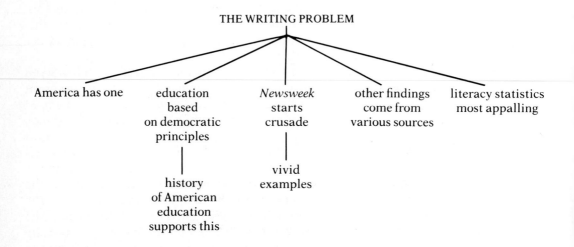

THE WRITING PROBLEM

America has one   education based on democratic principles   *Newsweek* starts crusade   other findings come from various sources   literacy statistics most appalling

history of American education supports this

vivid examples

The writer's intended tree

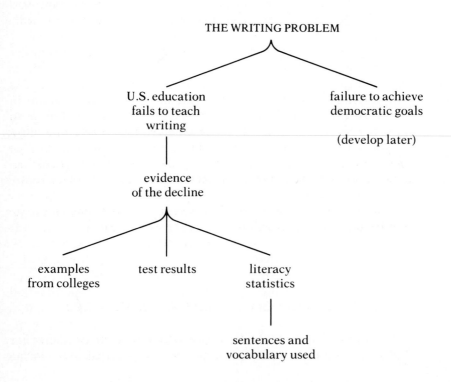

THE WRITING PROBLEM

U.S. education fails to teach writing   failure to achieve democratic goals

(develop later)

evidence of the decline

examples from colleges   test results   literacy statistics

sentences and vocabulary used

was spent on his major, top-level topics. In the process of composing, the writer remembered a number of interesting ideas about television and other media, so his ideas did seem to "flow" as he wrote. But in sketching the tree, he realized that he had given too much space to one supporting idea (watching television) and little or no space to his points that schools neglect basics and that changes in social values are causing the decline.

Example 6   *Revised Draft with a Strong Focus*

<u>The Writing Problem:</u>
<u>A Failure of American Education</u>

According to the startling <u>Newsweek</u> article of 1975 (''Why Johnny Can't Write''), the U.S. educational system is failing to equip its students with sound writing skills. The article displayed a number of examples of poor writing from colleges all over the country. But more definitive support came from test results reported by the National Assessment of Educational Progress, the Department of Health, Education, and Welfare, and the College English Education Board. These were supported by the even more appalling statistics on basic literacy itself; for example, the majority of Americans use only the simplest sentence structures and the most elementary vocabulary.

Figure 7-6 gives a vivid picture of the structure of this paragraph and places it in the context of the other major points the writer wanted to cover, in both the paragraph and the entire paper. As you can see, he intended to focus on American schools and education, but the interesting topic of television simply ran away with his paragraph.

Whether you actually sketch a tree or read your prose looking for its underlying hierarchical structure, you can use this technique to test for the focus and connections your reader is likely to see.

USING QUESTIONS TO DEVELOP AN ISSUE TREE

Sometimes a writer will develop a skeleton of an issue tree but not know where to go from there. One way to break this block is

Figure 7-6   *The second paragraph: a runaway branch*

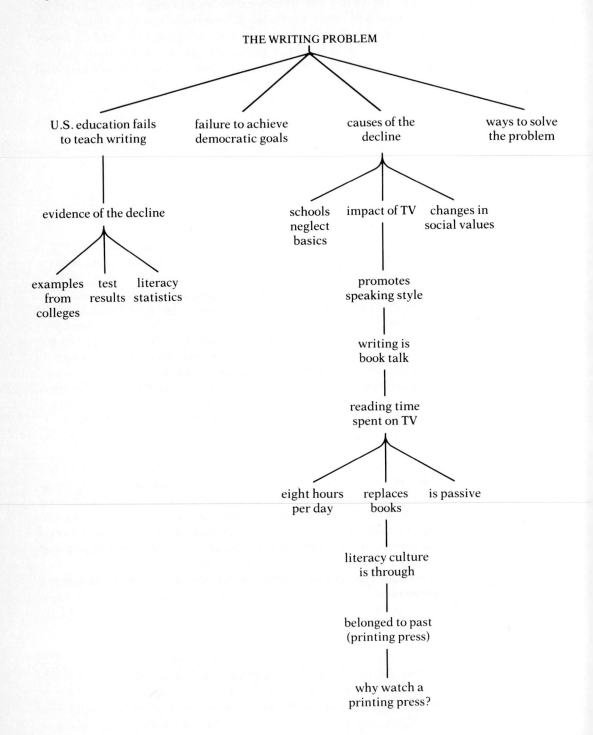

chapter seven / Organizing Ideas

to start asking questions about each item in the tree. This method simply makes a natural process more systematic. When you write you are often carrying on a question-and-response dialogue with your reader or yourself. Children, as we all know, can build endless chains of reasoning with the single question "Why?" or "How?" Other questions that frequently arise in a reader's mind are "What do you mean?" (which asks for a more expanded definition) and "Such as?" (which is a reaction to a vague, overly abstract idea that lacks supporting examples). As a writer, you can anticipate the reader's questions, as well as generate more material, by asking such questions of yourself. Some useful ones are:

What do you mean?
How so?
How do you know?
Such as?
Why?
Why not?
So what?

The questions that are most applicable will depend on the type of paper. A journal article exploring a question of scientific fact will rely heavily on the question "What evidence?" ("How do you know?"), whereas one concerned with pragmatic or technological issues would probably concentrate more on asking "How?" "Why?" and "So what?" Figure 7-7 shows how a writer has used the questioning method to develop ideas for a paper on running. Notice how each new point is a response to the point above it. Unlike an outline, an issue tree allows you to keep adding more points one under the other, in any direction you wish.

This technique, also called *issue analysis*, is often used in a formal, systematic way to examine large policy questions such as "Should we build more nuclear power plants?" Issue trees help people deal with such enormous problems because they offer a way of systematically stating and organizing all the major points such a decision should cover. In addition, a systematic use of questions such as "Why?" and "So what?" helps people to reason carefully about an issue by considering it from a variety of viewpoints.

PROJECTS AND ASSIGNMENTS

1 Use the strategies in Step 4, "Organize Your Ideas," to help test and improve the first draft of a paper on which you are currently working.

   a. *Expand code words.* Go through your first draft and circle three or four words that are functioning as code words for you. Then, on a

Figure 7-7   **A tree generated through the questioning method**

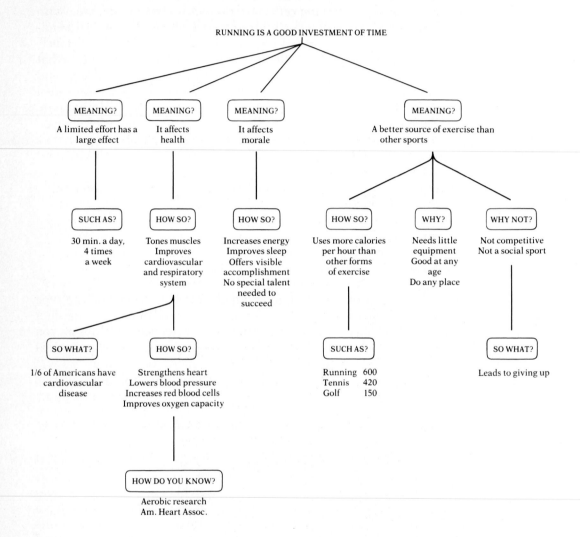

separate sheet, brainstorm all the things that come to your mind when you use those expressions. Use your brainstorming to go back and develop and clarify those ideas for your reader.

b. *Nutshell and teach your ideas.* Try to state the main points of your paper in a nutshell, then try to teach those ideas to another person. You might also test how well you communicated by having your listener tell you back, in his own words, what he thought you meant. If he didn't see your point, try again. Then use this experience and your own new ideas to go back and focus your paper better for a reader.

c. *Develop an issue tree.* On a separate sheet of paper, do an issue of the draft you have just written. Then find someone who is fa-miliar with the issue-tree concept and ask him to read your paper and from it develop his own tree. Tell him to write items down in his own words as much as possible and to tree your argument as he sees it on the first reading. If he is at all confused in trying to follow the paper, you want his tree to reflect that. Ask him not to put down any of his own ideas on what he thinks you should have said. Then compare the two trees and try to account for the differences. What happened and why?

2 *Checklist: Recognizing Code Words.* Only you can tell your own rich code words, but here are some words and phrases you should test for hidden, unexpressed meanings:

☐a. Important-sounding, three-syllable words with Latinate endings (such as *-ion, -ment, -ance)*, since these are often abstractions (for example, a performance situation)

☐b. Good sounding but vague phrases (for example, relevant and diverse areas)

☐c. Important words you would emphasize or pause after in speaking but haven't developed in the text (for example, break-through)

☐d. Words that name a list of things your reader might want the specifics of in addition to your generalization (for example, problems encountered in research)

☐e. Words that say a lot to you when you read the text (if someone asked, you could give a five-minute, on-the-spot elaboration).

3 Take a controversial question such as "Should smoking be allowed in public places?" Or, "Is a liberal arts education still one of the best preparations for any career?" Do a systematic analysis of the issue, using the questioning method ("How so?" "Why?" and so on) out-lined earlier. Make sure your analysis looks at both the pros and the cons. Then write a short paper that takes a stand and argues for one side while acknowledging the strengths of the other. Use an issue tree to focus and organize your ideas, and be sure to give your reader an introductory problem/purpose statement that previews your paper (see Chapter 5).

4 *Checklist: The Overall Structure of a Paper*

☐a. *Problem/Purpose Statement.* Have I given the reader an introduc-tory problem/purpose statement that sets up a problem or thesis on which my paper will focus? (This idea will be at the top of your issue tree. Also review the problem/purpose statement checklist in Chapter 5.)

☐ If I talk about various aspects of a problem, have I signalled what I see as the *central* conflict or issue?

☐ If I make a number of assertions, is my *major* claim or thesis signalled?

☐b. *Paragraph Focus.* Is each paragraph organized around an idea, not just a list of facts? (If not, you can use an issue tree to help create the missing, higher-level concept under which all your points will fit.)

☐ Have I used a topic sentence or some other convention to signal my main idea in each paragraph?

☐ If it is a complex idea, have I stated the gist directly at some point?

☐c. *Overall Hierarchy.* Can you and your reader see the overall hierarchical structure of your paper? Does each section, paragraph, and idea fit into the structure in a logical way? (If it doesn't, you probably need to rethink some of your top-level unifying ideas. Try using an issue tree to play with other possible organizations and concepts.)

5 The organizing techniques in this chapter, such as nutshells, issue trees, and questions, are really techniques for making sense out of the unstructured pool of ideas people often bring to writing. The following is an example of just such a body of data on the topic "Time Management and Efficient Student Strategies." It comes from two sources: List A, the "Real Experience" data, is based on students' comments about their own problems managing time for studying and writing papers. It lists the things people really do. List B, the "Good Advice" data, lists a number of suggestions for managing time. When you have read and thought about a topic for a while, your own knowledge may look like these rich but unordered lists of ideas. You know a lot, but you need to organize it in order to make meaning.

Real Experience	**Good Advice**
Once it's read, forget it.	Don't procrastinate!
Do what's due.	Set a sub-deadline; make a commitment to someone.
Do it all in one sitting.	The Executive Move: What is the best use of my time right now?[1]
Postpone big tasks.	
Don't reread notes until finals week.	Plan around special times or places.
Wait for inspiration.	Pace yourself.
Use minimal estimates of the time it takes.	"Planning is decision-making."[2] So decide how to use your time.

[1] Alan Lakein, *How to Get Control of Your Time and Your Life* (New York: New American Library, 1973), p. 109.
[2] Lakein, p. 109.

Real Experience	Good Advice
Don't talk to the teacher.	The Judo Move: Use fear constructively: What knowledge or action would neutralize it?[3]
Never mark up a book.	
Don't eat breakfast; stay up all night.	Have a positive attitude.
Assume you will understand sooner or later.	Learn your learning style.
	Pace yourself!
Panic!	Confer!
Remember: You hate school!	The Swiss Cheese Strategy: Identify and do one tiny task each day; reduce your mountain to a Swiss cheese by biting off small bits whenever you have a minute.[4]
Wait for the weekend.	
Avoid courses with writing or math.	
Reread texts for tests.	
Create a crisis.	Planning can be as important as doing.
Teachers never want as much as they ask for.	Set priorities.

a. As you read the "Real Experience" list for problems, you probably noticed that they fall into clumps. For example, some of the data clump together as a low-payoff, low-probability strategy that could be called:

"Lie to Yourself a Little"
Allow minimal time.
Assume you'll know it later.
Teachers don't want as much as they ask for.

What would be some other ways of grouping these experiences into an issue tree? (You may want to add some new "Real Experience" data of your own.) Give an appropriate title to each new group or tree. Notice how your title forms the top-level node on your small issue tree.

b. Look at your series of small issue trees and try to sum up each one in a nutshell. Then look at the larger picture: can you say how these strategies are related? Try to sketch an issue tree (you will probably have to think up your own top-level ideas) that brings your previous ideas or trees together and shows one way they could be related to each other. Test your new tree by trying to explain, in a nutshell, to someone else how you see this problem of managing time. (Do you predict that your nutshell will be the same as other people's?) You have now organized that unorganized list of experiences into a meaningful analysis of a problem.

[3] Lakein, pp. 131–132.
[4] Lakein, pp. 100–105.

c. Now look at that "Good Advice" column. What items of advice seem to you most useful in addressing the experience problems that you're working with? Take one of the pieces of good advice. Imagine that you could interview the person who gave this advice and ask questions about that strategy, for example, How does it work? and Why should I use it? Try the questions discussed on page 129, and use an issue tree to keep track of your points.

d. You have now analyzed the problem as "Real Experience" sees it and have explored and developed what some of the "Good Advice" could mean. Now try to put these two groups of ideas together in a brief paper. What good advice might help solve the problems you have defined? In organizing your ideas, look for ways to relate these ideas as cause and effect or a problem and solution. (Use issue trees to try out different possible organizations.) Then consider how you want to present the whole discussion—what is your own top-level organizing idea for understanding the problem of "Time Management and Efficient Student Strategies"?

IF YOU WOULD LIKE TO READ MORE

If you would like to know more about strategies for organizing ideas, see:

Simon, Herbert. "The Architecture of Complexity." *Proceedings of the American Philosophical Society*, 106 (December 1962), 467–482. Reprinted in Herbert Simon, *The Sciences of the Artificial*. Cambridge, Mass.: M.I.T. Press, 1969. / This essay, by one of the creators of information processing theory, discusses the role of hierarchical structures in human thought.

Wojick, David. "Planning for Discourse." *Water Spectrum*, Winter, 1975–76 and Summer, 1978. / This offers an introduction to issue trees in their original setting, the analysis of complex policy issues.

chapter eight

Analyzing a Problem and Building a Thesis

WHY WRITE? ONE OF THE most basic reasons for writing, which students, academic writers, journalists, and business people share, is to discuss and deal with problems. This chapter will explain how to go about analyzing a problem, then show you one way to express your thinking in a written problem analysis, and finally, show how you can use the process of problem analysis to develop the thesis of an expository or persuasive paper.

Problems occur when you are in one state, or at some Point A (let's say you are broke and have two papers to write) and you want to be in another state, or at a Point B (let's say you want to take off for spring break next week). What is the real problem: money, time, your priorities, your work habits? People define their own problems and good answers depend on a good analysis of the problem.

Defining and solving is also a major part of many jobs. If you have ever been a group leader, teacher, or a coach, you have probably been in a situation in which something—as yet undefined—wasn't going as well as it should. And it was your job to understand or define that problem and solve it—to move the situation from point A to a new, better point B.

Understanding a problem often means discovering a conflict that creates the problem or that keeps you from your goal. However, the conflict or critical issue at the heart of a problem is often hard to see. For example, why isn't your club working up to its potential? What is the conflict that underlies the situation? Do its members have multiple goals that don't mesh? Or take a famous problem raised in Shakespeare's *Hamlet*, namely, why does Hamlet delay? For years people have tried to define the social and psychological conflicts within Hamlet that prevent him from revenging his father's death. We can ask a similar question about Shakespeare himself: What broad human problems in his own mind was Shakespeare trying to dramatize when he wrote the play? Finally, what problems does *Hamlet* raise for us as readers; what unresolved issues does it create in our own minds? The play *Hamlet*, then, really involves a set of problems and conflicts existing in the minds of Shakespeare the author, Hamlet the character, and each of us as readers.

In literature, history, science, or education, much of the writing people do is an attempt to put their finger on the key issues in a situation involving a conflict. They write to define and help solve a problem. Whether you are a historian studying urban decay, or a hospital administrator writing a proposal to reorganize county clinics, or a student in either field, you will often depend on the skill of problem analysis. In this chapter we will look at a five-step process you can use to analyze problems and to communicate your understanding to a reader.

FIVE STEPS IN ANALYZING A PROBLEM

Problem analysis is a form of detective work. It is the act of discovering key issues in a problem that often lie hidden under the noisy details of the situation. The process of analysis begins when people encounter what is called a "felt difficulty." That is, you feel that something doesn't fit, you feel a conflict. Sometimes that conflict is obvious: two people disagree, or you discover that you yourself hold two contradictory ideas on a subject such as marriage. Many times both sides of a conflict will have merit, as in the federally required testing of new drugs for long-term dangers, which prevents their immediate use by those who would benefit. At other times the conflict will be harder to see; for example, you may feel that there is some as yet unspecified "organizational problem" at the place you work or in an organization to which you belong.

The question in all of these cases is, "What exactly is the problem?" In trying to answer that question an analyst would normally do the following five things:

1. Define the Conflict or Key Issue

A problem analyst's first job is to discover the critical conflict or key issue that lies at the heart of any felt difficulty. In trying to understand a problem, bear in mind the difference between defining a problem (finding a conflict) and merely stating a topic or describing a situation such as "pollution." Although everyone might agree that pollution is harmful and unpleasant, there was a time when it was seen not as a problem but as a sign of industrial prosperity. Problems are only problems for someone. Pollution is only a problem when people want clean air but drive cars that pollute, or when society wants both a clean environment and maximum industrial productivity.

An even clearer example is the much publicized "energy problem." Energy per se is not a problem; it is a topic. Even the dwindling supply of fossil fuel is only a situation. However, when we juxtapose this supply against the American tradition of high consumption at low cost, we have begun to isolate a problem. We have found one of the central conflicts that create a problem.

We often like to think of a conflict in terms of good versus evil, but in most human organizations it is a conflict between two goods (a high standard of living and a beautiful environment) or between the legitimate needs of two groups (the farmer versus the food consumer). This is what makes real problems so hard to solve.

2. Place the Problem in a Larger Context

As we have seen, the first step in problem analysis is to zoom in on a problem for a close-up look at its critical issues. The second step is to pull back for a broader view. Now you must try to see the problem in a larger context and fit it into a category of similar problems. This will let you describe the same problem at two different but complementary levels: close up and in context.

Sometimes the larger problem will seem obvious or implicit—for example, making a good career decision. But it is always important to look at the big picture, not just the immediate conflict. For example, is the "energy problem" a technological problem (production can't meet demand) or a social and economic problem (our wasteful consumption endangers our balance of trade)? The context you choose—and you may see more than one—will have an enormous impact on the solutions you propose. For example, should we treat energy as a technological problem and pump money into developing solar energy for the year 2020, or tackle the social problem and start rationing gasoline tomorrow?

Another way to step back and put your problem in perspective is to look for a larger concern you and your reader share. For example, the student whose paper compared statistics textbooks (page 14) saw a conflict between what students needed and what textbooks offered and placed this problem in the context of trying to get through a statistics course. If she had been writing to a group of teachers, she might have defined the problem in terms of effective teaching. Either way, her approach would be to step back and put the textbook problem in a broader perspective.

In a sense, students do the same thing when they step back to get perspective on an assignment an instructor has given. They may ask themselves "Why was I assigned this paper?" or "What is the point behind this lab experiment?" or "What is the larger issue or question my work should address?"

3. Make Your Problem Definition More Operational

Steps 1 and 2 help you create a two-level definition that defines a conflict or key issue and puts it in its larger context. If your goal is to understand a complex phenomenon, such as a Shakespearean play, these are the crucial steps.

But perhaps your problem is a practical one: Someone needs to act, or you wish to persuade him or her to act. Here you can improve your analysis by making your definition more *operational*. This means stating the problem or your goals as specific operations—as actions or tasks you could actually perform. An operational problem definition is more useful than an abstract one because it suggests possible courses of action or the features of a good solution. For example, you could make an abstract definition—such as "The problem is that Americans need to lower their energy consumption"—more operational by saying, "The problem is, how can we lower consumption by increasing fuel prices, without at the same time putting an unacceptable burden on the poor?"

Sometimes an operational problem definition contains details that work as miniature plans for tackling the problem. Let's compare different ways a smoker could define his problem:

1. My problem is cigarettes. (overly abstract problem definition; no identification of conflict or key issue)

2. My problem is that I want to cut down on smoking but just can't do it. (more specific problem definition with identification of conflict)

3. My real problem is how to stop smoking at parties or when I'm out with friends. (more operational definition)

4. My real problem is how to break a long-standing habit of smoking around my friends without feeling left out or unsociable. (an operational definition that suggests a number of places to act)

In defining your problem, try to make the conflict and context as operational as you can.

Note: The series of boxes in this chapter give guidelines for turning the ideas you generated through problem analysis into written form.

The format of a written problem analysis follows the thinking process in a number of ways. The format treated here, which we will call the basic problem analysis, is widely used in business and organizational communication (examples on pages 7–9). In addition, the elements of a basic problem analysis are the core of most research papers, essays, and reports, although the elements are often rearranged and subordinated to a thesis.

Writing a Problem Analysis

State Your Operational, Two-level Problem Definition at the Beginning

In writing a basic problem analysis, give your reader a clear, two-level definition of the problem somewhere near the beginning of your paper. In a short, one- or two-page paper, most readers will expect you to define the problem (on both levels) in the very first paragraph. Come immediately to the point so your reader will know the key issue. This is also the place to reveal the purpose or point of your paper. Stating this directly at the beginning isn't always easy to do, but your reader will be looking for it.

In many cases you will want to present the larger context or shared problem first, as a way of orienting the reader or catching his attention with a subject you and he care about. Then state the key conflict or issue that is at the heart of your problem.

Here is an example of an operational, two-level problem definition written as an introduction to a paper on creativity. Although this example makes the problem definition more operational by adding detail in an example, the question "How operational is my problem statement?" applies to the whole statement. It is a relative judgment about how easy it would be to act on the problem as you have defined it.

According to Brewster Ghiselin *(The Creative Process)*, "One might suppose that it is easy to detect creative talent and to recognize creative work. But the difficulties are considerable." Because every creative act in some way violates an established order, it is likely to appear eccentric, if not patently unreasonable, to most people. How, for example, could anyone be sure Freud's insights into the human mind weren't motivated—like the bizarre "insights" of his patients—by hidden psychological forces? And how could his contemporaries judge the validity of such startling and novel explanations of behavior? The careers of Sigmund Freud and Karl Marx show us how society deals with this problem of recognizing creative work.

Writing a Problem Analysis

Isolate and Define the Major Subissues or Subproblems Within the Problem

Make the overall hierarchical structure of your discussion clear. Once you have told the reader what the problem is, you will need to discuss it in more detail. However, instead of simply describing the situation, organize your discussion and your paragraphs around a set of subissues or subproblems within your problem. In other words, you should be able to name the major issues your analysis will address and the reader should be able to see which issue each paragraph or set of paragraphs is talking about.

In a short paper, you might use this organization:

First paragraph: TWO-LEVEL PROBLEM DEFINITION

Body of paper: Issue Issue Issue

Final paragraph: CONCLUSION

Notice that by defining a problem and a set of subissues or subproblems, you have created a hierarchical organization of ideas. Your problem definition is the top-level, most inclusive statement. The discussion and subproblems or subissues grow out of it, and your conclusion at the end will work like a new top-level idea in that it will respond to the entire discussion. Make sure your reader sees this hierarchical organization of your ideas.

---

4. Explore the Parts of the Problem

Once the problem is defined you need to explore the various subissues or subproblems within it. This helps you break a complex problem down into manageable parts. For example, a smoker might decide that the major subissues within the problem of stopping smoking are "health," "costs," "strength of habit," "social pressure," and so on. In isolating subproblems the analyst needs to see how they fit into the hierarchy as parts of the larger problem.

5. Come to an Open-Minded Conclusion

In the conclusion, you come to a solution or a new definition of the problem. But you will know whether your answer is best only if you have considered other good answers. The chief weakness of most problem solvers is that they leap too quickly to a solution. Upon seeing the first strong alternative, they breathe a sigh of relief, say "this is it," and look no further. However, your conclusion will look strong to your readers only if they know you have considered and rejected with reason other logical solutions or ways of viewing this problem. For example, some people feel that

---

Writing a Problem Analysis

Tie Your Conclusion to the Problem and to the Foregoing Analysis When Appropriate, Show that You Recognize Alternatives, Assumptions, and Implications

Your conclusion will be a new idea, but one that takes account of all the discussion that has gone before. Make sure your conclusion isn't simply a package plan you tack onto the end. It should be directly related to the problem *as you defined it*—and you should make that connection clear to the reader. Show how your conclusion deals with the problem and with the subissues or subproblems you defined. In your conclusion you must take a stand, which means offering a solution or presenting a summation of your new view of the problem. You can support your conclusion not only by offering evidence but by showing the reader that you have given open-minded consideration to alternatives and the implications of your own position.

smoking should not be viewed as a public health issue at all but as an example of the exercise of individual rights. Show that you have seriously considered the alternatives.

A good conclusion takes a stand, but it is open-minded in yet another way. It recognizes that any position has its own assumptions and implications. Real problems rarely go away; current solutions are often only a temporary fix. Your conclusion stands on a precarious boundary between a problem clamoring for a solution and the *implications* and consequences of that solution stretching out into the future. A solution with unrecognized implications may only be a new problem in the making. Your job as an analyst is to alert your reader to those implications that he or she must foresee if your solution is to have a real and beneficial impact. For example, giving up smoking can lead to an increase in eating and frequently cause withdrawal symptoms. Prepare your reader to deal with these implications.

To write a good conclusion, then, you must do three things: (1) seriously consider alternatives, (2) recognize the implications of your own position, and (3) then take a reasoned, open-minded, but solid stand. It can be uncomfortable to live with the knowledge that no response is absolutely right, but real problems rarely have simple answers. So decide what you think, even if no answer is perfect, and support it with the best evidence you can find.

EVALUATING YOUR FINAL WRITTEN PROBLEM ANALYSIS

Sometimes people have an intuitive understanding of a problem and arrive at a well-supported solution, hypothesis, or new view of the problem. But in actually sitting down to write the paper, they may let intuition take over and lose sight of the reader's probable reactions. It is one thing to understand a problem intuitively and well. However, if you want your understanding to make any difference, you must be able to communicate it to someone else. Having a good or even the "best" solution to a problem only matters if your analysis convinces someone else. A written analysis, unlike an intuitive one, demands both conceptual clarity as a thinker and rhetorical skill as a writer.

Use the checklist below to evaluate your written analysis. How well have you handled each of the following seven important features a reader will expect?

THE PROBLEM DEFINITION
1. Is there a shared problem or larger context?
2. Is the central conflict or key issue defined?
3. Is the problem definition operational?

1. Are specific subissues or subproblems clearly defined?
2. Is the overall hierarchical structure of the discussion clear?

THE CONCLUSION
1. Does the conclusion reflect an active consideration of alternatives and an open-minded sense of the assumptions and implications of your own position?
2. Is the solution clearly tied to the problem defined initially and to the bulk of your discussion?

Often, consulting such a checklist can help you see weaknesses or missing portions of your basic problem analysis. Here is a first draft of a problem analysis written by a student who had worked for two summers at a firm called Timmerman Landscape Company:

Where is the problem?

Timmerman Landscape is a local nursery that has recently moved into doing landscaping. They have a year-round staff of around ten people, but in the summer they hire a lot of summer help to meet peak summer workloads. Most of the summer help are college students. There is a waiting list for these jobs because the pay is good and the work is outdoors but not as heavy as construc-

Subproblem

tion work. Or at least it shouldn't be. But because many new summer workers don't know how to move large trees, the best ways to handle the equipment, handle the

Is this the key issue or conflict?

trucks, or the large plants, or dig holes, their job is much harder. But Timmerman does little to help summer employees in these areas.

Subproblem

One problem is that unloading large trees and shrubs can be difficult, even dangerous if you don't know how to position the truck and use the planks. And positioning large plants in the hole is very time-consuming if you don't know how to gauge depth and position before

Subproblem?

unloading. Word-of-mouth publicity is very important to Timmerman, but when neighbors come over to ask summer help about the names of plants, conditions they like, or care they need, the new workers usually have no idea, or make a blind guess.

**Subproblem?
Conclusion—not tied to problem definition; doesn't recognize alternatives and implications**

By my second summer, I had learned a lot about plants and realized that many, even expensive, trees and shrubs were damaged by incorrect rough handling and incorrect planting—in holes too shallow, too close to a house, with air left around the roots. In conclusion, I think Timmerman should develop a handbook for new employees that would be used as part of a brief orientation program for new summer workers.

In analyzing his draft, the writer realized that his problem definition was too long in coming and did not convey the conflict underlying the problem, nor was it very operational. He found that his subproblems were not organized hierarchically; one even appeared before the problem definition. He also decided that his conclusion seemed "tacked on": It did not clearly proceed from what had come before or recognize the alternatives and implications of his proposed solution. Here is his revision:

Larger problem
Operational problem definition including identification of conflict

Timmerman Landscape is a local nursery that has recently moved into doing landscaping. In the summer they need to hire extra help--many of them college students--to meet peak workloads during that season. Most summer workers like the job because the pay is good and the work is outdoors, but problems arise because Timmerman, in order to save money, spends no time on training them in procedures and techniques that would make them more efficient.

Subproblem

This lack of training affects both the students themselves and Timmerman's profitability. The work is hard for summer employees if they don't know the best ways to move large trees, handle the equipment and trucks, handle large plants, or dig holes. It can even be dangerous, if someone is unloading large trees and shrubs and doesn't know how to position the truck and use the planks.

Subproblem

Further, the lack of training causes reduced productivity, plant damage, and loss of business for Timmerman. Untrained workers waste a lot of time: for example, positioning a large plant in a hole is very time-consuming if you don't know how to gauge depth and

Subproblem

position before unloading. Many trees and shrubs, including expensive ones, are damaged by incorrect rough handling or incorrect planting--in holes too shallow or too close to a house, or with air left around the roots.

Subproblem

Finally, Timmerman depends on word-of-mouth publicity, but when neighbors come over to ask summer help about the names of plants, conditions they like, or care they need, the new workers usually have no idea, or make a blind guess.

Recognition of alternatives	Apparently Timmerman cannot afford to have its regular help spend much time training summer workers. I
Conclusion	think the best solution is for Timmerman to develop a handbook for new employees that would be used as part of
Recognition of implications; conclusion tied to problem definition	a brief orientation program for summer workers. While this would involve some time and expense, it is a one-time project that could help both the nursery and the new summer workers.

PITFALLS IN PROBLEM ANALYSIS

In trying to write a good analysis, people may encounter difficulty in any of the three major areas: problem definition, structure, or conclusion. Here are some examples of typical pitfalls to watch out for in your own writing. These come from responses to the assignment, discussed in Chapter One, on analyzing textbooks.

The Definition Pitfall

Instead of defining a problem, the writer in Example 1 is simply discussing his topic and describing a situation. He is telling us what he observed, instead of presenting key issues and concepts.

EXAMPLE 1: Of the three textbooks I surveyed, Brace's offers the most detailed coverage of modern history—1340 pages to carry every day. Howard's book is easier to read and half the length. Unlike most history books, it is organized around topics rather than strict chronology. Levine's is the oldest and is outdated on some recent topics. Each book has unique features.

The Structure Pitfall

The writer of Example 2 has given us a useful top-level idea: The book fails to provide background. However, the rest of the paragraph is simply a list of facts, all of which seem equally important but unrelated. The writer needs to reorganize this list into two or three major subproblems, such as the book's lack of social, biographical, and literary contexts, and then use the facts to support her organizing ideas.

EXAMPLE 2: The poems in this anthology are harder to understand and remember because the book doesn't provide any context for them. There are no footnotes to say when a poem was written and only a sentence or two about the author. Many poems refer to historical events or unfamiliar customs that most students wouldn't know about.

If you wonder about why the poem was written, or why it was written the way it was, the anthology offers no help. Although it has a large number of sonnets, it never mentions the nature of sonnets, what kinds of people wrote them, or when.

The Conclusion Pitfall

The writer of Example 3 started with a well-defined problem: The current French text is not organized for easy review, even though that is a necessary part of learning the material. But her conclusion shows two common pitfalls. First, the solution is a prepackaged, unrelated assertion that does not address the problem she defined. Secondly, it is the kind of conclusion that "can't go wrong." As with a statement supporting Mom and apple pie, no one will probably disagree with it, but then no one will bother to listen either.

> EXAMPLE 3: In conclusion, students need to be able to learn at their own pace and still cover the material required by the course. For many students this will involve not only more time spent studying, but more chance to speak and use French in the classroom.

MOVING FROM A PROBLEM TO A THESIS

In this chapter we have been discussing the art of problem analysis—the art of thinking through a complex situation. You may now be asking, "How does problem analysis help in writing a typical college paper in which you must state and support a thesis?"

Problem analysis can help in two ways. First, the thesis of many papers is simply a claim that a problem or an issue exists, that the conflict is important, interesting, unnoticed, or that we should do something about it. As you can see in the examples following, this claim or thesis is put in the spotlight and the paper is organized around it. But the main parts of a problem analysis are still the core of the paper as you discuss this problem and its sub-issues.

Writers can move from a problem to a thesis in another way. If pondering over and analyzing a problem has led you to a conclusion, a solution, or a new idea, that conclusion can become your thesis. Notice the irony in this: In order to find a good thesis (and to write the first paragraph of your paper which contains the thesis) you may need to write much of the paper first. That is, you may need to do a problem analysis in order to arrive at your conclusion. But when you do, that conclusion can be moved to the head of your paper as the thesis you want to support. In fact, this is how experienced writers often work. They may start with only a vague or tentative thesis; however, they fearlessly write this tentative thesis down simply to get started. Their first paragraph may say nothing more elegant than: "This paper is going to argue that . . . (a sketchy thesis). . . ." This lets them start writing about their problem and in the process come to a conclusion that will become the thesis.

It is important to recognize the difference between a topic, a problem, and a thesis. In the textbook assignment discussed on page 13, the topic was "textbooks and the differences among them." A topic simply names a field, a body of knowledge, or a situation (for example, textbooks differ). Given only a topic, you could simply write a description of different textbooks. But what would you choose to say, how would you order it, and why would you be writing (other than to turn in the paper on time)?

By contrast, when you define a problem *within* the topic, you are identifying a key issue or conflict that you and your reader care about. For example, in writing about textbooks you might define the problem as "Textbooks often don't meet students' needs." A problem analysis is, by definition, an exploration of a problematic situation. As a result of such an analysis, you might conclude that textbook writers are making the wrong assumptions and thereby making their books hard to use; that textbooks should build on the students' existing skills; or that the current statistics course is a failure. It is at this point that you have a thesis.

A *thesis* can be defined as an assertion about a topic that you believe to be true and that you intend to support and explain in your paper. If we could follow the thinking process of a writer, we would see that it often follows this path from topic to problem to thesis. The following examples show three ways in which writers turned the fruits of a problem analysis into a thesis. The first two kinds of theses focus on the problem itself, the third on its solution.

Theses that assert that a problem exists:
   The textbook in our course is causing real difficulty for many students.

   The continued fruitless search for the "missing link" in man's evolution suggests that the theory of slow, steady evolution needs to be reconsidered.

Theses that assert a hypothesis or new understanding of the problem:
   Students are failing to grasp the basic principles in our course because the textbook tries to build on knowledge most students don't have.

The relatively sudden and widespread appearance of early man eliminates the possibility that man evolved by the time-consuming mechanism of competition and survival of the fittest.

Theses that assert a solution to a problem:

Instructors of large, required courses should consider pretesting their texts with a representative group of students.

In order to unlock the mysteries of man's development, we should explore the genetic factors that govern two key features of man: the rapid growth of the brain and the slow process of maturation.

THE PROCESS OF BUILDING A THESIS

What happens when you have to build a thesis from scratch? Let me sketch a typical process writers go through and describe some milestones to look for in your own process. Although your path on a given paper may look quite different, this example shows some of the decisions that often go into creating a good thesis.

The assignment we will work with is an open-ended one which reads:

> College students have to move among many different discourse communities which include those created by family and friends, by college organizations, by classes. Students must operate not only within the academic discourse community itself but within the special discourse of different fields, different professions, and even different courses. Moving among these groups can be like going to a foreign country. When you cross the border both the language and the expectations of the audience change.
>
> The fact that different discourse communities exist is, of course, only a situation. Does this situation ever create a problem for students as writers or readers? What does it mean to enter or succeed in a given discourse community at your school?
>
> Write a paper on this issue, using your reading and own observation to develop and support a thesis. Define the audience you will address as a part of your plan.

How might you go about developing the thesis this situation calls for?

At the Beginning

1. Although the assignment requires a thesis, no one would expect you to have a claim already in mind, unless you had been previously working on the problem. So in fact, the best place to start is with your own experience and intuitions about the *problem*. For example, have you ever seen a problematic situation in

which a student was trying to talk with a professor or in which an expert was trying to explain her knowledge? Do the writing strategies that work in one class work in all? In your own major, do people write and talk in special ways? Have you ever seen the fact of discourse communities create a problem you would like to understand?

Here is where all your skills of problem analysis play a role. Build a picture of a problem you want to discuss.

2. In addition to exploring your own knowledge, explore the *assignment* and think about what your thesis will need to accomplish. As an academic writer, you will be expected to add something new to the conversation—not a staggering new theory, but an interesting idea based on your own close observation and outside reading. And because a thesis makes a claim, your readers will be looking for evidence and arguments that support your claim. But remember that academic readers also put special value on a skeptical argument that recognizes evidence on both sides of a question—so you can present a qualified thesis if you are not sure a flat assertion is really true. Your goal is to add to the conversation, not end it.

Along the Way

3. Don't go with the first attractive thesis that comes along. As you start to read a lot, to gather data and think a lot, a number of possible claims will occur to you. But chances are you will need to go through a longer thinking process before you see a thesis that can do justice to your best ideas. This is normal, and waiting is a smart way to proceed.

4. Decide on your *preliminary definition* of the problem. What is the issue here; what is the conflict you see? What is at stake? And what are some of the subproblems? (See the checklists on p. 99 and pp. 142–143.)

5. Create a *tentative thesis*. You probably won't keep this one, although some writers find it very difficult to give up their first idea or feel afraid they may not get another one. But doing research means you will learn so much that your later vision of the problem and your thesis are likely to be much better. However, this tentative thesis plays a big role in reaching the next two milestones.

Testing a Thesis

6. Given your sense of the problem and your tentative thesis, see if you can now describe your *purpose and audience* in writing.

You will have passed an important milestone when you know what you want to accomplish. Do you want to create a controversy, help professors understand students, help students enter the conversation, figure out what makes the discourse in your field distinctive or . . . ? Where are you headed? Who would appreciate your discovery? Who needs to hear about it?

7. Once you have a tentative thesis you can read in a more purposeful way: look for connections which will support it and look just as energetically for ideas which will test it. Finding evidence against your tentative thesis does not spell doom. It only makes you wiser. In the process of testing you are likely to see ways to *qualify or change your thesis.* You may even discover a whole new way of seeing the situation. If so, cheerfully abandon your tentative thesis—it did its work—and tell the reader about your new, more carefully tested and qualified claim and the evidence that makes it worth considering.

This process of *developing* a thesis—of starting with a problem or issue, of resisting the first idea that comes along, and of changing your tentative thesis until it fits your purpose and your evidence—means you spend a little more time planning and less time throwing away text that didn't work. As you probably know, leaping into writing with a "good" idea that fizzles out because it is too small to support a full argument can guarantee frustration. Having a thesis you have tested and having a purpose behind that thesis can make the time spent writing not only more productive but personally satisfying.

Here are excerpts from two papers stimulated by the assignment to explore a discourse community. Is it possible to locate both a thesis and a problem definition in each of these papers or not? Notice the form these statements take.

WRITING WITHIN IN A DISCOURSE COMMUNITY

When writing for a certain discourse community such as chemistry, does the author accommodate a text to the type of audience that is going to read it? To answer this question, I took three introductory textbooks in chemistry and compared them to two advanced textbooks. Does the writer of the simplified textbook, while "watering down" the information keep the basic principles intact, or will the reader have to relearn the information when he moves to a higher level book? I found that the authors definitely structured the books to simplify the text and theories for the novice reader. But they distorted the information as little as possible by simply leaving certain things out.

The first difference between the introductory and advanced books can be seen by just looking at them. The easier books are not as thick and have much simpler covers. A very thick chemistry textbook with fine print, lots of detail, many charts and tables, and atomic diagrams on the cover will most likely scare off the first-time chemist.

C. S. WORLD

The bright gray, black, and white screen flashes highlighted parts of the program I just typed and prints the message **PROGRAM NOT COMPILABLE** at the bottom. Clicking through the list of problems it has found, I see the computer is giving me messages that have become too familiar: **This is not a Val Parameter, This is Not an Expression, Type Clash and Mismatch.** I re-compile the program I am trying to write, to find yet more errors revealed. I clench my fists and stiffly beckon to one of the tutors in the room while contemplating breaking the little machine in front of me and taking the course next semester. The small, possibly cute screen has added a new and potent source of stress to my relatively new life as a college student.

The tutor understands his job too well and answers by asking me a question: What type of parameter do you think needs a Var or Value?" The tutor uses words like "program decomposition" and "control structures" that I don't recall being in the reading assignment. I ask a student who is typing away confidently next to me if he could help me with my program for a minute. I remember having seen him in some of my other classes and thinking that he was rather quiet. I was surprised at how talkative, confident and comfortable he seemed in the computer science world. He knew Pascal and told me what to type, but gave no explanation for what I was punching into the computer. The program worked, so I handed it in and closed the door to the sound of typing without a sense of accomplishment.

Computer science, since its birth, has created and refined a language that is unique for a reason. It is cryptic to an outsider, but it has a definite purpose as a useful tool in its world. . . .

These two writers relied on different conventions for combining a problem analysis with a claim or thesis. Look back to find as many different conventions used here as you can (see the glossary below for ideas). On the basis of your list, would you conclude that both of these papers are examples of academic discourse or not? Do they speak to the same community? (If you and other members of your class disagree, you might want to compare how you are defining a discourse community.)

PROJECTS AND ASSIGNMENTS

1 *A literary problem.* Many works of literature show us two sides of an important question—two conflicting attitudes toward love or honor or madness or imagination. Or they embody, in two characters, alternative ways of feeling or acting. In a book you are reading, describe this conflict—that is, what is at issue either within the world of the book, within the author's point of view, or within you as a reader?

2 *A personal problem.* Michael B. is a college sophomore who commutes to school. He feels he is missing much of the experience of college by living at home with his parents and seeing primarily high school friends who didn't go to college. He wants to live on campus next year but knows that if he does that, he will have to ask for the money from his father, who feels Michael should be working instead of going to college, and saving money rather than spending it. The conflict has left Michael unable to act. Can you analyze this problem and offer useful suggestions?

3 *A professional problem.* Jim Grayson and Tom Brand both work for the Ford Motor Company in Chicago. One is a spot welder on the assembly line, the other a plant manager. In his book *Working*, Studs Terkel interviewed both men, asking them to talk about their jobs, and turned up some interesting contradictions.[1] You have been hired as a trouble-shooter and consultant by Ford with the long-range goal of satisfying the needs of both the employees and management. These interviews, on pp. 164–68 and 171–81 of *Working* are your raw data. Analyze them and write a one-page problem analysis to the vice-president in charge of production. No one expects the problem to be a simple one; at the same time, your reader needs to be able to act on the recommendations you give.

Alternatively, you could read the interview with Steve Carmichael, also in *Working* (pp. 341–43), and write your own analysis of this situation in a one- to two-page report to the district superintendent, who needs to act on this personnel problem.

4 *Your own problem.* Generally the most fruitful problems to analyze are your own. Think of a problematic situation in which you find yourself right now. Remember, a problem is only a problem when someone feels caught between two sides of a question. Examine the key conflict in your situation and write an analysis of the problem, giving alternatives, assumptions, and implications.

5 The set of six projects and assignments which follow suggest various ways you can analyze problems and develop your own theses about how people use language. You can use one or more of these projects as a "method" to collect information for the discourse community assignment described on page 148. If you choose to address your paper to someone other than those of us already interested in how discourse communities work, indicate who your reader is.

Here is a brief glossary of terms you may find helpful in researching that topic. Add to this glossary some important terms from the discourse community you are observing or elaborate this glossary with specific examples from your area.

discourse: language in use, both written and spoken.
discourse community: a group of people who can comfortably use the conventions of a particular discourse and who share certain expectations about content, language, and style (see Chapter 1).

[1] Studs Terkel, *Working* (New York: Pantheon, 1972).

discourse convention: a familiar pattern or feature of a text which writers and their readers recognize as meaningful. Such convention range from the discipline-specific patterns expected in scientific argument, to general rhetorical patterns such as comparisons and examples, to text features such as topic sentences, thesis statements, and italics (see Chapter 1).

academic discourse: a set of conventions used to carry out and to share the results of research and scholarship and to carry on conversations about ideas. Different disciplines create their own communities within academic discourse (see Chapter 5).

problematic situation: a situation which contains some conflict, often in people's goals, values, or expectations.

problem definition: a statement which locates and describes the conflict itself or which defines the issue or question which underlies a problematic situation.

thesis: a statement or a claim, usually made in response to a problem or an issue, that will be supported with evidence.

preliminary problem definition and tentative thesis: good ideas created on the way to better ones.

6 Create a list of technical terms or confusing concepts from a course you have taken. In "Politics and the English Language," George Orwell argues that language is an instrument people create and use for their own purposes. In "If Black English Isn't a Language, Then Tell Me, What Is?", James Baldwin takes a less neutral stance; he argues that language is a political instrument; it is both a means and proof of power.

Consider these ideas as tentative theses and at the same time find out more about your chosen terms. Then develop and support your own thesis on how these words *evolved* or how they *work* within their discourse community.

7 Have you ever noticed what happens when insiders and outsiders to some discourse meet? Try to overhear (or stage) such an encounter and write a dialogue of your own which portrays the situation. Then take on the hat of a drama critic and write a short review that interprets and comments on your scene. (You may need to read some examples of both dialogues and drama reviews to sound like an insider yourself.)

8 Find two discussions of the same topic in a popular and a technical source (for example, a discussion of a historical event, a book, or a new product in a magazine article and a professional journal). Or compare the presentation of a concept in an introductory and advanced textbook. Use these comparisons to draw a portrait of the readers in each group: what do they know; what do they seem to expect; why?

9 In her article "Teacher Talk," Shirley Brice Heath says that teachers have special ways of asking questions that aren't really questions, but requests or commands. Her research suggests that questions are used to teach and socialize children into the appropriate patterns of response expected in school. John Braxton and Robert Nordvall claim that you can characterize a college by whether its teachers ask "why" and "how" questions (which he sees as desirable) or "what" questions (which simply ask students to parrot information). How do questions function in your classes? Can they tell you anything about how the discourse in those classes operates?

You can use some of the standard methods of classroom research to analyze teacher/student discourse. On two different days keep a detailed log on every exchange in a 10-minute period. Set up a system to note who initiated the exchange; who talked; what was the purpose; and what was the outcome. If you picked a course that causes difficulty for some people, you might ask: Did teachers and students seem to have the same expectations about this discourse? [Sources: S. B. Heath, "Teacher Talk: Language in the Classroom," *Language in Education: Theory and Practice 9* (Washington D.C.: Center for Applied Linguistics, Georgetown University, 1978). S. B. Heath, "Questioning at Home and School: A Comparative Study," ed. George Spindler, *Doing the Ethnography of Schooling* (New York: Holt, Rinehart & Winston, 1983). J. Braxton & R. Nordvall, "Selective Liberal Arts Colleges: Higher Quality as Well as Higher Prestige?", *Journal of Higher Education 36* (Sept.–Oct. 1985), pp. 538–54.]

10 Do different readers really see the same thing when they read a text outside their experience? Do your own observational research to get an answer. You will need a short (1 page) but demanding article from your field, a reader from outside the field, and a tape recorder. Give your reader the following instructions:

I'm going to give you a passage from _____ (a drama review, an automotive road test, an economics text). I would like you to read it out loud and say, as far as possible, whatever you are thinking as you read. After every few sentences I will also ask you to stop and tell me how you interpret the passage so far. At the end I will ask you a few questions about what you have read. Don't worry about "getting it wrong" or not understanding what the passage means. The purpose of my observation is to explore *different* ways readers interpret what they read.

Ask your reader how he or she "interprets" the text every few sentences, and if the reader falls silent, prompt your reader with, "Can you tell me what you are thinking now?" but don't interfere or explain. At the end you might ask your reader to summarize the text or to explain its main points to check his or her comprehension. For comparison, you may wish to repeat your observation with a reader in your field.

Look at your data. What did your reader do? Does this close look at the interpretive process help you see any problems readers might have who are trying to "enter the conversation of a field" as we talked about in Chapter 1? Use your data and any other information you have to analyze that problem.

11 Many of the preceding assignments ask you to experiment with different kinds of discourse, to collect and ponder information in order to understand a problem or develop a thesis. This gives you a good opportunity to observe your own process unfold. Keep a log in which you track how your definition of the problem and your thesis develops. Each time you work jot down a note about:

1a. Date   Time   Hours worked

1b. My *current* sense of the problem/my purpose/my tentative thesis is:

1c. What I Did/Interesting Observation:

When you are done, write a journal commentary on how your ideas seem to develop.

IF YOU WOULD LIKE TO READ MORE

If you would like to know more about problem analysis and designing your written analysis for a professional audience, see:

Mathes, J. C., and Dwight Stevenson. *Designing Technical Reports: Writing for Audiences in Organizations*. Indianapolis: Bobbs-Merrill, 1976. / This book shows how to use problem analysis to write effective technical reports within an organization. It gives an excellent introduction to professional writing in all kinds of organizations.

Young, Richard, Alton Becker, and Kenneth Pike. *Rhetoric: Discovery and Change*. New York: Harcourt Brace Jovanovich, 1970. / The authors of this important book on rhetoric explore the entire process of problem analysis and inquiry. They analyze what it means to think about problems through the act of writing, and in doing so they lay the groundwork for a modern theory of rhetoric.

chapter nine

Designing for a Reader

STEP 5   KNOW the needs of your reader

The first step in designing your writing to be read is to understand the needs, attitudes, and knowledge of your particular reader, and to help that reader turn your written message into the meaning you intended.

Strategy 1   ANALYZE YOUR AUDIENCE

Strategy 2   ANTICIPATE YOUR READER'S RESPONSE

Strategy 3   ORGANIZE FOR A CREATIVE READER

First drafts are often satisfying; they seem to say just what one meant. But when writers come back a day, a week, or a year later, they often discover a gap between what they were thinking and what their writing actually conveyed. If you are writing to be read, it is what you communicate to your reader that finally counts—not what is in your head. If you want to be understood, it is usually not enough simply to *express* your ideas. One of the secrets of communicating your ideas is to understand the needs of your reader and to transform writer-based thought into reader-based prose. The next two chapters will help you design your writing so someone else not only will read it but will understand and remember it.

In trying to design for the reader, one question people often ask is "How soon should I start thinking about my reader? Where does this step fit into the total writing process?"

The answer is that it can fit nearly anywhere. It may occur during planning, when you try to identify the audience; during idea generation, when you may develop your code words to help the reader understand; and during organizing, when you nutshell and teach your ideas with the reader in mind. Thus, designing for the reader occurs during many stages of the writing process. It could be said that this step is nested, or embedded, within other phases, much as a set of Chinese boxes is nested with one another.

Nesting also occurs on a broader level. The general steps of planning, generating, organizing, and editing are often performed "out of order" or one within the other. As you know from your experience, writers use the steps we have been discussing in this book but do not always use them in a 1, 2, 3 order like stair steps to a finished paper. They may generate ideas first, then go back to plan, then organize and edit while revising some of their plan, and so forth.

The process of designing for a reader, which will be discussed in this and the following chapter, is one that occurs throughout the act of writing. You may use the process as part of one particular step, such as planning, or you may stop between steps—say, between generating and organizing—and decide to focus on your audience before proceeding further. Therefore, designing for a reader is nested not only within each writing step but within the total writing process; you turn to it whenever you feel a need to pause and concentrate in depth on your reader. That moment could come in the middle of planning, while you are organizing ideas, or before you begin the second draft of the paper. Whenever such a time comes, Steps 5 and 6 will help you think and write for your reader.

STEP 5   KNOW the Needs of Your Reader

The goal of the writer is to create a momentary common ground between the reader and the writer. You want the reader to share your knowledge and your attitude toward that knowledge. Even if the reader eventually disagrees, you want him or her to be able for the moment to *see things as you see them.* A good piece of writing closes the gap between you and the reader.

Strategy 1   ANALYZE YOUR AUDIENCE

The first step in closing that gap is to gauge the distance between the two of you. Imagine, for example, that you are a student writing to your parents, who have always lived in New York City, about a wilderness survival expedition you want to go on over spring break. Sometimes obvious differences such as age or background will be important, but the critical differences for writers usually fall into three areas: the reader's *knowledge* about the topic, his or her *attitude* toward it, and his or her personal or professional *needs*. Because these differences often exist, good writers do more than simply express their meaning; they pinpoint the critical differences between themselves and their reader and design their writing to reduce those differences. Let us look at these three areas in more detail:

1. *Knowledge.* This is usually the easiest difference to handle. What does your reader need to know? What are the main ideas you hope to teach? Does your reader have enough background knowledge to understand you? If not, what would he or she have to learn?

2. *Attitudes.* When we say a person has knowledge, we are usually referring to his conscious awareness of explicit facts and clearly defined concepts. This kind of knowledge can be easily written down or told to someone else. However, much of what we "know" is not held in this formal, explicit way. Instead it is held as an attitude or image—as a loose cluster of associations. For instance, my image of lakes includes associations many people would have, including fishing, water skiing, stalled outboards, and lots of kids catching night crawlers with flashlights. However, the most salient or powerful parts of my image, which strongly color my whole attitude toward lakes, are thoughts of cloudy skies, long rainy days, and feeling generally cold and damp. By contrast, one of my best friends has a very different cluster of associations. To him, a lake means sun, swimming, sailing, and happily sitting on the end of a dock. Needless to say, our differing images cause us to react quite differently to a proposal that we visit a lake. Likewise, one reason people often find it difficult to discuss economics and politics is that terms such as "capitalism" conjure up radically different images.

As you can see, a reader's image of a subject is often the source of attitudes and feelings that are unexpected and, at times, impervious to mere facts. A simple statement that seems quite persuasive to you, such as "Lake Wampago would be a great place to locate the new music camp," could have little impact on your reader if he or she simply doesn't visualize a lake as a "great place." In fact, many people accept uncritically any statement that fits in with their own attitudes—and reject, just as uncritically, anything that does not.

Whether your purpose is to persuade or simply to present your perspective, it helps to know the image and attitudes that your reader already holds. The more these differ from your own, the more you will have to do to make him or her *see* what you mean.

3. *Needs.* When writers discover a large gap between their own knowledge and attitudes and those of the reader, they usually try to change the reader in some way. Needs, however, are different. When you analyze a reader's needs, it is so that you, the writer, can adapt to him. If you ask a friend majoring in biology how to keep your fish tank from clouding, you don't want to hear a textbook recitation on the life processes of algae. You expect the friend to adapt his or her knowledge and tell you exactly how to solve your problem.

The ability to adapt your knowledge to the needs of the reader is often crucial to your success as a writer. This is especially true in writing done on a job. For example, as producer of a public affairs program for a television station, 80 percent of your time may be taken up planning the details of new shows, contacting guests, and scheduling the taping sessions. But when you write a program proposal to the station director, your job is to show how the program will fit into the cost guidelines, the FCC requirements for relevance, and the overall programming plan for the station. When you write that report, your role in the organization changes from producer to proposal writer. Why? Because your reader needs that information in order to make a decision. He may be *interested* in your scheduling problems and the specific content of the shows, but he *reads* your report because of his own needs as station director of that organization. He has to act.

In college, where the reader is also a teacher, the reader's needs are a little less concrete but just as important. Most papers are assigned as a way to teach something. So the real purpose of a paper may be for you to make connections between two historical periods, to discover for yourself the principle behind a laboratory experiment, or to develop and support your own interpretation of a novel. A good college paper doesn't just rehash the facts; it demonstrates what your reader, as a teacher, needs to know—that you are learning the thinking skills his or her course is trying to teach.

Effective writers are not simply expressing what they know, like a student madly filling up an examination bluebook. Instead they are *using* their knowledge—reorganizing, maybe even rethinking their ideas to meet the demands of an assignment or the needs of their reader.

Sometimes it is also necessary to decide who is your primary audience as opposed to your secondary audience. Both may read your paper, but the primary audience is the reader you most want to teach, influence, or convince. When this is the case, you will want to design the paper so the primary reader can easily find what he or she needs.

A SAMPLE AUDIENCE ANALYSIS

Margo Miller, a college student who works in the bookstore at her university, has been asked by the new store manager to write a job description of her position as an administrative assistant in the paperback department. The manager, Dot Schwartz, said she wanted to know what tasks the position involved and needed information that would help in evaluating Margo's performance and in hiring and training an eventual replacement should Margo leave the position. Dot mentioned that new trainees might be shown the description for guidance in performing the job.

Margo's audience chart in Figure 9-1 pinpoints the critical features of her primary reader, the store manager, Dot Schwartz. Although there is much more Margo could find out about Dot, such as age and education, and so forth—observe how her notes and thinking focus on the critical facts—the facts most relevant to her purpose in writing.

KNOWLEDGE: Dot Schwartz, the new manager, knows a lot about bookstore operations in general, but she probably doesn't know what, exactly, I do as an administrative assistant and what tasks I've added to my job since I've been here. In terms of the tasks I've added, the amount of *new knowledge* I'll need to convey will be rather small, so that aspect of the report should be easy to handle.

ATTITUDES: When I took this job it was mostly a matter of typing and filing. However, through my own efforts I've now often become

Figure 9-1   *Audience chart for primary audience: the new store manager*

CRITICAL FEATURES OF THE READER

KNOWLEDGE	ATTITUDES	NEEDS
Has general knowledge of bookstore operations but not a detailed understanding of how things work here.	Sees it as a student job—no responsibility.	General list of tasks.
	Assumes I'm a temporary.	Time they take.
Doesn't know what tasks I've added to my job description.		Background or experience required.
		Needs info to give new trainees.

responsible for dealing with salespeople, ordering certain paper-backs, and designing window displays. I suspect Dot's image of my job is an inadequate one that doesn't recognize the importance of what I'm doing. She may see it as simply a part-time student job, but I see it as a training position that's allowing me to gain increased experience and responsibility. This difference in our images of the job could be critical when I ask for a raise in the fall. So in this report I need to revise Dot's inadequate image of my job and close the gap between our differing attitudes.

NEEDS: If asked, I could give a very detailed account of my job: exact facts, figures, people, and procedures. But I don't think that's what my reader needs. Dot asked for the report in order to carry out her overall job as a bookstore manager, not to get involved in minutiae. She's interested in the basic tasks involved, how long they generally take, and, since trainees may be coming in, what kinds of background or experience to look for.

Clearly the reader's needs here dictate a quite special organization of Margo's knowledge.

Margo also has a secondary audience for this report: the new trainee who will eventually read it. This reader is quite different in some ways from the manager, as Margo's audience chart in Figure 9-2 shows. Again, here are Margo's notes and thinking:

KNOWLEDGE: This reader probably won't know the difference between a back order and an O. P. title, so I'll need to explain procedures and terms in more detail.

ATTITUDES: Given the official description of this as a part-time job, a new trainee may not realize the opportunities it offers or the amount of planning and organization required to do it well.

NEEDS: The new assistant may be using this report to learn the job, so, unlike the manager, he or she will need a report organized around when and how to do things. However, since the manager is still my

Figure 9-2   *Audience chart for secondary audience: the new trainee*

CRITICAL FEATURES OF THE READER

KNOWLEDGE	ATTITUDES	NEEDS
Probably won't know basic terms or procedures.	May think of it as a "simple" part-time job.	Needs to know what to do and how to do it: an operational description of the job.
	Might not recognize the opportunities or demands really involved.	

primary audience, I probably should put this detailed information in a chart or separate section at the end.

By analyzing her audiences and their particular needs, Margo now knows enough to design a report that not only will achieve her ends but will be effective for her two quite different readers.

What about other situations, when you must write for a general reader? In the following example, Margo has decided to adapt her thoughts about her job to a very different use. She wants to submit an article to the *University Times* for a series the paper is running on jobs at the university. Even though this audience represents a cross-section of the university's students, faculty, and staff, Margo's audience analysis turns up some concrete ideas that will help her plan the paper. Here are her thoughts about the article:

> *These readers may have a limited knowledge of what it means to run a bookstore beyond selling books* (knowledge). *Furthermore, as with the store manager, their image of my job will be colored by their conception of part-time jobs* (attitudes). *Since I want to show how part-time jobs can be good career training, I'll have to deal directly with those attitudes. Finally, these readers will also need or expect something from the article* (needs). *Some people might want to learn things relevant to themselves, or might simply want some entertainment. Many people are reading the series in order to find out about various types of jobs they might like to apply for. It may be possible to meet all these needs if I structure the article well.*

Margo also needs to keep in mind her secondary audience, the *University Times* editor. Although the editor is himself seeking to meet the needs of his audience, he also has special requirements the writer must meet. For example, he needs articles under 1,000 words that are focused on the series topic and are written in an engaging, partly journalistic style. To be successful with both her audiences, Margo needs to meet them halfway.

We can sum up this discussion of audience analysis by noting three things you can do:

1. Find out who your reader will be. If you have more than one, decide which audience is primary. Which reader or kind of reader will your paper be designed primarily for?
2. Then begin to explore what you know about your reader's knowledge, attitudes, and needs. Locate these characteristics of your reader that will be critical in light of your purpose in writing.
3. Then plan how you are going to close the gap between you and your reader to make your paper effective.

⤴ Strategy 2   ANTICIPATE YOUR READER'S RESPONSE

Let us now shift focus from a particular audience or type of audience to the reader's actual process of understanding. When you think about it, we ask a great deal when we expect people to translate a few words presented on a page into a complex meaning or an image that resembles what we originally intended. As we all know, merely reading a message is not the same thing as understanding, much less remembering, it.

The question then is, what happens when a reader tries to turn a *message* into a *meaning?* And what can a writer do to increase the chances that the reader will comprehend and retain the *writer's* meaning?

HOW DOES THE COMMUNICATION PROCESS WORK?

We often talk about communication as if it were a physical process rather like sending goods in a delivery truck to the reader. We say that a writer *conveys* his message, *expresses* his ideas, or *gets* his point *across.* In this view, the writer's duty is simply to pack all his meaning into the message before it is delivered. Then the reader supposedly gets the message and sees the writer's point of view. Figure 9-3 depicts this concept of communication.

One problem with this model is that it turns the writer into a delivery boy. Communication, it seems to say, is the same as simply expressing what's on your mind. If your meaning has been placed (somewhere) in the message, then the reader can dig it out. But unfortunately readers can, and quite often do, read information yet fail to get your meaning or your point. This model of the communication process misleads us by suggesting that a writer's meaning or ideas can simply be transferred intact to someone else.

Figure 9-3   *Delivering an idea: a simplified model of communication*

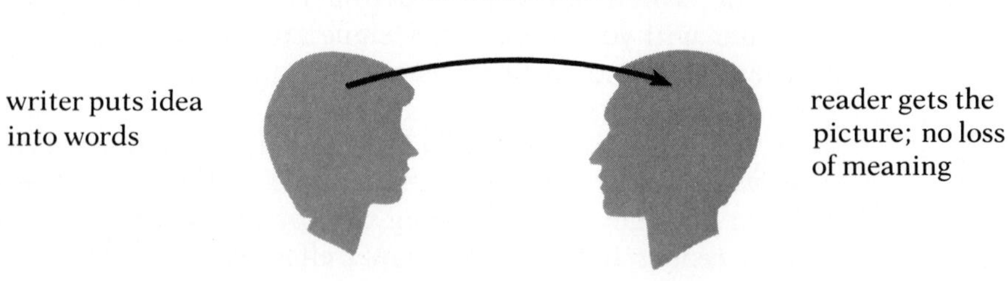

idea transmitted to reader

writer puts idea
into words

reader gets the
picture; no loss
of meaning

Figure 9-4   *A model based on communication theory*

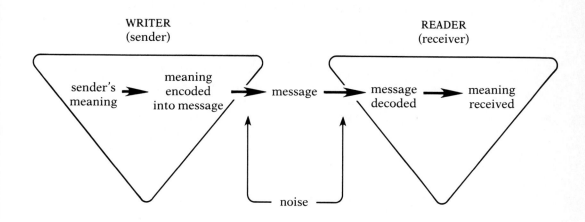

During World War II a more sophisticated version of the communication process was developed by electrical engineers who were trying to increase the amount of information transmitted through electronic equipment such as radios and telephones. This model of how communication works (see Figure 9-4) depicts the writer as a combination of a radio announcer and a transmitter that sends the messages out on air waves.

In this model the writer, or sender, has a meaning in mind. He "encodes" that meaning into a message, and it is this message that is sent to the reader. The message could take the form of a signal sent out on air waves, a hastily scrawled note tacked on the back door, or a twenty-page paper with pictures and graphs. The point is that the sender has to *encode* his meaning in some form in order to send it. And some senders are better at turning meaning into code than others. A powerful radio transmitter sends off a good-quality signal; a good writer is able to send messages that accurately express his or her meaning. The first hurdle in the communication process, then, is turning meaning into a message.

This model also reminds us that there are many opportunities for *noise* or interference in this process. While the radio operator may worry about thunderstorms, the writer must worry about everything from misspellings and bad grammar to poor organization and fuzzy thinking—all the things that make his coded message a little less clear.

When the message finally reaches the reader, he, like a radio receiver, must repeat the process of decoding the message back into a meaning. The reader, like a secret agent with a cryptogram, must interpret a meaning. And again the chance for noise enters; if the reader is tired, is confused by the subject, or misses a key word, the communication process breaks down a little more.

As you can see, it is a long way from the meaning the sender had in mind to the meaning that the receiver eventually decodes at the end of the line. The value of this model is that it graphically demonstrates that no matter what you *mean*, and even no matter what message you *send*, all that finally counts is the decoded meaning that the reader finally *receives*.

This model, however, has a limitation: It can't help us understand how readers actually decode messages. To know that, we would need a cognitive or mental model that describes some of the thinking strategies readers use to transform messages into meanings as they read. The discussion that follows will show that readers are not passive recipients who simply *see* the writer's point. In order to comprehend a message, they actually create a meaning in their own mind.

THE CREATIVE READER

What happens when readers go about decoding messages and creating meanings? The first thing to notice is that they just don't *remember* all the things we tell them. (Imagine trying to repeat every major and minor idea that was presented in the preceding chapter of this book.) Instead of remembering all the details, readers do something much more creative—they draw inferences as they read and use the writer's ideas to form their own concepts. In other words, readers remember not what *we* tell them, but what they tell *themselves*. You can demonstrate this process for yourself with the following exercise.

Here is an excerpt from the "Personal Experience" section of Henry Morris's application for a summer job in accounting. As personnel director, you have been asked to evaluate six such applications. Your job is to read each one and come up with a set of distinctive qualities that characterize each candidate. How would you characterize Henry Morris from his statement below?

> During high school I managed the concession stand for our home basketball games. Later I worked at the nearby A & W Root Beer stand during summers, and for three years I kept the books at my father's local soda bottling plant. I have taken a number of math courses and have had two courses in acounting. I am currently taking courses in small business managment.

Before reading further, write down several sentences that you would use to characterize this applicant.

You now might want to compare your reactions to those of a group of students who were shown the statement. First they listed

Figure 9-5 **Drawing Inferences From Facts**

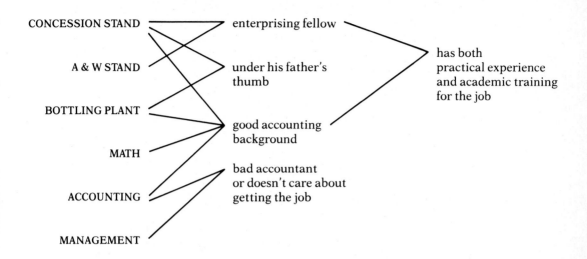

in the left column the main facts about Henry they all agreed were important (see Figure 9-5). Then everyone proceeded to describe the Henry they had just read about. Here are some of the conclusions they reached about Henry:

LISA: He seems like a good bet for the job—first, because he's had a lot of practical accounting experience. And then he's had a couple of courses on the subject, plus the math. On top of that, he seems pretty enterprising to have taken all those courses and gotten himself those summer jobs.

JOSE: It sounds as if he's had accounting experience all right, but all he's done is work at his father's plant. And maybe he only had the job at the concession stand because of his father's plant. He doesn't seem very enterprising if he hasn't gone out and found another accounting job to get more varied experience.

TIM: His accounting experience does look impressive: three years is a lot of experience for a young guy coming into a summer job. But his application is so sloppy. He misspelled both "accounting" and "management" in just that one paragraph. Accountants are supposed to be good with details. Maybe he didn't proofread the statement before he sent it, but in that case he seems very careless or not really interested in the job.

Note that from even small details in the text, such as misspellings, the students had arrived at some sweeping conclusions. Furthermore, the chances are good that a real personnel director might have the same response. As you can see from this example, when

167

people are trying to understand a passage, they constantly are drawing inferences and making their own meanings.

This experiment demonstrates two things. The first is that readers do not passively absorb a writer's information; they make meaning as they read. Second, the meanings they make are often surprising leaps of imagination. The obvious question, then, is why are readers so creative with our prose? Why must they draw inferences and form concepts?

The Problem of Conscious Attention

One reason for this phenomenon is the limitation of our conscious attention, which forces us to "chunk," or group, information in order to understand it. When it comes to reading, or in fact processing any kind of new information, people are remarkably inefficient. This is because our conscious attention (or short-term, working memory) can handle only a limited number of inputs at one time. This is in contrast to the apparently unlimited storage capacity of long-term memory.

Imagine yourself sitting in a lecture. All incoming information—the voice of the speaker, the words on the blackboard, that idea you were trying to remember, and the person smiling at you across the room—all this information clamors for a portion of your limited conscious attention. We are often caught like jugglers with too many balls in the air.

To test the limits of your own short-term, working memory, multiply 12×14 in your own head. Now try multiplying 789×678 in your head. Do it now.

Notice how difficult it is to keep track of your partial answers, carry-overs, and the current multiplication task at the same time. You can see why one of our major limitations as thinkers and problem solvers is the nature of our short-term memory. Although we must deal with highly complex problems, we are unable to actively hold in mind and consider more than a few separate items at a time. Cognitive psychologists set the critical limit at 7 ± 2 bits of information.

Furthermore, in comparison with other processing systems, such as a computer, we are neither particularly fast nor accurate. As a communication channel the human voice can process 25 "bits" of information per second, whereas most electronic channels are designed to process between 10^4 and 10^5 bits in that same second. According to cognitive psychologist George Miller, it is a charity to call us a channel at all. We are more like a bottleneck.

Fortunately, we human beings have another trick up our sleeve that makes us remarkably good at thinking. This is the ability to "chunk" information—to look at a whole milling array of facts and perceptions, all shouting for immediate individual attention, and to reduce that throng to a single chunk. ("Oh, that's one of those whatchamacallits again.") A chunk may be a concept, a category, a term—anything that enables a person to organize miscellaneous data. Telegraph operators use this process when they learn to perceive a string of rapid dashes and dits as meaningful chunks such as words and phrases. You and I do it when, instead of thinking "There are forty-eight individual cars (in Aztec Red, Seafoam Green, Harvest Gold, and so on) jammed up around the 5th and Penn Avenue intersection honking their horns at 5:34 P.M. Tuesday afternoon . . . ," we simply think to ourselves, "rush hour traffic jam," and go on with our conversation. In order, then, to compensate for the limitations of short-term memory, people sort information into chunks they can manage.

Drawing Inferences/Remembering Gists

One way to make a chunk is to draw an inference. An inference is a new idea *we create* from previous ideas. (Sometimes, however, people such as the résumé readers may not realize they have drawn an inference and think they are simply stating the facts.) In slow motion, the process would look like this: We look at two or more facts or ideas and ask ourselves, "What single new idea (or chunk) would connect (or contain) those facts?" Our inference, such as "he's a good accountant," is a creative interpretation of the information. Another way to chunk information, which we have already discussed, is to summarize it into a gist. These inferences and gists often form the top-level ideas in a hierarchy. And these top-level ideas are what readers remember best.

But what determines *how* the reader will chunk new information and *which* inferences they will draw? We naturally like to think that readers carefully mine our prose for *the* meaning we intended. But much recent research in psychology shows that it is more accurate to think of readers as hard at work using our information like a set of tinker toys, to build an idea structure of their own. And if our writing doesn't help them build it, that final structure may or may not resemble our own. In attempting to read and understand a message—to make meaning—a creative reader

1. *Uses context.* The reader will try to fit your new information into a context or framework he or she already knows.
2. *Makes predictions.* Readers make predictions about what should follow, and they use these expectations to interpret the text—even when they are wrong.

3. *Creates gists.* Readers consolidate new information into more manageable packages or chunks. These gists are what they remember.
4. *Organizes ideas.* Readers sort and structure ideas into an unconscious hierarchical structure built around key concepts or gists (as they see them).

Let us look at these processes of the reader in more detail.

Readers need a framework, or context, for new ideas. In 1938, Orson Welles threw thousands of people into panic with a radio broadcast reporting a Martian invasion of New Jersey. Why? Because his audience had the wrong framework. Those who tuned in during the middle thought they were hearing a news broadcast, not a mere radio drama called "The War of the Worlds."

Readers make sense out of new information by putting it into context. When they aren't given a clear context for such information, they are likely to do two things. First, they supply their own context. A worried reader, anticipating disagreement and afraid that no one likes him, will interpret your helpful suggestion as yet another criticism. Second, they will not understand you at all. Even the simplest information may be hard to understand and impossible to remember if the reader has no context for making sense out of it.

To demonstrate this for yourself, try this experiment. Read the following passage through once (and only once).

> The procedure is actually quite simple. First you arrange things into different groups. Of course one pile may be sufficient depending on how much there is to do. If you have to go somewhere else due to lack of facilities that is the next step, otherwise you are pretty well set. It is important not to overdo things. That is, it is better to do too few things at once than too many. In the short run this may not seem important, but complications can easily arise. A mistake can be expensive as well. At first the whole procedure will seem complicated.
>
> Soon, however, it will become just another fact of life. It is difficult to foresee any end to the necessity for this task in the immediate future, but then one never can tell. After the procedure is completed, one arranges the materials into different groups again. Then they can be put into their appropriate places. Eventually they will be used once more and the whole cycle will then have to be repeated. However, that is a part of life.[1]

Now shift your attention for a minute or so by saying the alphabet backwards or reading a page at random from this book.

[1] John D. Bransford and Nancy S. McCarrell, "A Sketch of a Cognitive Approach to Comprehension," in *Cognition and Symbolic Processes*, ed. Walter Weiner (Hillsdale, N.J.: Erlbaum, 1974).

Then, without looking at the passage again, try to write down all you can remember about the passage.

How much did you remember? When psychologists John Bransford and Nancy McCarrell ran this experiment they found that their subjects did very poorly, even though the passage describes a very common activity for which everyone has a framework: washing clothes. When another group of subjects was given the passage and told at the beginning that it was a description of washing clothes, the subjects had an immediate framework. Not only did they appear much less frustrated with the task, but they remembered much more of the passage. By creating a context for their readers, Bransford and McCarrell were able to more than *double* their readers' comprehension and recall.

Professional writers and magazine editors often go to great lengths to establish a context for their articles. Consider the article shown below, from the March 1979 issue of *Ms.* magazine. It creates a context in five different ways, each one more specific than the last.

1. The heading tells us we are reading the magazine's monthly column on *money.*
2. This month it will be on money and *housing*, the picture says.
3. In particular it's on *buying* your own house, we learn from the title.
4. Buying, that is, with a *low down payment*, the subtitle adds.
5. And it is especially pertinent if you are a *woman*, we learn in the first sentence.

1.

2.

3.

4.

5.

MONEY

How To Buy A House on Your Own...with a Little Help from Uncle Sam

Under one government program, you can buy a house for $1 down.

I never dreamed that as a single woman I would ever be able to own a house. Like many women, I assumed that on my salary (about $14,000 a year) and with today's staggering new-home prices, I would continue to be a "renter" all

BY EMILY VAN NESS

my adult life—unless I struck it rich or decided to get married and pool my resources.

Then, while apartment-hunting last year in New Jersey, I came

across an ad in a local paper for a three-story, brick house in Trenton for only $30,000, 10 percent down, and an unbelievably low 7½ percent mortgage. (Today most conventional lenders are requiring a cash down payment of at least 20

Consider the difference if the article had had an ambiguous title or heading and had started out with "While apartment hunting last year in New Jersey, I came across an ad in a local paper for a three-story brick house in Trenton. . . ." Unless you knew it was a short story (and had faith that it would get better soon), your reaction would probably have been "So what? Why should I read this?" As you can see, a context not only helps a reader make sense of things, it also creates expectations that lure him or her on. And this brings us to the second point about readers.

Readers develop expectations and want those expectations met. General context, as we have seen, gives readers a rough idea of what is coming by setting up a framework with empty slots waiting to be filled. Sometimes the very type of article or paper arouses firm expectations. For example, whenever I read a movie review I expect to find some discussion of the theme or plot, some background on the actors, and an evaluation by the critic—but not a description of the ending. If you depart too greatly from your genre—whether it is a stockholders' report, a highly structured essay assignment, or a résumé—you are likely to confuse or disorient your reader.

Although you can sometimes use expectations readers already have, as a writer you also have the power to create expectations in the reader's mind. Exam graders, for example, are strongly influenced by a dazzling first answer or a weak beginning. If an article or paper begins in a vague fashion, the reader's expectation may be: "This paper sounds as if it's going to be full of hot air, so I can just skim." Perhaps the writer is building slowly up to a point or plans to save his best ideas for last, but it is hard to overcome the powerful effect of a reader's initial expectations.

Cues in the text—whether they are key words you introduce, "teaser" sentences that suggest interesting material to come, or simply a preview of the contents—help generate expectations. But cues can backfire, too. In Henry Morris's accounting application (see page 166), certain readers saw Henry's misspellings as evidence that he would be a poor accountant. Readers often generate expectations from relatively small, and sometimes inadvertent, cues in the text. These expectations may be so strong that the reader simply won't see what you have to say.

Once a reader's expectations are aroused, they actively clamor to be fulfilled. So it is important to follow through on what your initial paragraphs promise. A reader quickly becomes impatient with wandering prose that seems not to be moving toward the points initially previewed.

Setting up and fulfilling expectations also serve another very important function—they make people remember things. The best way to make your point vivid and memorable is to set up a strong expectation and then fulfill it. Expectations are a valuable way of circumventing short-term memory. If you know what you are looking for, it is much easier and faster to process all that information. Plus, by giving the reader a context and building up expectations, you are equipping him with a set of hooks for retaining what you want him to know.

Readers organize ideas into gists and natural hierarchies. A final way readers understand and remember what you tell them is by organizing your discussion in a general hierarchical way. If you don't do it for them, they will do it themselves—and the result may be far from what you had intended.

The important things about hierarchies, as you know, are that they create a focus by distinguishing major points from minor ones and they show how ideas are related to one another. In general, a reader will want to get a feel for the structure of any discussion very quickly; it is hard to hold many unrelated ideas in mind for long. A writer, on the other hand, might want to present all the facts first and then reveal his point, hoping the reader will keep everything in mind until he does so. Unfortunately, when readers don't see the focus and structure of your ideas, they will probably just build an organization of their own to comprehend the discussion. And the structure they build may not be the one you had in mind at all.

To demonstrate for yourself just how creative readers can be, try the following "headless paragraph" experiment. The six sentences listed below come from a paragraph written by a student on the topic of "The Writing Problem of College Students." Without a topic sentence and without the transitions and connections between the sentences, it is hard to see just how the ideas in this paragraph were organized. Read the six sentences and then jot down in a sentence or two what you think the main point of the paragraph was.

The Headless Paragraph

Students aren't practicing.
College atmosphere produces tension.
Students are afraid of getting a "D."
Writing is time consuming.
Writing is usually done under time pressure.
Writing courses are not required, so students must take a heavy
    course load to learn how.

When this experiment was conducted with a group of eighteen college sophomores, the results were surprising to the student who had written the paragraph containing these ideas. Out of eighteen readers, no one came up with the same organizing idea she had had in mind. Three had concepts that accounted for much of the paragraph, such as: "Students have difficulty in writing due to the pressures imposed upon them by grades, time, and the tension of college life." Three other readers focused on an inclusive or high-level idea, pressure, but neglected other points such as practice.

Altogether, only six of the eighteen came up with an organizing idea that could incorporate most of the information in the paragraph. Of the other twelve readers, four came away with concepts that accounted for only a limited part of the paragraph, such as "Students don't have enough time." And seven ended up with ideas that were not contained in the sentences at all! For example, these readers thought the topic sentence should be "Students aim to please teachers," or "There is too much competition in college," or "Writing should not be required," or "Writing should be required in college." These readers simply took the writer's information and hooked it onto a framework of their own. They used it to support something they already believed. The final reader in this group of eighteen even dropped the subject of writing altogether and said that the major idea of the paragraph was that "Students are more interested in grades than in learning. Their selfishness produces artificial pressures." This statement came as quite a shock to the original author.

As you can see, some readers created a focus or structure that was at least close to what the writer had intended. Their topic sentence created a tree that was at least able to account for most of the information. But some of the readers, in their need to create some sort of organization, interpreted the paragraph in unexpected, even drastic ways.

Here, for comparison, is the paragraph that the writer finally developed after receiving input from her classmates. Note how she employed a topic sentence to create expectations and used cues along the way to show how the ideas were related.

> Students often have trouble writing in college because of a combination of bad habits and high pressure. To start with, students don't practice. This is partly because of time limitations: learning to write is time consuming, and since writing courses are not required, students have to take a heavy load in order to learn how. Some students do have the time to practice but fail to do so because writing in the high-pressure atmosphere of college produces anxiety and tension. Many students are so afraid of getting a "D" that they avoid writing altogether—until the day before the paper is due. Furthermore, college papers are usually done under time pressure, which simply increases the tension of writing.

✍ Strategy 3   ORGANIZE FOR A CREATIVE READER

Creative readers are a fact of life, because reading, like writing, is an active process of making meaning. For example, I expect you, my reader, to mentally rewrite this book as you read, making it your own with your own examples and associations and using it for your own purposes. On the other hand, I want my version of the ideas to be clear to you, too—even if you choose to remember your own. As writers, one of the major tools we have for speaking to our creative readers and for helping and guiding them as they read is organization. A clear organization lets readers do three of the four actions described on pages 169–70: make predictions, create gists, and organize ideas.

In the next few chapters we will look closely at ways to plan and test for a coherent and reader-based organization. But of all the techniques we will look at, probably the three most time-tested rules of thumb are the following ones:

1. State Your Main Idea Explicitly in the Text.

This is harder than it sounds, because it often means that you must look at a paragraph and say, "What is my main idea?" You have to create the gist you want the reader to remember. You can place this main idea in various places. The most common ones in a paragraph are at the beginning and at the end. Notice, however, the distinction between a mere *topic* and a *gist*.

A topic merely names the subject or issue you are talking about. In the student example above, the topic is "students' writing troubles." A topic sentence that names the topic is indeed helpful to the reader, but that is not the same as stating your main idea.

A main idea or a gist is a statement about the topic—that is, it makes a claim or a comment on the topic of "writing troubles." The main idea or gist of the paragraph above is that these troubles are caused by bad habits and high pressure. In our example paragraph, the topic sentence not only announces the topic but summarizes the main idea of the entire paragraph in explicit terms and then places that statement of the gist in the powerful first-sentence position. When you test your own paragraphs, don't confuse a mere topic with an explicit statement of your main idea—your comment on that topic.

2. Focus Your Paragraph on the Topic or Main Idea.

Assume that the reader will try to see each paragraph as one chunk. Are all the sentences connected to your main idea, and can they be summed up into a single gist? If not, you may have a headless paragraph the reader will rewrite.

3. Use a Standard Pattern of Organization.

You can help the reader make good predictions by organizing your ideas into a familiar paragraph pattern. Such patterns, which are discussed in Chapter 12, include these ways of organizing:

Describe something: Stick to your topic if you use this one. Compare two things: Show how they are alike and different. Show cause or effect: You can work backward or forward. Present a problem and a solution: This can be dramatic.

The following set of data presents a real-life problem in doing all the things discussed in this chapter. This is part of a survey conducted among students to discover their assumptions about writing and to see whether their assumptions had any relation to the kind of writing they did. What does it mean? In order to understand these data, we will walk through some of the things you as a writer might do:

1. Chunk related facts together and draw an inference.
2. Group those inferences together in order to interpret each student's assumptions about writing in physics.
3. Compare those assumptions to each other, to the instructor's assumptions, and to the student's success in writing in physics.
4. Build your own interpretation and set of main ideas or inferences from these data.
5. Apply your inferences, if you wish, to related kinds of writing.
6. Present your main ideas to a reader, using the data and your inferences to support your interpretation, and creating a context and a structure the reader can follow.

JOE'S SURVEY PROJECT

Professor Grapevine, a teacher of freshman composition, has asked her students to do a survey among the students in some class that has writing assignments (other than freshman composition), for the purpose of learning on what standards the students in that class think their work is being evaluated. Dr. Grapevine wants her students to compare, as far as possible, their view of what teachers look for when they evaluate writing with the views of the students in the course being investigated.

Joe Scholar, a student in Dr. Grapevine's class, has decided to use a section of Physics 50, taught by Professor Orangeblossom, for his survey project. Joe has chosen Physics 50 because he took the course last semester and he has dark memories of struggles with lab notebooks and written explanations of homework problems. Since it is early in the semester, Joe wonders whether this group of students is having the same difficulties he had. After considerable thought, Joe produced the following form.

```
            Pilot Survey for Physics 50


What 2-4 things in writing lab reports for Physics 50
have hurt your grade the most?
1.
2.
3.
4.
What is your grade in Physics 50 so far?  _____
What is your academic major?  _____
What is your grade in school?  (circle one)
Fresh  Soph  Jr  Sr  Grad
Is this your first physics course?  (yes/no)  _____
```

When Joe begins to read the data from his pilot survey, he finds a sheet with the following responses on it. From these data, what inferences could you draw about either Student S or about what effective writing means in Physics 50?

```
                 Student S


1. didn't use graph paper
2. didn't use two-column data/comment format
3. didn't number the steps
4. used #4 pencil
Course grade so far: D
Academic major: Criminal Justice
Year in school: Freshman
Is this your first physics course?  yes
```

How did you interpret that set of facts? How did you, as a creative reader, arrive at your interpretation? In this case study of

Joe's project, we are going to walk through the process of looking at facts (or statements or observations) and then draw an inference that will sum up or interpret those facts with a new idea. We will try to slow down this process of inference making, which normally happens so quickly that we don't even realize we have done it. As we follow Joe's inference-making process, bear in mind that there are no right or wrong answers. We are looking at his interpretation. We are watching a writer in action.

From these data on Student S, Joe draws several inferences. First, he notices that Student S's comments all deal with matters of form: using certain paper, using a soft lead pencil, using columns, and so on. (The little ⇒ is a symbol for an inference, which you can read as "means.")

· wrong paper	(means)
· wrong format	⇒ form matters most
· unnumbered steps	(inference)
· wrong pencil	

Apparently Student S believes that the most important feature of well-written homework is its form, or that form is what Professor Orangeblossom is grading for. Joe's inference, to the right of the arrow, sums up S's four comments with the phrase "form matters most."

Having taken Physics 50, Joe remembers that the theory "form matters most" was one that many freshman students held at the beginning of the year. However, looking back, he realizes that it is possible to draw a different inference (or interpretation) about what Professor Orangeblossom was looking for if one thinks about other possible causes for the same results. Here are Joe's inferences, which add up to a very different conclusion:

(means)
· unnumbered steps ⇒ the order of the discussion
is hard to follow
(inference 1)

clearly showing
the steps in your
⇒ solution matters
(inference 3)

· #4 pencil ⇒ the fuzzy handwriting
is hard to read
(inference 2)

We now have two conflicting sets of inferences: those Joe attributes to Student S and his own. How do we know which is best? Inferences are interpretations that both writers and creative readers constantly make in order to make sense out of things. But what makes a good or a better inference? Here are two rules of thumb you can use to test your own inferences.

1. A good inference accounts for all (or more) of the data.
2. A good inference follows closely from the facts.

Put in the negative, if you have to make a large leap of imagination to get from observation to inference, or if someone else has trouble seeing the connection, be suspicious. You may have made a greater inference (a bigger leap) than the facts allow.

At this point Joe asks himself whether the rest of the data support his current inference. For instance, what might be the relevance of the two-column data/comment format? Here is his interpretation:

	S gave either no	showing
· no data/comment format ⇒	comments or	your reasons
	very brief comments ⇒	matters
	(inference 4)	(inference 5)

In support of this theory, Joe remembers that when he began learning physics principles, he often misapplied them because he didn't understand how questions about different parts of the same problem could call for the application of different principles. When he wrote out his reasons for choosing a principle and his decisions about how to use it, he learned a great deal, especially when he read Professor Orangeblossom's comments. Joe remembers that Orangeblossom gives credit for a reasonable solution process even if you get the wrong answer.

Putting together all these observations and inferences, Joe has come up with his own theory about what effective writing means in Physics 50:

· showing the steps matters	showing your thinking and having
· showing reasons matters ⇒	a clear problem-solving process
· a good attempt counts	matter most in physics writing
	(inference 6)

How well do you think these inferences account for the data?

Here are three more sets of data, from Students Y, Z, and Q. What inferences can you draw about why each student is earning the grade reported on the form? If you look at all four sets of data, what inferences can you make about Professor Orangeblossom's grading standards?

<u>Student Y</u>

1. late papers
2. used wrong principals for the problems
3. mispelled physics terms
4. coments to short
Course grade so far: C—
Academic major: engineering
Year in school: freshman
Is this your first physics course? no

<u>Student Z</u>

1. Although I can usually think of 2 or 3 ways to approach a problem,
2. I can't always tell why one is better than the others.
3. Also, I frequently can't make any one of them work.
4. When an approach does work, I'm not always sure why
   it worked when another one didn't.
Course grade so far: B—
Academic major: Chemistry
Year in school: Freshman
Is this your first physics course: no

<u>Student Q</u>

1. bad math
2. bad handwriting
3. diagrams unclear
4. personality conflict with teacher
Course grade so far: C—
Academic major: Math
Year in school: Freshman
Is this your first physics course? no

After conducting his survey and tabulating the results, Joe decided to interview Professor Orangeblossom to learn what criteria
he used when grading and how well his criteria matched those of
his students. Here is how Dr. Orangeblossom answered the survey:

1. mechanical, unthinking approaches to problems; no explanation of why a particular approach was chosen
2. not showing clearly all the steps of the work
3. sloppy work—leaving out steps, writing hard to read, solution spread haphazardly all over the page and out of order
4. late papers

Regarding his first answer, Dr. Orangeblossom said,

> I suppose it's cheating to give two answers to #1, but the first thing is what I encounter in all students. To get them past it, I have to insist on explanations for approaches and on clearly presented problem-solving processes. Of the two, the explanations are more important because they are where I can make the most direct contact with the students' minds, where I can comment in ways that will teach them how to think about physics problems. I had to mention late papers because I get so many of them that I have to grade down for lateness, but really, that doesn't matter to me as much as the first three answers matter. They are about communication, or failure to communicate. That's what really bothers me about students' writing, failure to communicate.

Then Joe gave Dr. Orangeblossom a list of the problems most commonly cited by students in the survey and asked him to rank them. Here is his ranking:

1. not showing all the steps of the work
2. giving few comments
3. using physics terms incorrectly
4. getting wrong answers or using incorrect principles
5. using incorrect format (for example, numbering the steps of solutions to physics problems)
6. using the wrong kind of pen or pencil
7. misspelling words

You have now seen a sample of the data from Joe Scholar's study, "Writing in Physics." As you have probably noticed, it is included in this chapter because it raises two questions about writing for a reader.

Problem 1: In Writing for a Physics Professor or Writing Lab Reports, What Matters Most?

To answer this question, you must examine the rest of the data, just as Joe did, and draw your own inferences. Remember, an *inference* is a new idea that connects or accounts for previously learned facts. But notice that a good inference must account for a number of facts. *A good inference is supported by the evidence.*

The following questions might help you draw inferences as you examine the data in this problem (that is, the comments by four students, Joe's inferences, and the professor's input).

1. How consistent are the subjects' grades with Dr. Orangeblossom's comments? Does Orangeblossom really seem to be grading for the things that he says he's grading for?
2. How does Dr. Orangeblossom's comment about communication help explain his answers to the two survey forms? What inferences can you draw?
3. Certain things appear to matter very much to Dr. Orangeblossom, and other things matter relatively little. What can you reasonably suppose are the reasons for this?
4. Why do some things that are important to Dr. Orangeblossom not even appear in the pilot survey results? And why do Orangeblossom's students place so much emphasis on matters that their teacher thinks are fairly trivial?
5. What attitudes, theories, and features of the writing itself matter most in writing for physics?

If you draw an inference that you think is right but don't have enough evidence to support it, you can try to get more information. When Joe asked Dr. Orangeblossom to explain his comment about communication, he received the following answer. How does it affect your reasoning about the last question?

> You see, Joe, physics is as much a way of thinking about the relationships among forms of matter and energy as it is knowing sets of facts. In fact, the thinking may be more important. I'm trying to teach people how to think about these relationships. I can't show them how to improve their thinking if they don't tell me *what* they're thinking. That's why I give up to 80 percent credit to an answer that is mathematically wrong if it's well thought out and clearly expressed—that is, if the student used the appropriate physics principle for the right reasons in the right ways. I believe that if you can't express what you're thinking, then you don't really *know* what you're thinking.

Problem 2: Writing for Your Own Reader

After thinking about this material, could you give Students S, Y, Z, and Q some advice on how to raise their grades on the physics lab reports in Dr. Orangeblossom's class?

Remember, you have creative readers who want to see the main ideas and see the relevance to themselves. As you write for these readers, think about their attitudes and needs:

1. What do some of your readers already believe?
2. How can you present and support your own inferences or top-level ideas? Help your readers to see not just the facts but your interpretation of them.

PROJECTS AND ASSIGNMENTS

1 Thinking about the reader while you are composing is a good way to make decisions about what to include, what to emphasize, and how to organize it. The writer in the following transcript is using the reader for that purpose as he composes a section of a new staff handbook for the Timmerman Landscape Company. This section will introduce inexperienced summer staff to the surprisingly complex task of planting a tree. (You can see the original proposal for this project in Chapter 8.) As this writer uses the audience in this planning, he also creates a slowly growing portrait of those readers—as he sees them. Using his comments, try to reconstruct this writer's "mental image" of his readers.

First, you might look at which of the readers' features he actually considers: knowledge, attitudes, or needs. (The initial episodes in his planning have already been annotated.) Then compare his assumptions about his readers to the discussion on pages 158–160. Does he see his audience as creative readers? How does he expect them to read or process information or to respond to what they read?

Draw a verbal portrait of the reader (as this writer sees him). Then decide whether this is a realistic portrait. Will his plans, based on that reader, work?

Transcript About Writing a Manual

reader's knowledge	OK, the most important thing in this manual is how to plant trees. And I don't want people to make the mistakes that Larry and I made.
need to know	Our biggest problem was the holes—we made them too small.
reader's response/ need to know	And here I wonder if it will confuse people to have different directions for evergreens and deciduous trees right together? Or if I give separate sets of directions, will they read the first set and miss the second set? Hmm. The only difference is the treatment of the root ball. So maybe I'll keep all that together and just give separate directions at that one point, and use big labels.
	OK, now, the hole. I'm going to need a drawing. I can tell them to make the hole twice as big as the root ball, and I will tell them in what

183

order to put in the drainage stuff, manure, and dirt. But a drawing is clearer, it lets you see everything in proportion to the tree.

OK, what else? The dirt—it has to be new dirt, not the customer's subsoil. I have to explain that. And we supply it.

Oh yes. CALL THE CUSTOMER! Essential step; I'll have to put it early in the manual. So why is it an essential step? They'll need a list of reasons here:

—to verify the order
—to make sure he's home when they deliver
—so he can supervise where they dig the hole
—so he can call someone if they hit a pipe, or there's some other kind of trouble
—so he can pay them and save us sending a bill.

That reminds me—I have to explain about not planting trees too close to the house, the street, the driveway.

This could be long. Will they read it? Diagrams—they'll look at pictures with big headings and not much print. So I'll also need a diagram for bushes—or maybe combine bushes & trees into one diagram? Yeah—make this one chapter on planting bushes *and* trees. Because who needs different chapters for every little thing?

OK, good. Now, the list of stuff for the truck: wire cutters, spade, pick, canvas, stakes, pieces of garden hose. Burlap, twine, wire, pruning hooks, clippers, bucket, 2 hoses. I should say that they can't expect to use the customer's things, or even expect the customer to have a hose. Most of this is pretty obvious. Except maybe the canvas. If I tell them step by step how to plant and stake the tree, they'll see why they need these things. So I won't explain; this will be a checklist they can use when they go out on jobs. So it will go up at the top, even before calling the customer. And the step-by-step directions will be real short.

I wonder if I'll need a picture of how the tree should look when they've wrapped the trunk and staked it?

2 You are writing an article on eating out for people who are following a low-carbohydrate diet, and you plan to include a paragraph on fast-food restaurants. Use the data in the following table for source material, and write a paragraph tailored to your audience. How will you chunk the data? What inferences can you draw?

chapter nine / Designing for a Reader

NUTRITIONAL CONTENT OF POPULAR FAST FOODS

Item	Calories	Protein (grams)	Carbohy-drates (grams)	Fat (grams)	Sodium (milli-grams)
HAMBURGERS					
McDonald's Big Mac	541	26	39	31	962
Burger Chef Hamburger	258	11	24	13	393
FISH					
Arthur Treacher's Fish Sandwich	440	16	39	24	836
Long John Silver's Fish (2 pieces)	318	19	19	19	not available
OTHER ENTREES					
McDonald's Egg Muffin	352	18	26	20	914
Taco Bell Taco	186	15	14	8	79
Dairy Queen Brazier Dog	273	11	23	15	868
SIDE DISHES					
Burger King French Fries	214	3	28	10	5
Arthur Treacher's Cole Slaw	123	1	11	8	266
McDonald's Chocolate Shake	364	11	60	9	329
McDonald's Apple Pie	300	2	31	19	414

Source: The New York Times, September 19, 1979. Copyright © 1979 by The New York Times Company. Reprinted by permission.

Now use the table for a different purpose. You are giving a talk to a group of heart patients who must follow a low-fat, low-salt diet, and you plan to mention fast food. Write a paragraph advising them of good and poor fast-food choices. A third way you could chunk the information in this table is in terms of food value per dollar. A survey of fast-food places in Pittsburgh in April of 1984 and again in January of 1988 turned up these prices (1988 prices are in parentheses): a Big Mac is $1.30 ($1.54); Arthur Treacher's Fish Sandwich is $1.19; Long John Silver's Fish is $1.81 ($2.10); an Egg McMuffin is $.99 ($1.16); a Taco Bell taco is $.73 ($.79); and a Dairy Queen Brazier Dog is $.79 ($.79). Write a discussion of fast foods in terms of the best food for your money.

IF YOU WOULD LIKE TO READ MORE

If you want to know more about readers and how to design your writing with them in mind, see:

Bransford, John D. *Human Cognition: Learning, Understanding and Remembering.* Belmont, Calif.: Wadsworth Publishing, 1979. / This is an excellent introduction to the most recent research and theories about human thinking processes.

Farnham-Diggory, Sylvia. *Cognitive Processes in Education.* New York: Harper and Row, 1972. / This book offers a good introduction to the many psychological issues that affect education and learning.

Mathews, J. C. and Dwight Stevenson. *Designing Technical Reports: Writing for Audiences in Organizations.* Indianapolis: Bobbs-Merrill, 1976. / This book gives excellent guidance on professional writing in all kinds of organizations, with special emphasis on the writing of technical reports. It also offers a very detailed and effective way of analyzing one's readers in a technical organization.

Miller, George. "The Magical Number Seven, Plus or Minus Two: Some Limits on Our Capacity for Processing Information." *Psychological Review*, 63 (March 1956), 81–96. In *The Psychology of Communication*, New York: Basic Books, 1967. / This is a witty and well-written introduction to the research that has been done in information processing, authored by one of the pioneers in the field.

chapter ten

Writing Reader-Based Prose

STEP 6   TRANSFORM writer-based prose into reader-based prose

Use your knowledge of the reader's needs to develop a strategy for communicating, not just expressing, your ideas. By identifying a goal you share with the reader and adapting your knowledge to your reader's needs, you can also achieve your own goals as a writer.

Strategy 1   SET UP A SHARED GOAL

Strategy 2   DEVELOP A READER-BASED STRUCTURE

Strategy 3   GIVE YOUR READER CUES

Strategy 4   DEVELOP A PERSUASIVE ARGUMENT

As we saw in Chapter 9, simply expressing yourself isn't always enough; it's no guarantee that you are actually communicating with someone else. This chapter will focus on specific rhetorical strategies you can use to design your writing for a reader.

Some people are rightly suspicious of the notion of rhetorical strategy when they equate it with such things as "mere rhetoric," empty eloquence, or the sophist's art of persuading by any means available. The rhetorical strategy we will discuss is, instead, an attempt to fulfill your goals by meeting the needs of your reader. It is, in essence, a plan for communicating.

Why is such a strategy necessary? We have already looked at one reason: The creative reader needs the help of a context, a clear structure, and guiding expectations to effectively read your prose. Writing a message down is one thing; communicating your meaning is an art that requires planning. Shortly we will look at a second reason for conscious strategy, which grows out of the private nature of the writer's own composing process.

STEP 6   TRANSFORM Writer-Based Prose into Reader-Based Prose

Good writers know how to transform writer-based prose (which works well for them) into reader-based prose (which works for their readers as well). Writing is inevitably a somewhat egocentric enterprise. We naturally tend to talk to ourselves when composing. As a result, we often need self-conscious strategies for trying to talk to our reader.

⇐ *Strategy 1*   SET UP A SHARED GOAL

The first strategy for adapting a paper to a reader is to create a shared goal. Try to find a reason for writing your paper and a reason for reading it that both you and your reader share. (Remember that your desire to convey information will not necessarily be met by your reader's desire to receive it.) Then organize your ideas and your arguments around this common goal. You will need to consider the knowledge, attitudes, and needs of your reader, as discussed previously.

A shared goal can be a powerful tool for persuasion. To illustrate, try this exercise:

> You have just been commissioned to write a short booklet on how to preserve older homes and buildings, which the City Historical Society wants to distribute throughout a historical section of the city in an effort to encourage preservation. Most of your readers will simply be residents and local business people. How are you going to get them, first, to read this booklet and, second, to use some of its suggestions?

Take several minutes to think about this problem, then write an opening paragraph for the booklet that includes a shared goal.

To test the effectiveness of your paragraph, consider the following two points about shared goals:

1. A shared goal can *motivate your audience* to read and remember what you have to say. Does your paragraph suggest that the booklet will solve some problem your reader faces or achieve

some end he or she really cares about? An appeal to vague goals or a wishy-washy generalization such as "our heritage" is unlikely to keep the reader interested. Use your knowledge to fill some need your reader really has.

In a professional situation think of it this way: Your reader has ten letters and five reports on her desk this morning. Your opening statement with its shared goal should tell her why she would want to read your report first and read it carefully.

2. A shared goal can *increase comprehension.* People understand and retain information best when they can fit it into a framework they already know. For example, the context of "home repair" and "do-it-yourself" would be familiar and maybe attractive to your readers. In contrast, if you defined the goal as "architectural renovation" or "techniques of historical landmark preservation" you would make sense to members of the historical society but would have missed your primary audience, the local readers. They would probably find that context not only unfamiliar but somewhat intimidating.

Offer your readers a shared goal—one for which they already have a framework—that helps them turn your message into something meaningful to them.

Here are examples of three different introductory paragraphs written for this booklet. After reading each one, consider how you would evaluate its power to motivate and aid comprehension. Then read the reaction of another reader, which follows each paragraph.

1. This booklet will help you create civic pride and preserve our city's heritage. In addition you will be helping the Historical Society to grow and extend its influence over the city.
   A reader's response:
   I suppose civic pride is a good thing, but I'm not sure I'd want to help create it. This paragraph makes me feel a little suspicious. What does the Historical Society want from me? I'll bet this is going to be a booklet about raising money so they can put up city monuments.
2. This booklet is concerned with civic restoration and maintenance projects in designated historical areas. It discusses the methods and materials approved by the City Historical Society and City Board of Engineers.
   A reader's response:
   I guess this is some booklet for city planners or the people who want to set up museums. "Methods and materials" must refer to all those rules and regulations that city contractors have to follow. I wouldn't want to get mixed up with all that if I were doing improvements on my own home.
3. If you own an older home or historical building, there are a number of ways you can preserve its beauty and historical value. At

the same time you can increase its market value and decrease its maintenance costs. This booklet will show you five major ways to improve your building and give you step-by-step procedures for how to do this. Please read the booklet over and see which of the suggestions might be useful to you.

A reader's response:

This might be a good idea. I don't know if I'd want to buy the whole package, but I think I'll read it over. What is it—five things I could do? I might find something useful I could try out. I'm particularly concerned about the maintenance costs. Maybe I can find something here on insulation.

Note that in the final example the writer not only has identified shared goals but has given the reader a sort of mental map for reading and understanding the rest of the booklet.

Sometimes a shared goal is something as intangible as intellectual curiosity. But it is the writer's job, in whatever field, to recognize goals or needs that his reader might have and to try to fulfill them. Philosopher Bertrand Russell set forth his shared goal in this way in his introduction to *A History of Western Philosophy:*

> Why, then, you may ask, waste time on such insoluble problems? To this one may answer as a historian, or as an individual facing the terror of cosmic loneliness. . . . To teach how to live without certainty, and yet without being paralyzed by hesitation, is perhaps the chief thing that philosophy, in our age, can still do for those who study it.[1]

To sum up, the first step in designing your paper for a reader is to set up a shared goal. Use it in your problem/purpose statement, and you might also use it as the top level of your issue tree when you generate ideas. A good shared goal will motivate your reader by providing a context for understanding your ideas and a reason for acting on them.

☜ Strategy 2   DEVELOP A READER-BASED STRUCTURE

Most of us intend to write reader-based prose, to communicate with our reader. But for various reasons, people often end up writing writer-based prose, or talking to themselves. For example, the following excerpts are from letters written by students applying for summer jobs. They had been asked to include some personal background and experience.

Do some detective work on these paragraphs and try to describe the hidden logic that you think is organizing each one.

[1] Bertrand Russell, *A History of Western Philosophy* (New York: Simon and Schuster, 1945), p. xiv.

Compare the paragraph to some other way you could write it. Why did the writers choose to include the particular facts they did, and why did they organize them in these particular ways?

Terry F.:
I was born in Wichita, Kansas, on December 4, 1962. After four years there my family moved to Topeka, Kansas, where I attended kindergarten. The next year my family moved to Rose Hill, Iowa. I went to first grade there and my family moved again. I started second grade in Butler, Pennsylvania, and finished it in Pittsburgh, Pennsylvania, where I still live today. . . . I took the college curriculum in high school, which included English, history, science, French, and mathematics, and am currently a college sophomore.

I would like this job for two reasons. First, I could use the money for school next year. Second, the experience would be very helpful. It would help me get a job in that specific area when I graduate.

Katherine P.:
As a freshman I worked as a clerk in a student-managed store, Argus. . . . I became acquainted with the university personnel manager and was offered the position of Argus personnel manager for the semester beginning August, 1979. I accepted and held the job until December of 1979, when a managerial position was eliminated. With managerial staff reduced to two people, responsibilities were adjusted and I was offered the position of purchasing agent. Again I accepted.

Notice that in these examples there is a logic organizing each paragraph, but it is the logic of a story, based on the writer's own memories and, in Terry's case, personal needs. The needs of the reader have not been considered. This is writer-based prose—writing that may seem quite clear and organized to the writer but is not yet adequately designed for the reader. In each case, the potential employer probably wants to know how the applicant's background and experience could fit his or her needs. But neither paragraph was organized around that goal.

Why do people write to themselves when they are ostensibly writing to a reader? One reason is a natural mental habit that psychologists call "egocentrism": thinking centered around the ego or "I." Egocentrism is not selfishness but simply the failure to actively imagine the point of view of someone else as we talk or write. We see this all the time in young children who happily talk about what they are doing in a long, spirited monologue that has many gaps and mysterious expressions. They may speak in code words or private language that, like jargon in adults, is saturated with meaning for the user but not for the listener. Although a bystander may be totally in the dark, the child seems to assume everyone understands perfectly.

Part of the child's cognitive development is growing out of this self-centeredness and learning to imagine and adapt to another person's state of mind. But we never grow out of our egocentrism entirely. When adults write to themselves, it is usually because they have simply forgotten to consider the reader.

There is another very good reason adults write writer-based prose. If you are working on a difficult paper, it is often easier to discover what you know first and worry about designing it for a reader later. An interesting study called the New York Apartment Tour experiment demonstrated people's tendency to explain in a self-oriented way.[2] The experimenters, Charlotte Linde and William Labov, posed as social workers and asked a number of people to describe their apartments. They found that nearly everyone gave them a room-by-room verbal tour and used similar procedures for conducting it. Although neither the experimenters nor the speakers were actually in the apartments, the descriptions were phrased as though they had been. For example, the description typically starts at the door; if the nearest room is a big one, you go on in ("from the left of the hall you go into the living room"); if the nearest room is small, the speaker merely refers to it and makes a comment ("and there's a closet off the living room"). Then the speaker suddenly brings you back to the entrance hall ("and on the right of the hall is the dining room"), without having to retrace steps or repeat previous rooms. The intuitive, narrative procedures used in conducting this verbal tour were very efficient for remembering all the details of the apartment.

Linde and Labov found that 97 percent of the people questioned used this sort of *narrative* tour strategy. Only 3 percent gave an *overview* such as "Well, the apartment is basically a square." The reason? The narrative tour strategy is a very efficient way to retrieve information from memory—that is, to survey what you know. In this case it allows you to cover all the rooms one by one as you walk through your apartment. Yet it is almost impossible for another person to reproduce the apartment from this narrative tour, whereas the overview approach, which only 3 percent used, works quite well. As in writing, an organization that functions well for thinking about a topic often fails to communicate that thinking to the listener. A strategy that is effective for the speaker may be terribly confusing to a listener.

Note, however, that in draft form, writer-based prose can have a real use. Since this type of writing comes naturally to us, it can be an efficient strategy for exploring a topic and outwitting our nemesis, short-term memory. If a writer's material is complicated or confusing, he may initially have to concentrate all his attention on generating and organizing his own knowledge. He might

[2]Charlotte Linde and William Labov, "Spatial Networks as a Site for the Study of Language and Thought," *Language*, 51 (1975), pp. 924–39.

simply be too preoccupied to simultaneously imagine another person's point of view and adapt to it. The reader has to wait. But you don't want to make the reader wait forever.

You can usually recognize writer-based prose by one or more of these features:

1. An *egocentric focus* on the writer
2. A *narrative organization* focused on the writer's own discovery process
3. A *survey structure* organized, like a textbook, around the writer's information.

There are times, of course, when a narrative structure is exactly right—if, for example, your goal is to tell a story or describe an event. And a survey of what you know can be a reasonable way to organize a background report or survey. But in most expository and persuasive writing, the writer needs to *reorganize* his or her knowledge around a problem, a thesis, or the reader's needs. Writer-based prose just hasn't been reorganized yet.

A READER'S TEST

Following are two drafts of a report that will be used as a test case. The writers were students in an organizational psychology course who were also working as consultants to a local organization, the Oskaloosa Brewing Company. The purposes of the report were to show progress to their professor and to present a problem analysis, complete with causes and conclusions, to their client. Both readers—academic and professional—were less concerned with what the students had done or seen than with *how* they had approached the problem and *what* they had made of their observations.

To gauge the reader-based effectiveness of this report, read quickly through Draft 1 and imagine the response of Professor Charns, who needed to answer these questions: "As analysts, what assumptions and decisions did my students make? Why did they make them? And at what stage in the project are they now?" Then reread the draft and play the role of the client, who wants to know "How did they define the problem, and what did they conclude?" As either reader, can you quickly extract the information the report should be giving you? Next try the same test on Draft 2.

As a reader, how would you describe the difference between these two versions? Each was written by the same group of writers, but the revision came after a discussion about what the readers really needed to know and expected to get from the report.

Let us look at the three things that make Draft 1 a piece of writer-based prose.

Draft 1

Group Report

(1)   Work began on our project with the initial group decision to evaluate the Oskaloosa Brewing Company. Oskaloosa Brewing Company is a regionally located brewery manufacturing several different types of beer, notably River City and Brough Cream Ale. This beer is marked under various names in Pennsylvania and other neighboring states. As a group, we decided to analyze this organization because two of our group members had had frequent customer contact with the sales department. Also, we were aware that Oskaloosa Brewing had been losing money for the past five years, and we felt we might be able to find some obvious problems in its organizational structure.

(2)   Our first meeting, held February 17th, was with the head of the sales department, Jim Tucker. Generally, he gave us an outline of the organization, from president to worker, and discussed the various departments that we might ultimately decide to analyze. The two that seemed the most promising and more applicable to the project were the sales and production departments. After a few group meetings and discussions with the personnel manager, Susan Harris, and our advisor, Professor Charns, we felt it best suited our needs and Oskaloosa Brewing's needs to evaluate their bottling department.

(3)   During the next week we had a discussion with the superintendent of production, Henry Holt, and made plans for interviewing the supervisors and line workers. Also, we had a tour of the bottling department that gave us a first-hand look at the production process. Before beginning our interviewing, our group met several times to formulate appropriate questions to use in interviewing, for both the supervisors and the workers. We also had a meeting with Professor Charns to discuss this matter.

Draft 1 (continued)

(4)   The next step was the actual interviewing process. During the weeks of March 14–18 and March 21–25, our group met several times at Oskaloosa Brewing and interviewed ten supervisors and twelve workers. Finally, during this past week, we have had several group meetings to discuss our findings and the potential problem areas within the bottling department. Also, we have spent time organizing the writing of our progress report.

(5)   The bottling and packaging division is located in a separate building, adjacent to the brewery, where the beer is actually manufactured. From the brewery the beer is piped into one of five lines (four bottling lines and one canning line) in the bottling house, where the bottles are filled, crowned, pasteurized, labeled, packaged in cases, and either shipped out or stored in the warehouse. The head of this operation, and others, is production manager Phil Smith. Next in line under him in direct control of the bottling house is the superintendent of bottling and packaging, Henry Holt. In addition, there are a total of ten supervisors who report directly to Henry Holt and who oversee the daily operations and coordinate and direct the twenty to thirty union workers who operate the lines.

(6)   During production, each supervisor fills out a data sheet to explain what was actually produced during each hour. This form also includes the exact time when a breakdown occurred, what it was caused by, and when production was resumed. Some supervisors' positions are production-staff-oriented. One takes care of supplying the raw material (bottles, caps, labels, and boxes) for production. Another is responsible for the union workers' assignments each day.

       These workers are not all permanently assigned to a production-line position. Men called ''floaters'' are used, filling in for a sick worker or helping out after a breakdown.

(7)   The union employees are generally older than thirty-five, some in their late fifties. Most have been with the company many years and are accustomed to having more workers per a slower moving line. . . .

Draft 2

MEMORANDUM

TO: Professor Martin Charns

FROM: Nancy Lowenberg, Todd Scott, Rosemary Nisson,
      Larry Vollen

DATE: March 31, 1977

RE: Progress Report: The Oskaloosa Brewing Company

Why Oskaloosa Brewing?

Oskaloosa Brewing Company is a regionally located brewery manufacturing several different types of beer, notably River City and Brough Cream Ale. As a group, we decided to analyze this organization because two of our group members have frequent contact with the sales department. Also, we were aware that Oskaloosa Brewing had been losing money for the past five years and we felt we might be able to find some obvious problems in its organizational structure.

Initial Steps: Where to Concentrate?

After several interviews with top management and a group discussion, we felt it best suited our needs, and Oskaloosa Brewing's needs, to evaluate the production department. Our first meeting, held February 17, was with the head of the sales department, Jim Tucker. He gave us an outline of the organization and described the two major departments, sales and production. He indicated that there were more obvious problems in the production department, a belief also suggested by Susan Harris, the personnel manager.

Next Step

The next step involved a familiarization with the plant and its employees. First, we toured the plant to gain an understanding of the brewing and bottling processes. Next, during the weeks of March 14–18 and March 21–25, we interviewed ten supervisors and twelve workers. Finally, during the past week we had group meetings to exchange information and discuss potential problems.

Draft 2 (*continued*)

<u>The Production Process</u>
Knowledge of the actual production process is imperative in understanding the effects of various problems on efficient production. Therefore, we have included a brief summary of this process.
The bottling and packaging division is located in a separate building, adjacent to the brewery, where the beer is actually manufactured. From the brewery the beer is piped into one of five lines (four bottling lines and one canning line) in the bottling house, where the bottles are filled, crowned, pasteurized, labeled, packaged in cases, and either shipped out or stored in the warehouse.

<u>Problems</u>
Through extensive interviews with supervisors and union employees, we have recognized four apparent problems within the bottling house operations. The first is that the employees' goals do not match those of the company. . . . This is especially apparent in the union employees, whose loyalty lies with the union instead of the company. This attitude is well-founded, as the union ensures them of job security and benefits. . . .

Narrative Organization

The first four paragraphs of the draft are organized as a narrative, starting with the phrase "Work began. . . ." We are given a story of the writers' discovery process. Notice how all of the facts are presented in terms of *when* they were discovered, not in terms of their implications or logical connections. The writers want to tell us what happened when; the reader, on the other hand, wants to ask "why?" and "so what?"

A narrative organization is tempting to write because it is a prefabricated order and easy to generate. Instead of having to create a hierarchical organization among ideas or worry about a reader, the writer can simply remember his or her own discovery process and write a story. Papers that start out, "In studying the economic causes of World War I, the first thing we have to consider is . . ." are often a dead giveaway. They tell us we are going to watch the writer's mind at work and follow him through the process of thinking out his conclusions.

197

This pattern has, of course, the virtue of any form of drama—it keeps you in suspense by withholding closure. But only if the audience is willing to wait that long for the point. Unfortunately, most academic and professional readers are impatient and tend to interpret such narrative, step-by-step structures either as wandering and confused (does he have a point?) or as a form of hedging.

Egocentric Focus

The second feature of Draft 1 is that it is a discovery story starring the writers. Its drama, such as it is, is squarely focused on the writer: "I did/I thought/I felt." Of the fourteen sentences in the first three paragraphs, ten are grammatically focused on the writers' thoughts and actions rather than on the issues. For example: "Work began . . . ," "We decided . . . ," "Also we were aware . . . and we felt. . . ." Generally speaking, the reader is more interested in issues and ideas than in the fact that the writer thought them.

Survey Form or Textbook Organization

In the fifth paragraph of Draft 1, the writers begin to organize their material in a new way. Instead of a narrative, we are given a survey of what the writers observed. Here, the raw facts of the bottling process dictated the organization of the paragraph. Yet the client-reader already knows this, and the professor probably doesn't care. In the language of computer science we could say the writers are performing a "memory dump": simply printing out information in the exact form in which they stored it in memory. Notice how in the revised version the writers try to *use* their observations to understand production problems.

The problem with a survey or "textbook" form is that it ignores the reader's need for a different organization of the information. Suppose, for example, you are writing to model airplane builders about wind resistance. The information you need comes out of a physics text, but that text is organized around the field of physics; it starts with subatomic particles and works up from there. To meet the needs of your reader, you have to adapt that knowledge, not lift it intact from the text. Sometimes writers can simply survey their knowledge, but generally the writer's main task is to *use* knowledge rather than reprint it.

To sum up, in Draft 2 of the Oskaloosa report, the writers made a real attempt to write for their readers. Among other things the report is now organized around major questions readers might have, it uses headings to display the overall organization of the report, and it makes better use of topic sentences that tell the reader what each paragraph contains and why to read it. Most important, it focuses more on the crucial information the reader wants to obtain.

Obviously this version could still be improved. But it shows the writers attempting to transform writer-based prose and change their narrative and survey pattern into a more issue-centered hierarchical organization.

Consider another example of how a writer transformed a writer-based paragraph into a reader-based one. The first draft below is full of good ideas but has a narrative organization and an egocentric focus. We can almost see the writer reading the book. Her conclusions (which her professor will want to know) are buried within a description of the story (which her professor, of course, knows already).

Writer-based draft:
In *Great Expectations*, Pip is introduced as a very likable young boy. Although he steals, he does it because he is both innocent and good-hearted. Later, when he goes to London, one no longer feels this same sort of identification with Pip. He becomes too proud to associate with his old friends, cutting ties with Joe and Biddy because of his false pride. And yet one is made to feel that Pip is still an innocent in some important way. When he dreams about Estella, one can see how all his unrealistic, romantic illusions blind him to the way the world really works.

We know from this paragraph how the writer reacted to a number of things in the novel. But what conclusions did she finally come to? What larger pattern does she want us to see?

Reader-based revision:
In *Great Expectations*, Pip changes from a goodhearted boy into a selfish young man, yet he always remains an innocent who never really understands how the world works. Although as a child Pip actually steals something, he does it because he has a gullible, kind-hearted sort of innocence. As a young man in London his crime seems worse when he cuts his old friends, Joe and Biddy, because of false pride. And yet, as his dreams about Estella show, Pip is still an innocent, a person caught up in unrealistic romantic illusions that he can't see through.

The revised version starts out with a topic sentence that explicitly states the writer's main idea and shows us how she has chunked or organized the facts of the novel. The rest of the paragraph is clearly focused on that idea, and words such as "although" are used to show how her observations are logically related to one another. From a professor or other reader's point of view, this organization is also more effective because it clearly shows what the writer learned from reading the novel.

Below is a good example of a writer who has focused all his attention on the object before him. He has given us a survey of what he knows about running shoes, although the ostensible purpose of the paragraph was to help a new runner decide what shoe to buy.

Writer-based draft:
Shoes are the most important part of your equipment, so choose them well. First, there are various kinds. Track shoes are lightweight with spikes. Road running flats, however, are sturdy, with ½″ to 1″ of cushioning. In many shoes the soles are built up with different layers of material. The uppers are made in various ways, some out of leather, some out of nylon reinforced with leather, and the cheapest are made of vinyl. The best combination is nylon with a leather heel cup. The most distinctive thing about running shoes is the raised heel and, of course, the stripes. Although some tennis shoes now have such stripes, it is important not to confuse them with a real running shoe. All in all, a good running shoe should combine firm foot support with sufficient flexibility.

In this draft the writer has focused on the shoe, not the reader who needs to choose a shoe. How would we decide between leather, nylon, and vinyl? Or judge what is "sufficiently" flexible? Why does it matter that the soles are layered; was the writer trying to make a point?

Reader-based revision:
Your running shoe will be your most important piece of running equipment, so look for a shoe that both cushions and supports your foot. Track shoes, which are lightweight and flimsy, with spikes for traction in dirt, won't do. Neither will tennis shoes, which are made for balance and quick stops, not steady pounding down the road. A good pair of shoes starts with a thick layered sole, at least ½″ to 1″ thick. The outer layer absorbs road shock; the inner layer cushions your foot. Another form of cushioning is the slightly elevated heel, which prevents strain on the vulnerable Achilles tendon.

The uppers that will support your foot come in vinyl, which is cheaper but can cause blisters and hot feet; in leather, which can crack with age; and in a lightweight but more expensive nylon and leather combination. The best nylon and leather shoes will have a thick, fitted leather heel cup that keeps your foot from rolling and prevents twisted ankles. Make sure, however, that your sturdy shoes are still flexible enough that you can bend 90° at the ball of your foot. Although most running shoes have stripes, not all shoes with stripes can give you the cushioning and flexible support you need when you run.

chapter ten / Writing Reader-Based Prose

Notice how the revision uses the same facts about shoes but organizes them around the reader's probable questions. The writer tells us what his facts *mean* in the context of choosing shoes. For example, vinyl uppers mean low cost and possible blisters. And the topic sentence sets up the key features of a good shoe—cushioning and support—which the rest of the paragraph will develop. The reader-based revision tells us what we need to know in a direct, explicit way.

CREATING READER-BASED PROSE

In the best of all possible worlds we would all write reader-based prose from the beginning. It is theoretically much more efficient to generate and organize your ideas in light of the reader in the first place. But sometimes that is hard to do. Take the assignment "Write about the physics of wind resistance for a model airplane builder." For a physics teacher this would be a trivial problem. But for someone ten years out of Physics 101, the first task would be remembering whatever they knew about wind resistance or friction at all. Adapting that knowledge to the reader would just have to wait.

In general, write for your reader whenever you can, but recognize that many times a first draft is going to be more writer-based than you may want it to be. Even though the draft may not work well for your reader, it can represent a great deal of work for you and be the groundwork for an effective paper. The more complex your problem and the more difficult your material, the more you will need to transform your writer-based prose to reader-based prose. This is not an overly difficult step in the writing process, but many writers simply neglect to take it.

In order to transform your paper to more reader-based prose, there are four major things you can do, all of which should be familiar by now:

1. Organize your paper around a problem, a thesis, or a purpose you share with the reader—not around your own discovery process or the topic itself.

2. With a goal or thesis as the top level of your issue tree, organize your ideas in a hierarchy. Distinguish between your major and minor ideas and make the relationship between them explicit to the reader. You can use this technique to organize not only an entire paper but sections and paragraphs.

3. If you are hoping that your reader will draw certain conclusions from your paper, or even from a portion of it, make those conclusions explicit. If you expect him or her to go away with a

few main ideas, don't leave the work of drawing inferences and forming concepts up to your reader. He or she might just draw a different set of conclusions.

4. Finally, once you have created concepts and organized your ideas in a hierarchy focused on your reader and your goals, use cues—which we will discuss shortly—to make that organization vivid and clear to the reader.

⬅ Strategy 3 GIVE YOUR READERS CUES

Part of your contract with a reader, if you seriously want to communicate, is to guide him or her through your prose. You need to set up cues that help the reader see what is coming and how it will be organized. This means, first of all, creating expectations and fulfilling them so that when your point arrives, your reader will have a well-anchored hook to hang it on. This was discussed in Chapter 9 (on pages 172–173). In addition, you want the reader to know which points are major, which are minor, and how they are related to one another. By using various kinds of cues and signposts, you can guide the reader to build an accurate mental tree of your discussion.

Readers, of course, come to your prose with built-in expectations about where these cues will be. For example, they expect to find

1. the most important points of a discussion stated at the beginning and summarized in some way at the end.
2. a topic sentence that tells them what they will learn from a paragraph.
3. the writer's key words in grammatically important places such as the subject, verb, and object positions.

It is to your advantage to fulfill these expectations whenever you can.

Writers have a number of tools and techniques they can use to *preview* their meaning, *summarize* it, and *guide* the reader. Figure 10-1 lists some of the most common. Check this list against the last paper you wrote. How many of these tools did you take advantage of?

The conventions of format on a page also work as familiar cues to the reader. Figure 10-2 shows a typical format for papers and reports.

Draft 2 of the Oskaloosa Brewing memo (pages 196–197) is a good example of how headings, topic sentences, and previews of conclusions can provide reader cues. Here is another piece of

Figure 10-1   *Cues for the reader*

Title
Table of contents
Abstracts
Introduction } *Cues that preview your points*
Headings
Problem/purpose statement
Topic sentences for paragraphs

Sentence summaries at ends of
   paragraphs } *Cues that summarize or illustrate your points*
Conclusion or summary sections

Pictures, graphs, and tables
Punctuation
Typographical cues:
   different typefaces,
   underlining, numbering } *Cues that guide the reader visually*
Visual arrangement:
   indentation, extra white space,
   rows and columns

Transitional words
Conjunctions
Repetitions } *Cues that guide the reader verbally*
Pronouns
Summary nouns

writing that was designed with the reader in mind. It comes from Thomas Miller's book *This Is Photography*, in a chapter called "Action."[3] One of the first previews the reader sees on the page is a photo of a pole vaulter effortlessly sailing over a bar and a place kicker completely off the ground with his right foot at the top of his kick. The caption reads, "These look like top speed but. . . ."

In the passage below, I have italicized and footnoted certain portions for discussion later. As you read the italicized parts, try to figure out what effect the writer was hoping to have on you by using the cues he did.

Poised Action[1]
In many sports,[2] particularly in races, movement is constant enough to permit picture making in terms of calculated speeds. *But there are other sports*[2] in which the action is spasmodic, defying calculation. *In those sports,*[2] the instants when action is poised are, pictorially, just as vivid and interesting as the moments when action is wildest.

[3]Thomas Miller and Wyatt Brummitt, *This Is Photography* (Rochester, N.Y.: Case Hoyt Corp., 1945).

Figure 10-2   *Common Format for Typewritten Paper*

```
          THIS IS A TITLE: THE SUBTITLE QUALIFIES IT


    The first sentence in this paragraph is a topic sen-
tence, which announces the topic and previews the argu-
ment or point of the paragraph.  The remainder of the
paragraph often previews the rest of the paper, intro-
ducing the main points to be covered.


THIS IS A MAJOR HEADING

    Major headings are placed flush left, often set in
caps, and, in typewritten manuscript, usually under-
lined.  In print they are often set in boldface type.
Ideally a reader should be able to see the shape of your
discussion simply by reading the title and major head-
ings.  Make the wording of major headings grammatically
parallel, if you can, as the major and minor headings
are in this example.


    This Is a Minor Heading

    Unlike a major heading it is indented and typed in
capital and lowercase letters.  It should be clearly and
logically related to the major heading that pre-
cedes it.

         The fact that this passage is indented
         says it is either a long quotation or an
         example.  The additional space around it
         and the single spacing signal that it is a
         different kind of text, and let readers
         adjust their reading speed and expecta-
         tions.
```

Take pole vaulting, for instance.[2] At the very top of the vault, with the vaulter's body flung out horizontally over the bar, action is relatively quiet—yet it's the best pictorial moment in this field event. This peak instant can be "stopped" with much less shutter speed than either the rise or fall.

Baseball[3] has a number of moments which are full of *poised action.*[3] The pitcher winds up and *then*[4] unwinds to throw his speed-ball. *In that instant*,[4] between winding and unwinding, action is suspended, yet a picture of it tells a story of speed and power. *An instant later,*[4] having released the ball, the pitcher is *again*[4] poised—all his energy having gone into the delivery. *There's another pictorial moment.*[5] *To picture either of these moments you need to work swiftly, but a high shutter speed is less important to your success than an understanding of the sport and of the personal style of the athlete before your lens.*[6]

Even in boxing,[7] a good photographer gets his pictures as the blows land, not as they travel. *There was that famous instance*[8] at the Louis-Nova fight in '41. Two photographers, on directly opposite sides of the ring, saw a heavy punch coming and shot just as it landed. Both used Photo-flashes, of course, but one of the lamps failed to work. The photographer whose light had failed discovered, on developing the film, that he had a picture—a most unusual and vivid silhouette—*made by the light of his competitor's flash.*[9] The fighters hid the other man's flash bulb, so the silhouette effect was perfect—and dramatic. *The only moral to this yarn*[10] is that experience teaches pressmen and other pro's that there are right instances for any shots. The photographers on opposite sides of the ring were right—and right together, within the same hundredth of a second.

Here are comments on the writer's cues:

1. In the original, this heading is set in boldface type.
2. These cues make the relationship between each of the sentences explicit. They lead us along; many sports are contrasted to other sports. We are told something additional about "other sports" and then given an example.
3. A topic sentence ties a new subject, "baseball," to the old topic, "poised action."
4. These words and phrases reinforce our sense of the timing and sequence of the action.
5. The writer recaps his discussion by redefining it not just as an action but in the larger context now of photographs representing "pictorial moments."
6. This sentence is a recap on an even larger scale. In it the writer draws a conclusion based on both this paragraph and the preceding one, and ties the paragraphs to the larger goal of the book and the chapter: how to take good action photographs.
7. This topic sentence and its introductory phrase are performing two functions: They introduce a new subject, boxing, and tie it neatly to the old framework with the words "even in."
8. We are told to see this as an example of the writer's point. He doesn't let us simply be entertained by the story; he uses it.
9. This line was also in italics in the original, to emphasize how unusual the occurrence was. Note that in the phrase just before this one—"a most unusual and vivid silhouette"—the

writer used dashes to highlight the significance of the facts. Both italics and dashes are attention-getting cues, though they can be overdone.

10. The writer draws a particular conclusion from all of this that is tied to the point of his book, and he signposts his conclusion quite clearly so we won't miss it: "The only moral to this yarn is . . ."

✐ Strategy 4   DEVELOP A PERSUASIVE ARGUMENT

People often write because they want to make something happen: They want the reader to do something or at least to see things their way. But sometimes expressing a point of view isn't enough, because it conflicts with the way the reader *already* sees things. We are faced with the same old problem of communication: Your image of something and your reader's are not the same. What kinds of arguments can you use that will make him or her see things *your* way? In this section we will look at the nature of arguments and at one type, the Rogerian argument, that can help you persuade another person to see things differently.

WINNING AN ARGUMENT VERSUS PERSUADING A LISTENER

When people think of arguments they usually think of winning them. And the time-honored method of winning an argument is by force ("You agree or I'll shoot.") or, in its more familiar form, by authority ("This is right because I [your mother, father, teacher, sergeant, boss] say it is."). The problem with force or authority is that, short of brainwashing, it often changes people's behavior but not their minds.

A second familiar form of argument is debate. Yet many people who learn to debate in high school discover that in the real world their debate strategies can indeed prove their point—but lose the argument. Debate is an argumentative contest: Person A is pitted against person B, and the winner is decided by an impartial judge. But in the real world, person A is trying not to impress a judge but to *convince* person B. The goal of such an argument is not to win points but to affect your listener, to change his or her image of your subject in some significant way. And, as you remember, that image may be a large, complex network of ideas, associations, and attitudes. The goal of communication is to find a common ground and create a shared image, but debate typically polarizes a discussion by pitting one image against the other.

Let us look for a moment at the possible outcomes of an argument or discussion in which the two parties have firmly held but differing images. Ann has decided to take a year off to work and travel before she finishes college and settles on a career. Her parents immediately oppose the idea. To them, this plan conveys an image of "dropping out" and wasting a year, with the possibility that Ann might not return to school. Furthermore, they have saved money to help put her through school and see this prospect as an indication that she doesn't value their plans, hopes, and efforts for her.

For Ann, on the other hand, taking a year off means getting time and experience that would enable her to take better advantage of college. She hopes it will help her decide what sort of work she wants to do, but more importantly she sees it as a chance to develop on her own for a while. In her mind, the goal of going to college isn't getting a degree but figuring out what things you want to learn more about.

Clearly Ann and her parents have very different images of taking a year off. Assume you are Ann in this situation. What are the possible outcomes of an argument you might have with your parents?

One outcome, and usually the least likely one, is that you will totally reconstruct your listeners' image so they see the issue just as you do. You simply replace their perspective with yours. Reconstruction can no doubt happen if your audience has an undeveloped image of the subject or sees you as a great authority, but argument strategies that set out to reconstruct someone else's ideas completely—to *win* the point—are usually ill-founded and unrealistic. They are more likely to polarize people than to persuade them.

A second alternative is to modify someone else's image, to add to or clarify it. You do this when you clarify an issue (for example, taking a year off is not the same as "dropping out") or when you add new information (Ann's college even has a special program for this and might give her some course credit for work experience). As a writer this is clearly the most reasonable effect you can aim for. In doing so you respect the other person's point of view while striving to modify those features you can reasonably affect.

The third possible outcome of an argument may be the most common: no change. Think for a minute of how many speeches, lectures, classes, sermons, and discussions you have sat through in your life and how many of those had no discernible effect on your thinking. If we think of an argument as debate in which a "good" argument inevitably wins, we forget that it is possible for even a "correct" argument to have absolutely no effect on our listener.

To sum up, the goal of an argument is to modify the image of your listener—and that this is not the same as simply presenting your own image. A successful argument is a reader-based act. It considers attitudes and images the reader already holds.

However, a great roadblock stands in the way of modifying a listener's image. Many people perceive any change in their image of things as a threat to their own security and stability. People's images are part of themselves, and a part of how they have made sense of the world. To ask them to change their image in any significant way can make people anxious and resistant to change. When this happens, communication simply stops.

Arguments that polarize issues often create just this situation. The more the speaker argues, the more firmly the listener clings to his own position. And instead of listening, the listener spends his time thinking up counter-arguments to protect his own position and image. So the critical question for the writer is this: How can I persuade my reader to listen to my position and maybe even modify his or her image without creating this sense of threat that stops communication?

ROGERIAN ARGUMENT

Rogerian argument, developed in part from the work of Carl Rogers, is an argument strategy designed not to win but to increase communication in both directions. It is based on the fact that if people feel they are understood—that their position is honestly recognized and respected—they may cease to feel a sense of threat. Once the threat is removed, listening is no longer an act of self-defense, and people feel they can afford to truly listen to and consider other ways of seeing things.

The goal of an argument, then, is to induce your reader at least to consider your position and the possibility of modifying his or her own. One way to make this happen is to demonstrate an understanding of your listener's position *first*. That means trying to see the issue from his or her point of view. For face-to-face discussions, Carl Rogers suggested this rule of thumb: Before you present your position and argue for your way of seeing things, you must be able to describe your listener's position back to your listener in such a way that he or she *agrees* with your version of it. In other words, you are demonstrating that you not only care about your listener's perspective but care enough to actively try (and keep trying) to understand it. So Ann in our example would have begun the discussion with her parents by exploring with them their response to her leaving college and the reasons behind their feelings.

What does this mean for writers who don't have the luxury of a face-to-face discussion? First, you can use the introduction to your paper, including your shared goal, to demonstrate to your reader a thorough understanding of his or her problems and goals. This is your chance to look at the question from your reader's point of view and show how your message is relevant to them.

Secondly, try to avoid categorizing people and issues. This puts people into camps, polarizes the argument, and stops communication. For example, Ann may well have felt that her parents were being old-fashioned and conventional to resist her idea, but establishing that point would have done little to change their minds. A Rogerian argument, by contrast, would begin by acknowledging the parents' plans and hopes for her and recognizing the element of truth in their fear of her "dropping out." They know that, despite good intentions, many people don't come back to college. In taking a Rogerian approach, Ann might also begin to understand the issues more clearly herself. One of the hidden strengths of a Rogerian argument is that, besides increasing one's power to persuade, it also opens up communication and may even end up persuading the persuader. It increases the possibility of genuine communication and change for both the speaker and listener.

The first draft of Ann's letter started like this:

```
Dear Mom and Dad,
    I wish you would try to see my point of view and not
be so conventional.  Things are different from when you
went to school.  And you must realize I am old enough to
make my own decisions, even if you disagree.  There are
a number of good reasons why this is the best decision I
could make.  First, . . .
```

Although this letter created a "strong" argument, it was also likely to stop communication and unlikely to persuade. Here is the letter Ann eventually wrote to her parents, which tries to take an open Rogerian approach to the problem.

```
Dear Mom and Dad,
    As I told you the other night on the phone, I want
to consider taking a year off from college to work and
be on my own for a while.  I've been thinking over what
```

you said because this is an important decision and, like you, I want to do what will be best in the long run, not just what seems attractive now. I think some of your objections make a lot of sense. After all the effort you've put into helping me get through college, it would be terrible to just ''drop out'' or never find a real career that I could be committed to.

I know you're also wondering if I recognize what an opportunity I have and are probably worrying if I'm just going to let it slip through my fingers. Well, in a way I'm worried about that too. Here I am working hard, but I don't really know where I want to go or why. It's time for me to specialize and I can't decide what to do. And it's that opportunity I'm afraid of losing. I feel I need some time off and some experience so I can make a better decision and really take advantage of my last year here.

But there's still the question of whether I would be dropping out. The college actually has a program for people who want to take a year off, and they even encourage you to enter it if you have some idea of what you'd be doing. So, as far as the school is concerned, I'd be in a well-established leave of absence program. But the fact is, people do drop out. They don't always come back. What would a whole year away from school do to me? You're right, I can't really be sure. But I think my reasons are good ones, and I'm working on a plan that would let me earn credit while I work and come back to school with a clearer sense of where I want to go. Can you offer me any more suggestions on ways I could plan ahead?

Love,
ANN

PROJECTS AND ASSIGNMENTS

1 Here are some mini-cases, dealing with a college environment, in which you need to create a goal that both you and your reader share. Write an introduction that sets up a shared goal and then discuss why you think it would work.

  a. You would like the chairperson of your department to contribute some money to a fund that would allow coffee hours and socials for majors in the department. You know she has a rather tight budget this year. What can you say to her?

  b. You would like the faculty members in your department to coordinate their exams and papers better so that students' work will be spread out more evenly over the term. For them, this would be just one more thing to try to plan their syllabus around. They have given you five minutes to talk at the faculty meeting.

c. You have been given the responsibility of getting voluntary compliance to the "no smoking" rule in the redecorated conference classrooms, which are rather small and cozy and used for group meetings. Find a shared goal.

2 The following paragraph comes from a student paper analyzing a form that was currently being used for student evaluation of the department's courses. See how many characteristics you can find that make this a writer-based discussion. Then reread the paragraph, decide what the main ideas are, and try to transform it into a piece of reader-based prose. Remember you will need a topic sentence that previews the main points for the reader and transitions that show how sentences are related.

> In order to improve the course evaluation form, it was first necessary to know how the current form is viewed by students and faculty, so the following survey of opinion was taken. From the faculty viewpoint, the form seems subjective. Many feel that the goals of their course are not as simple as the form sets them out to be. And the form has the aura of a popularity contest. When students were asked about the purpose of the form, a majority felt it was designed to mollify disgruntled students. Only a few marked the box "improves faculty performance" on the questionnaire. It also appeared that many students fill out the evaluation form just to let off steam. Attitudes about the form's effectiveness were further indicated by the questions students often asked while the survey was being conducted. The most common of these were "Why aren't the results published?" and "How does the administration use these evaluations?"

3 Write a brief narrative that describes your first experience with something new, such as moving into an apartment, going to a new class, joining Weight Watchers, or learning to play squash. Then think of some group of readers who might benefit from your experience. Contemplate what they are like and write a short, reader-based article or essay that adapts your knowledge and experience to their needs.

IF YOU WOULD LIKE TO READ MORE

If you want to know more about readers and their responses, see:

Clark, Herbert and Eve Clark. *Psychology and Language: An Introduction to Psycholinguistics.* New York: Harcourt Brace Jovanovich, 1977. / This is a readable and wide-ranging survey of the ways language works.

Holtzman, Paul. *The Psychology of the Speakers' Audience.* Glenview, Ill.: Scott, Foresman, 1970. / This writer describes communication in terms of the listener's experience.

Linde, Charlotte and William Labov. "Spatial Networks as a Site for the Study of Language and Thought." *Language,* 51 (1975), pp. 924–39. / This article contains the original discussion of the apartment tour experiment.

chapter eleven

Revising for Purpose and Editing for Style

STEP 7   REVIEW your paper and your purpose

Check over your paper in a goal-directed way, testing it against your plans and your reader's probable response.

    Strategy 1   REVIEW YOUR GOALS, GISTS, AND DISCOVERIES

    Strategy 2   DETECT, DIAGNOSE, AND REVISE

STEP 8   TEST and EDIT your writing

Edit your paper to achieve a clear, direct prose style.

    Strategy 1   EDIT FOR ECONOMY

    Strategy 2   EDIT FOR A FORCEFUL STYLE

Writers who depend on inspiration are often reluctant to reread their papers. Their image of the writing process assumes that when ideas finally come, they should not be altered or need improvement. Perfect-draft writers have spent so much time laboring over their sentences that they simply don't want to see them again. But a problem-solving writer treats editing and revising as useful steps in composing because they break the process up and make it much easier to handle. Many of the problems that could block a writer are easily solved when the writer returns to revise. Even more important, revising is an inexpensive method (in terms of time and effort) for making dramatic improvements in your writing. Like strategies for designing for a reader, revising lets you concentrate on *communicating*.

STEP 7   **REVIEW Your Paper and Your Purpose**

In no other area of writing does the difference between experienced and inexperienced writers seem so clear as it does in revision. A number of studies on writers suggest that the experts, the people with lots of experience, are simply giving themselves a different task to do than are the novices, the writers with less experience. Both say they are revising, but they do different things. Here is a brief profile of these two kinds of revisers. See where you fit.

The goals of a novice: Inexperienced writers often use revision to proofread, to clean up their prose, and to correct errors. Almost all of their revisions focus on individual words or phrases (rather than whole sentences, paragraphs, or the top-level ideas of the text). Their major technique is deleting words (rather than adding new material). The most common diagnosis or reason the writers give for the changes they make is that the current text "doesn't sound right" or that it is "incorrect."

The process of a novice: Inexperienced writers typically begin to revise as soon as they begin to read. They work through the text in a straightforward manner, diagnosing and revising word by word. This is a very methodical process, but it also means that they are usually looking at or evaluating small pieces of text, such as a sentence, rather than a whole idea, paragraph, or discussion.

The goals of an experienced writer: Experienced writers expect to rework a first draft, because the one-two combination of write-then-revise is the fastest way to produce a good paper. They are likely to see that draft as merely a springboard to the final text, using it to try out and develop ideas. In addition, they go into revising a first draft with the goal of expanding, reorganizing, or changing not just words and sentences, but the gist of a paragraph, an argument, or even the whole paper. Their attention is focused on the main ideas; their top priority is the organization and effect of the entire paper.

The process of an experienced writer: Because experienced writers divide their writing time between planning, drafting, and revising, they spend less time writing and perfecting the first draft. Because revising is a strategic move, they also make decisions about what to look for and how to go about it. They may decide to skim the whole text first for organization or persuasiveness, or to work in two passes, reading once for ideas and once for mechanics and style.

Experienced writers also divide their time between **global** and **local** revision. **Local** revision is the familiar process of evaluating individual words, phrases, and sentences. Local changes affect only a small, local part of the text. They don't alter the gist or the overall structure of the text. Even with extensive revision, the top levels of the issue tree stay the same. Local revision often makes a text more "correct" according to the rules of spelling, grammar, and punctuation, or it makes it fit the conventions of good usage and polished style, or the conventions of format and presentation a given discourse community expects.

Global revision affects how the paper works as a whole. Global revision (even if it physically alters only a few sentences) involves changes in the purpose, in the gist, or in the major ideas; it may alter the logic of an argument or the writer's stance toward the reader. These changes, which affect the gist, the structure, the overall tone, or purpose of the piece, may also involve a number of local changes. But the important thing is that they are all part of a more global plan of revision. Writers need both global and local revision strategies.

In order to do global revision, writers must have a clear sense of their own goals or purpose and of the gist of what they wanted to say. Only then can they compare the text they wrote to what they really intended. However, even at the end of writing a draft many writers still find it hard to say exactly what their purpose is or to state the gist of their paper. They have been so involved in writing individual parts, they would find it easier to describe all the details to you than to put it in a nutshell. How, then, can they do global revision? Experienced writers solve this problem by actually reviewing their own work like a new reader to get a sharper picture of their intentions, which in turn guides revision.

In the section that follows we will walk through a four-step procedure for revising that involves review, detection, diagnosis, and revision. Although I will present it as a step-by-step procedure to make the process clear, these strategies are meant to be customized and adapted to your own situation. You will need to develop your own ways to review and diagnose, and you must decide when a given strategy is likely to help. (Chapter 13 will give you another view of this process.) Remember, one thing experienced writers do is to manage and adapt the revision process to suit their needs.

✍ Strategy 1   REVIEW YOUR GOALS, GISTS, AND DISCOVERIES

In a nutshell, what is your plan for this paper? And how do each of these sections (or paragraphs) fit into that master plan?

The first thing to notice about this strategy for getting the big picture is that you may want to start by *not* looking at your text. You need a fresh look that isn't captured by the words on the page, and you need to resist the temptation to plunge into local revision. So to start out, sit back and think for a moment: What do I want to do or to say? What do I want my readers to think (and what do they expect)?

Since the plan you made earlier (see Chapter 5) may have changed, it helps to jot a few notes or sketch an issue tree. Or skim over the text quickly to review your plan. Or read the introductory section carefully and sketch the issue tree you have in mind and promised the reader. A more systematic approach for reviewing an argument or complex discussion is actually to make small notes on the gist or point of each paragraph or section of the paper right there in the margin. How good was your review? Test it by trying to give a three-minute overview of your purpose and your main points to someone else. Can you tell them how each paragraph or section is supposed to function in your plan?

Admittedly, reviewing before you revise may take four or five minutes and sometimes a little hard thinking, but it has some real rewards. First, you are now ready to test your paper against your personal goals, not just against the conventions and rules of standard usage. Secondly, you will often discover something in your own thinking that has developed during the process of writing. Look for conclusions, for observations, for inferences you have drawn as you wrote. These discoveries are often found at the end of a first draft, at the end of paragraphs, or even buried in the text or in your head. At the same time, look for ideas you now question, for contradictions you can now see. (Remember, recognizing ideas that seem to contradict or that let you qualify your argument is valued in academic discourse.) Discoveries made while writing often turn out to be important insights that let you organize the paper around your best ideas and your real purpose. Revising lets you move these ideas out of the writer-based position (where they occurred to you during writing) and promote them to a more clearly signalled position as an organizing idea, a topic sentence, a named concept, or a more fully stated conclusion. Small changes based on these discoveries often make a large difference to readers.

⬅ Strategy 2   DETECT, DIAGNOSE, AND REVISE

Some revisions are triggered by happy discoveries—you revise the text to fit your new vision of things. Most revisions are triggered by problems. But if you have only a vague intuition that something doesn't sound right, you may spend time rewriting but never find or fix the real problem. The three-step process of Detect, Diagnose, and Revise may help you turn your intuitions into a more workable, "operational' plan for revising. Detecting lets you find possible problems—ones you might overlook otherwise. Diagnosing helps you pinpoint the source of the problem and lets you revise to fix that problem rather than just rewrite and hope it goes away. (Again, I will present this as a step-by-step procedure for clarity, but expect to customize these strategies to fit your needs.)

STEP 1. DETECT

Assuming your review (above) has given you a good sense of your goals, now is the time to read through your text trying first to detect global problems. At this point all you need to do is to detect that a problem exists, not fix it. So read through at your regular speed like a first-time reader, try to follow the structure, listen to your argument unfold, note how you respond—and listen to your intuitions. Did you stumble anywhere, did you feel confused at the end of a sentence, did you reread, did something sound awkward, did one idea not follow the next here and there? If so, that's normal. Listen for any signal, even a faint one, that you have detected a problem and simply put a note in the margin, a bracket about a paragraph, or a line under a phrase and go on. These are the possible problem spots you will return to later.

Concentrating on detection *only* works well for both global and local problems. For instance, you may hear a faint warning bell for misspelled words and faulty punctuation, even when you don't know exactly what is correct. Just mark the spot as a possible detection and go on. But you will improve your chances of detecting problems if you concentrate on global and local problems in two separate passes. It is hard to see the big picture when your attention is riveted to spelling and equally hard to look closely at words when the argument is racing along.

Try reading the passage below like a detector, marking all the places you hear a faint signal of a possible problem. It is the second paragraph from a handout written to get undecided freshmen women involved in college sports. The first paragraph described available varsity sports, so think about the context and start your detector working as you begin the paragraph. Remember, mark global and local problems, but don't stop to fix them.

Problem text (paragraph 1 was about varsity sports):

I don't want to infer that the only chance women get for participating in sports is on varsity teams. Intramural sports are not quite the same as varsity sports, in which the rules are better, equipment is better, and with the techniques of the players being more developed. Irregardless, IM sports may be the choice for many women—they can be just as much fun and take less time.

If you can compare your problem spots with those of other people in your class, notice if you were near the group average in number of detections; were there common spots everyone chose? I will show you the choices of one experienced writer shortly. You may find that because readers bring different goals for what the text should do, they will agree on the local problems, but see quite different global ones.

STEP 2. DIAGNOSE THE PROBLEM

At this point in the process, some writers simply say to themselves, "that doesn't sound right" and they leap in and begin to rewrite. Leaping in can work well if you have a new discovery to add or need to experiment with language, or if you feel something is missing. But we have observed that rewriting without diagnosing often takes more time in the long run (especially for global problems); it can create new problems; and it may fail to solve the original difficulty.

Look back at all the problems you have detected on the intramural sports paragraph. Go through each one and try to diagnose what it was in the text that triggered your detection. What is the cause of the problem; what is its effect on the reader; is it a category of problem you recognize? A diagnosis is a descriptive analysis of the problem. Think of the difference between a mere detection and a diagnosis this way: If a friend looked at you and said, "Say, I think you need some rest," you might be happy he cared and even detected your terminal condition. However, if your doctor said the same thing after you had dragged your sorry case to her office, you might well be annoyed, since from a doctor you expect a *bona fide* diagnosis with specific information and a recommendation for what to do (such as, "You have infectious mononucleosis with a white blood count of 12,000. What you need is to have no alcohol and 10 hours of sleep a night for the next two weeks."). A diagnosis, in that setting, is a problem description that you would be willing to pay for.

Some local problems such as run-on sentences and wordiness become easy to diagnose once you know them by name and know how to spot them. We will look at some familiar problems of this sort later in the chapter. A handbook is another good source of diagnoses for standard, sentence-level problems. But as you will see in the sample diagnosis below, some diagnoses are really a theory about why this text won't meet its own goals or about how a reader might respond. In order to diagnose a global problem, you often have to go through the very process we discussed in Chapter 1 and Chapter 8—you have to become a problem solver, draw inferences, and define the problem for yourself. How does your diagnosis of the intramural sports paragraph differ from that of the writer below? Did you bring the same goals to your diagnosis?

> "Well, I tossed out infer because it's used incorrectly—just a matter of usage—"infer" for "imply." But the whole sentence is just so—so wordy. For instance, "not quite the same as" doesn't say a thing; in what way are they "not the same"? What's the point of making that kind of a remark? But what I really wanted to fix was all the negatives—the "don't infer," and "not the same" and that awful "irregardless." I think that's not the way a recruiting document should be. I think you should put in positive statements. Talk about positive things. Now secondly, both of these sentences are really lead-ins that don't get you anywhere. You want to get to where you tell what it is rather than what it's not. This sentence structure is just a delaying tactic. So what I tried to do was jump in and talk about what I was going to talk about, which is intramural sports, not varsity. And put the varsity stuff in a subordinate clause. These sentences are just on the wrong subject."

Notice some of the strategies that make this writer an expert reviser. Although he does know the rule about "imply and infer," he sees that error as secondary to the larger problem. He first diagnoses the problem with a maxim about style and "wordiness." But he then goes on to diagnose the real problem in terms of the goals of the text. Handouts, he thinks, should be positive; they should tell people what they need to know and get to the point. Notice, too, how this writer keeps thinking about the problem, trying to be more and more explicit. As his diagnosis develops, it becomes focused more and more on the text's more global purpose and problem. He then uses that diagnosis to plan his revision.

STEP 3. REVISE

Once you diagnose a problem, especially a global one, you often find there are multiple ways to revise it. You need to think about how the changes you make to a given paragraph might affect other parts of the text. Look at your options and plan the best revision you can think of. The important feature of this third step—revision based on a diagnosis—is that you are making changes for a reason. Here is our diagnoser's proposed revision for the intramural paragraph.

Proposed revision:

Even more than varsity teams, intramural sports attract a growing number of women. Intramurals focus on developing skills; they are less competitive and take less time, but they can be just as enjoyable and valuable as playing on a varsity team.

Can you think of another solution to the problem that might be equally good for different reasons? Other people revising this text certainly did. This revision reflects this writer's plan for what he thought the text should do. Although we don't see it here, his comments show that he had already done some thinking about the goals of the handout, and we can imagine him reading to get a sense of the gist. He then uses those goals and that gist to revise the paragraph. That is, he tries to make it sound like a recruiting document and to focus on the real topic, rather than just fix the errors. A second thing that makes him an expert is his ability to connect his general diagnosis (such as "negative" and "wordy") to specific parts of the sentence. This kind of concrete and operational diagnosis of how these words are working lets him zero in on the words and sentence patterns he wants to change. (In Chapters 12 and 13 we will look at some of these techniques for testing and modifying your language itself.) Experts like this one see global problems, but they also connect that diagnosis to actual parts of the text.

This three-step Detect, Diagnose, and Revise strategy helps you approach your text like a problem solver *when you need to.* Using this strategy lets you do each of these three quite distinct parts of the process better.

Working with a Collaborator/Imagining a Reader

Because only you know your own goals, you are the best detector for some problems. But if you know a topic too well or are new to the conventions of some discourse, it can be hard to read like your reader. For these and some other problems a collaborator is the best detector. And a collaborator may come up with a surprising diagnosis because he or she is bringing a different but valuable set of goals to the reading of your text. In addition, after working with a collaborator you begin to anticipate how other readers respond and become able to simulate a reader's response on your own when you need to.

Although you can always simply give your paper to a friend for response and advice, some times all people can say is how *they* would have written it. But their goals may not be yours. There are a number of ways to work with a collaborator that can be more informative. Here is the simplest: Ask your collaborator to go through your draft in the same way you did as a detector, marking places that cause confusion, break the flow, or seem somehow problematic as well as places with local problems and errors. Then ask your reader to say what he was responding to (but tell your friend that he doesn't have to say how it *should* be written or how to fix it!). Asking friends to work as detectors, not revisors, makes them willing to see you come back again.

However, if you are part of a writing group where everyone is working together, there are even more helpful ways to collaborate. Remember, you are managing this revision process to meet your own goals. So diagnose your own problems first and ask your collaborator to read with your goals and problem in mind. Some of the best collaboration comes when people put their minds to a common problem.

If you are feeling experimental, let your reader see only one paragraph at a time and ask her to tell you the gist of the paragraph and to predict what will come next. Are your signals to the reader clear enough that she gets it right? For an even more surprising test, feed the introduction out sentence by sentence asking your reader what she thinks the problem or issue or thesis is—at this point. Has she already come to a wrong conclusion before you get to your point?

Now consider the whole paper. Ask a friend to jot down two things: first, a nutshell or capsule statement of what he thinks you are trying to do or say (in his own words, not yours) and second, an outline or diagram of your major points and how they are related. If you are even more daring, have him try this some time after he has read the paper to see what really stands out in his memory.

Then, of course, you compare this reader's version against your own. To keep everything honest, you should jot down your own nutshell and outline *before* you read his. Bear in mind that there is always the chance your reader will misread or forget, but consider this as a signal that you need to increase your cues or redesign some part of your presentation. It also helps to know where your reader felt bored, because that is usually a signal that you have confused him or that your point is unclear.

If you don't have a live reader, you can simulate a reader's response in a number of ways. The simplest is to role-play, as was discussed in Chapter 6. Think yourself into the role of your reader responding to individual sentences in your text. What is she looking for, what does she need to do after reading this, and how would she react to what you just said? If you would like a more elaborate response, simulate a scenario in which you have a dialogue with the reader. Have her ask you questions such as "What do you mean?" "How do you know?" "Such as?" and "Why?" whenever your intuition tells you a real reader might do the same.

Many people find it very helpful to read their own writing out loud. Try it if you have some privacy. Listening to yourself out loud sometimes cuts out that private voice in your mind that fills in all the gaps between ideas and makes everything sound smooth and coherent. Reading out loud also helps you hear how your style sounds and see if your prose "flows" or doesn't.

Finally, if you are fresh out of friends, imagination, or privacy, there is a fourth technique called a highlighter test. You can simulate the comprehension process of a typical busy reader by going over your paper with a highlighter pen in hand and marking off all the titles, headings, and sentences to which convention or position in the paper give special significance. Assume that these are the major elements your reader will see and perhaps remember. Now check to see whether these highlighted parts contain the major information you want the reader to focus on and retain. Ideally the highlighted items will identify the goals of your paper and the top-level elements of your issue tree. If they don't, what have you given the reader instead?

The Revision Process in Action

Here is an example of a student writer's Review, Detect, Diagnose, and Revise process in action. As a reader, try to detect problems you see and make your own diagnosis before you read what the writer, another reader, and her instructor had to say. You may find yourself diagnosing some global problems differently than these readers. If so, ask yourself "why?" Take a look at your own assumptions or criteria for what this paper *should* do. Notice how a diagnosis is often based on the particular goals and criteria a person brings to reading. If you remember our earlier discussion of task representation in Chapter 5, you will see we have come full circle. The goals writers give themselves at the beginning define the task they are trying to do—the problem they try to solve. And those same goals will later dictate how they review their own text, what they even detect as a problem, and how they diagnose and revise the difficulties they do see.

Draft #1. A problem analysis: Black Students in the College
[Points at which readers detected a problem are numbered.]
More minority students need to be admitted[1] into the College for many reasons. One reason might be to get funds from the government which would benefit the school.[2] Another reason, this gives[3]

minorities a chance to learn in one of the best programs in the country. A final reason is to create a diverse social environment for everyone in the College. But right now this isn't happening.

One solution to the problem might be to create an environment more appealing to minorities socially and educationally[4] . . .

Review Goals and Gist

By the time she completed this first draft the writer, Desiree, was sure that the problem she really cared about was recruiting—not just why it should be done, but why it was so difficult to do at her predominantly white school. Notice how this affects what she detects.

Detect

1. "Admitted" is the wrong word.
2. This sentence seems inappropriate. Her reader also put a mark there and simply said, "this feels out of place here."
3. At this spot both Desiree and her readers had to stop and reread the sentence to get it to make sense.
4. The sentence sounds awkward at the end.

Diagnose

1. Desiree chose to write this paper because she wanted to say that the College should admit more blacks. But as she wrote, she discovered that the interesting topic—and the real problem—was recruiting. This early focus on "admitted" no longer fit her master plan. Her detection at #1 was a local, word-level problem in one sense, but she detected it because it jarred with her global plan. And its prominent location in the first paragraph meant it might mislead the reader, too.
2. People diagnosed the problem with this sentence in different ways. One reader said this idea seemed trivial compared to the other large social reasons, and the potential income was so small, it didn't even seem like a good argument. Another said it set up the wrong set of expectations at the beginning—it made the paper sound like the beginning of a financial analysis written from a company's point of view. These readers saw a relatively local problem with the sentence itself. But Desiree, as the writer, saw a more global problem and an opportunity because she had the big picture of her own goals in mind. Desiree's own diagnosis

triggered a whole new plan for revision: the funding sentence was "out of place" because what she really wanted the paper to do was to look at recruiting from a student's point of view and show what the problem was. By describing the problem (rather than giving "reasons") she wanted to show that the College needed a stronger social network for black students on campus first if it wanted to convince students even to apply. Trying to diagnose the feeling of a "misfit" created by this sentence helped her see her real purpose.

3. The instructor diagnosed the first phrase as a sentence fragment ("Another reason *[is that]*") spliced onto another sentence ("This gives . . ."). But the real problem to correct, she said, was faulty parallelism. Since the sentence is logically parallel with the other two sentences that give "reasons," it should be grammatically parallel; for example, "Another reason is to give . . ."

Desiree's diagnosis didn't use technical terms, but it also described the problem. "I started out making this sentence like the one before. But after, the 'another reason' I just started a new sentence. You can make it all make sense if you read it out loud with pauses and emphasis, but it won't work in writing."

4. This local problem was one Desiree didn't detect herself. But when a reader found it awkward she easily diagnosed the trouble. She knew that the words "educationally and socially" were supposed to modify the idea of "appealing," and she had placed them at the end of the sentence for emphasis. But that position made her adverbs appear to modify "minorities," the word to which they were closest. From a reader's point of view these two words were misplaced modifiers.

Revise

1. Although the word "admitted" appeared to be a local problem, Desiree's diagnosis called for a more global action than simply changing the word to "recruited." She wanted to show that there was, in fact, a problem with recruiting. As you will see below, she decided to replace her simple assertion ("minority students need to be admitted") with an introduction that *showed* why recruiting needed to be done and why the social environment made it difficult.

2. Diagnosing the global problems in sentences 1 and 2 actually helped Desiree form a new plan. She wanted her text to show how recruiting affected students. She considered simply asserting that it caused a problem, but she knew it would be much stronger if she could show the problem directly. So she decided to use her own experience to let the reader see the problem, too.

She knew she had two good "reasons" for recruiting blacks, but most readers would already agree with those. What she wanted to write about was her own sense of why ordinary recruiting wasn't working. So as you will see, she reorganized the paper around this new purpose.

3 and 4. Diagnosing these two awkward sentences made Desiree more conscious of some of the options for sentence structure: she could solve the problem by giving all three sentences about reasons a parallel form (for example, "one reason might be to get . . . ," "another reason is to give . . . ," and "a final reason is to create . . ."), and by placing her misplaced modifiers in front of "appealing." But she was smart not to spend time actually working on these two local problems because in her more global plans for revision both of these sentences disappeared, even though the ideas were used later in the paper.

Here is the revision that came out of her diagnosis and plan.

Draft #2 A Black Need

"When the fall comes, we won't be around each other all the time to help work things out. Sometimes we're just going to have to survive on our own." As I walked into Freshman Writing on the first day of classes, these words from a fellow student in our Pre-College Program echoed in my mind. I was suddenly hit with reality; not only was I in a room full of people that I had never seen before, but what was worse, I was the only black. This strong feeling of uneasiness was one of the many reasons that made me feel that more black students needed to be recruited for the College.

Even with increasing recruitment, the total number of black students who apply to the College is low. Last year, for instance, the number of black students admitted nearly doubled. But still only a small number (about 11%) of the applications come from black students.

Review, Detect, and Diagnose

In reading this new problem statement, how would you define the particular issue this text is presenting? To review her new draft, Desiree tried to play the role of reader and imagine your response, by asking herself, "what would I think at the end of this paragraph? How would I state the gist?" She predicted that most readers would see her first point—new black students face a real problem. But she realized that readers might *not* infer her second point—that in order to recruit minorities, the College needed a social community of black students first.

Detecting that something is missing in the text, when it is clear in your own mind, is one of the hardest problems to spot. Her reader helped by asking why she leaped into discussing applications in the second paragraph; it confused him. His diagnosis was, "This needs a transition." But Desiree diagnosed the real problem by comparing the gist she had in mind with what her text really said. Here is the sentence she added at the end of the paragraph. Does it change your picture of the problem?

> The College is a great school academically, but its predominantly white environment discourages many black students from even applying. It needs a stronger black social community already here as the first step in recruiting.

As a reader I find Desiree's revised paper far more significant and interesting; I learned something by reading it. But the important thing about her revising process is that it let her reach and actually discover *her own goals*. Desiree went at this problem like the experienced writers described at the beginning of this chapter. She didn't spend all her time perfecting a first draft nor correcting local, sentence-level problems when she detected them. She wrote a thoughtful first draft but used it as a springboard to revision which began when she reviewed her own goals and tried to state her gist to herself. This writer used a number of techniques to detect problems, including listening to real readers and simulating a reader's response in her own mind. But notice how important her own diagnosis was. As the writer she kept testing the text against her own goals, so she was able to see opportunities for global revision. And because she hadn't spent all her time writing sentences and perfecting the first version, she was happy to throw away her prose but keep her good ideas for the second draft.

Seeing Desiree's process as four different steps—Review, Detect, Diagnose, and Revise—makes her thinking look like a slow and formal process when in reality many of these decisions happened within minutes or even seconds of each other. But breaking the revision process up this way lets you see that there really are separate actions that you can choose to take or to skip. You obviously have to make a conscious choice to use the strategies of reviewing your goals and diagnosing, since these may require a few minutes of focused thinking. But bear in mind, experienced writers regularly use those strategies because a little extra thinking can often make a large difference in writing.

In the rest of this chapter, we will look at some other problem-solving strategies you can apply to more local problems of structure and style.

TEST and EDIT Your Writing

No matter how well they speak on their feet, few people can write their most vigorous, direct, or logical prose on a first draft. In fact, if you are working in an organization or attending an institution such as college, it may even seem natural to write in the padded style of organizational prose. If you are working with technical material, it may come naturally to write with a great deal of jargon or technical language. Or, if you are trying to juggle a number of facts and ideas, it may be easiest to write out a paragraph that looks more like a list than a well-balanced tree. When writing this way comes most naturally to you but you know it won't work for your reader, the most efficient procedure is to *write* it—however it comes—and then *edit*.

Some writers will ask, "Why not make each sentence and paragraph perfect the first time so you won't have to look at them again?" The answer is that if you separate the two operations of generating and editing, it is easier for you and you can get better results. The ultimate goal is always polished, reader-based prose. What changes are the immediate subgoals on which you choose to concentrate. Certain things, including organization and style, are sometimes better handled by an editor than an idea generator. *Editing can come at any point in the composing process*—after you have written a phrase, a sentence, a paragraph, or an entire draft. Sometimes editing is simply a final stage for fixing up details. But it is always a powerful strategy for writing.

The method is essentially the same one used in generating ideas and designing them for a reader. A writer-based prose style or unedited draft may be a reasonable and natural way to say what you have to say at that particular moment. Once your thoughts are out of short-term memory and down on paper, you can come back as an editor with a much clearer sense of where you are going and what you want those words to do.

The editing techniques you will learn in this chapter are not concerned with frills or with adding commas and dotting "i's." For an experienced writer, editing is a major tool for making meaning. A writer may in fact spend more time editing and restructuring a first draft than he or she did generating it. Once you know a few basic editing techniques, you will be able to transform sentences, paragraphs, and even entire discussions into far more effective statements of your meaning.

Knowing how to edit a first draft doesn't guarantee that you will produce elegant writing. But it does mean that you will be able to cope with three major problems professional writers have, and that you will be better able to write:

Economical prose that says exactly what you mean
Forceful prose that holds your reader's attention
Logical prose that expresses the hierarchical structure of your ideas

✒ Strategy 1   EDIT FOR ECONOMY

The goal of this editing strategy is to help you write clear, direct statements that come quickly to the point and say exactly what you mean. Probably the most frequent complaint made about college and professional writing is that it is stuffy and inflated or overly technical and full of jargon. And yet, it is often written by dynamic people who can think clearly and speak forcefully when they are face to face. These people often use inflated or "institutional" language because they hope it will sound more impressive.

The problem with institutional language is that it handicaps the writer who really has something to say, burying his or her point beneath a load of excess language. Think of all the college catalogues, final reports, or political statements you never finished reading. As readers of such institutional prose, we all know how readers respond to an inflated style. It makes us mentally rewrite sentences to find the point and we soon begin to skip, skim, and read with diminishing attention. If you really have something to say and want to keep a reader alert and reading, you need to write economical prose that comes to the point.

INSTITUTIONAL PROSE AND THE ABSTRACTION LADDER

A direct prose style is much like the style people use when they speak. One of the chief differences between an institutional style and a personal speaking style is the level of abstraction. In fact, one decision you make every time you speak or write is how abstract or concrete you want to be.

Say someone asks you, "What do you expect to be doing tomorrow afternoon?" There are a number of ways you could convey your situation, ranging from abstract at the top to concrete at the bottom:

Expect to still be living and breathing, if all goes well.
Will be busy.
Will be busy part of the afternoon.
Have a previous appointment at 4:30.
Have my Friday afternoon tennis match at 4:30 with Joyce at the Stanton Avenue courts.

The level of abstraction you choose in replying will depend on who asked you and why. For example, on the phone you might choose to tell Ms. Howard, the chairperson of a committee to which you belong, that you "will be unable to make the meeting because of a previous appointment at 4:30." However, ten minutes later when talking to a friend, you might translate that highly abstract "previous appointment" into: "Oh, I have my usual tennis match with Joyce at the Stanton courts." One difference between the two statements is their level of abstraction.

When you write you likewise have a range of options, going from general, abstract terminology at the top to specific, concrete information at the bottom. In choosing your abstraction level, each choice carries an advantage and a price. By going to the top of the ladder and using nice, fuzzy abstractions you gain the advantage of breadth—and if you are high enough it's hard to be wrong. Weather forecasters do this when they say, "Unfavorable weather patterns may materialize in the near future." However, the problem with abstractions is that they are likely to be misinterpreted or just plain ignored. If you say, "It's going to rain like hell between now and 3 A.M.," you've put yourself on the line, but you can be sure your listeners will pay attention. In writing, you'll usually get much better results with concrete language.

Likewise, a vivid, direct prose style works because it cuts out unnecessary padding and puts powerful words in powerful places. This lets the main words and major ideas stand out prominently and, because the prose is direct and to the point, encourages the reader to listen.

KEY-WORD EDITING

One method that can help you achieve such a style is key-word editing. The method has five steps:

1. Divide the sentence into meaningful units.
2. Identify the key words or phrases in each unit.

3. Cut out unnecessary words, and build your statement around the key terms.
4. Pack in more concrete words when possible.
5. Let the actors act.

Consider this verbose sentence from a student paper:

> The condition of excessive redundancy that exists in such a great degree in the academic paper assignments produced by members of the student body should be eliminated by grading policy and the example-setting capabilities that lie at the disposal of those who instruct such students.

The editor's first step is to divide the sentence into its natural, meaningful units. The next step is to pick out the key words and phrases in each unit—in other words, look for words that seem to be carrying the weight of the sentence's meaning. Thus:

> The condition of excessive *redundancy* / that exists in such a great degree in the academic *paper* assignments / produced by members of the *student* body / should be eliminated by *grading* policy and the *example*-setting capabilities / that lie at the disposal of those who *instruct* such students.

The third step is to cut out as much of the nonfunctional padding as possible and try to write a sentence around the key words.

> Redundancy in student papers should be eliminated by grades and the example set by the instructor.

The fourth step is to try to pack the sentence with concrete information where possible, replacing abstractions with more specific words. For example, since "redundancy" could mean wordiness or repetition or both, the writer needed to ask himself: "What exactly am I trying to say?" He decided he meant:

> *Wordiness and repetition* in student papers should be eliminated by grades and the example set by the instructor.

The final step is to let the actor act. Usually the person or thing that carries out the action of the sentence should also be the grammatical subject.

> *Instructors* should use grades and their own example to eliminate wordiness and repetition in student papers.

Here is another example. Try the key-word editing technique on this sentence, then compare your result to the revision that follows.

> In the event of your participation in a charter flight, the thing that should be noticed is the fact that there is a possibility of a change in fare necessitated by a last-minute change in fuel prices.

Steps 1 and 2: Divide into meaningful units; identify key words	In the event of your *participation* in a *charter flight* / the thing that should be *noticed* is the fact that / there is a *possibility* of a *change in fare* / necessitated by a *last-minute change in fuel prices*.
Step 3: Cut out unnecessary words; build around key terms	In participation in a charter flight, the possibility of a change in fare necessitated by a last-minute change in fuel prices should be noted.
Steps 4 and 5: Pack in more concrete words; let the actor act	When you sign up for a charter flight, remember that a last-minute change in fuel prices can increase your fare.

Note that in the final revision the writer realized that the real actor was "you," the passenger, and translated the vague "change in fare" into the concrete "increase your fare."

The primary goal of key-word editing is to *put powerful words in powerful places*. As you could see in the first-draft sentences, the words that carried the writers' meaning were buried in verbiage. The subject and verb are the two most powerful parts of a sentence, and as readers we rely on those parts to contain the writer's essential information. The object position is also a strong one. In the first draft of the airline paragraph, the words in the powerful subject, verb, and object positions only told us: "the *thing is* the *fact*."

Key-word editing, therefore, helps you say what you want to say by putting powerful words in these grammatically powerful places. Naturally you won't always want to use such a spare, economical style, but it is important to know how to write direct, concise sentences when you need them. When you try to write economical prose, think of yourself as giving a brief, well-prepared oral presentation. Imagine yourself in your reader's office: You have three minutes to tell him or her the gist of what you have to say. Concentrate on the essential points you want that person to remember. Think about the structure and emphasis of what you have to say, rather than making your phrases flow. You may well find that your key words are emerging, your excess words are dropping away, and you have become more direct and concrete.

➾ *Strategy 2*　EDIT FOR A FORCEFUL STYLE

If you still feel your writing sounds heavy-handed, indirect, or verbose, other trouble-shooting techniques may help. Try some of these editing approaches:

1. LOWER THE NOUN/VERB RATIO

Test the following sentence for vigor by counting the ratio of nouns to verbs: Nouns/Verbs = __/__. Then rewrite the sentence using more verbs and fewer nouns.

> The effect of the overuse of nouns in writing is the placing of excessive strain upon the inadequate number of verbs and the resultant prevention of the flow of thought.

Note that the original sentence contained one verb and eleven nouns, few of which were serving any useful purpose. Here is a revised version with a ratio of two verbs to seven nouns:

> Using too many nouns in writing places strain on verbs and prevents the flow of thought.

Note that in some sentences you simply have to use many nouns—for example, you have a compound subject involving four or more essential nouns. But if you improve the ratio of verbs to nouns as much as possible, your prose will be more forceful.

2. TRANSFORM HEAVY NOUNS BACK INTO VERBS

Many of the heavy, polysyllabic nouns that make prose hard to read were made in the first place by adding a Latin ending to a verb. Often, your sentences will improve if you transform these nouns back into their original form. The five Latin endings below are the most common ones to watch for.

Remove this Latinate *ending*	from a *noun*	to produce a *verb*
-tion	resumption	resume
-ment	announcement	announce
-ing	dealing	deal
-ion	decision	decide
-ance	performance	perform

3. AVOID WEAK LINKING VERBS

The verb "to be" can be used as a linking verb ("The water is hot") or as an auxiliary or helping verb ("The water is boiling furiously"). The verb can take these forms:

be	is	was	been
am	are	were	being

When used as linking (or state-of-being) verbs, these words are simply saying that "something = something else." They can't act. If you want to state a definition, linking verbs are often very powerful ("To be or not to be, that is the question"). If, however, you are discussing an action, whether it is physical, mental, or metaphoric, linking verbs can weaken your sentence.

For example, you might write: "Galileo's telescope was helpful in the explosion of the myth of an earth-centered universe." But by using a form of "to be" you waste some of the potential of the powerful verb slot in your sentence. To make the sentence more forceful, transform the words "helpful" and "explosion" into verbs: "Galileo's telescope helped explode the myth of an earth-centered universe." Look for ways to change linking verbs into action verbs.

4. TRANSFORM NEGATIVE EXPRESSIONS

Sentences containing several negative expressions ("No, I didn't know that the book was not on the shelf") are more difficult to comprehend than positive expressions ("I thought the book was on the shelf"). Negatives require increased mental processing time, and they decrease the chance that a person will correctly remember what he or she has read. Studies have even shown that implicit negatives such as "forgot" (didn't remember), "absent" (not present), and "hardly," "scarcely," and "few" have a similar effect.

Obviously, negative expressions are necessary at times. But remember that they can dilute the forcefulness of your statements and make your writing difficult to read. Test the following paragraph. Is the meaning clear on a first reading? How many negatives does the passage contain? Revise the paragraph and see how many negatives it is really necessary to use.

> To avoid assuming the rapid decrease in temperature implied by the weather charts described above, other factors, used to make a prediction from past data, were not ignored. We feel the method can scarcely fail to predict the direction of temperature change for the not-so-distant future.

According to the writer, who hoped that all these extra qualifications would make her prose sound more scientific, what she really meant was:

> In order to make a prediction from our past data and not simply assume a rapid decrease in temperature that the weather charts imply, we used a variety of factors in the calculation. We feel this method will effectively predict the direction of temperature change for the near future.

5. TRANSFORM PASSIVE CONSTRUCTIONS INTO ACTIVE ONES

Passive expressions, like negative ones, are harder to understand and harder to remember. The difference between an active and a passive construction is a simple one. In an active construction, the subject *acts:*

     s   v
Moe made a decision.

In a passive construction, the subject is *acted upon:*

     s   ⌐——v——⌐
A decision was made by Moe.

While this example was a simple one, complex passive constructions create problems. Often readers must mentally transfer such constructions into active ones as they are reading in order to comprehend them. If you use a number of passives, your reader may not be willing to put in that extra effort; furthermore, you are forcing him to waste energy on processing your prose when he should be concentrating on what you have to say. Passive constructions may also twist your meaning, because they push the actor, which should be the subject of the sentence, into a less significant grammatical position.

To transform a passive construction into an active one, try these techniques:

1. Find the hidden actor in the sentence and let him (or it) act.
2. Convert an important noun in the sentence into a verb.

Usually, going from passive to active means switching from an impersonal to a personal style.

Passive:
Negotiation of a contract with the Downtown Jazz Club was conducted by our agent after an initial booking was used to establish contact. Performances are planned to start in two weeks.

Active:
Our agent negotiated a contract with the Downtown Jazz Club after establishing contact through an initial booking. We plan to begin performing in two weeks.

There are, of course, many times when a Latinate noun, a passive verb, or a negative expression is exactly what you want to say. For example, passives let you put emphasis on the result of an action when the actor is not important, as in: "My telephone has finally been repaired." The important thing is to know how to make your prose direct and vigorous when you need to, and to recognize the effect your choice will have on a reader. A thank-you note that says, "The assistance received from the members of your department was appreciated," doesn't convey the warmth and sincerity of a more direct statement such as "I sincerely appreciated the help everyone in your department gave me."

If you believe in an idea and want to stand up for it—but still be serious and formal—you can do it in active, direct language. Which of these conclusions to a planning report would you be more likely to act on?

> The conclusions drawn from the Co-op Board's study indicate that it seems advisable under present circumstances to initiate the adoption of the new work-sharing plan. If a presentation of all the facts of the plan is duly made to the co-op members, our opinion is that their approval will be forthcoming.

or

> As a result of our study, we believe the Co-op Board should adopt the work-sharing plan. Once the members fully understand the plan, we think they will favor it.

PROJECTS AND ASSIGNMENTS

1 Give a 3-minute oral review of *your plan* for your paper based on reviewing your first draft. Ask your listeners what they want to know and what they expect to hear based on the plan you have in mind.

2 *Checklist: Using the Detect, Diagnose, Revise strategy with a collaborator.* Here is a systematic way to use this strategy.

☐a. Review your goals and review each major section of your paper for its gist in order to prime your detector.

☐b. Read your paper to detect and mark global then local problems.

☐c. Diagnose your global problems (writing down your analysis of the 2 or 3 most important ones) and try to diagnose or identify your local ones (here your handbook can help you figure out some diagnoses; you might wish to start a personal checklist of your most common problems).

☐d. Make a plan for revising that will solve your global problems (write your plan down for the 2 or 3 major ones) and make a note on how to fix your local ones.

☐e. Now you are ready to meet with a collaborator. Ask your reader to detect (anything) and to diagnose (1 or 2 global problems). Compare your reader's response with your own diagnosis and revision plan.

☐f. Then update your plan and revise.

3 Try the Detect, Diagnose, Revise strategy in a more informal way. Mark detections and jot only brief notes to yourself about your diagnoses and revision plans. (Is diagnosis more or less useful on different kinds of problems?) As you Detect, Diagnose, and Revise, test out two or three of the various techniques mentioned in the text, such as using a highlighter or a collaborator. Keep notes on how well those particular strategies worked for you *on this particular paper* and *why*. Write a brief (1–2 page) commentary on your decisions and on what you observed about your revision process to hand in with your revised paper.

4 Do you see different things in a text depending on your own role or your goals? Use the detect and diagnose steps as described in Assignment 2 (on a paper provided by your instructor) to respond *as a student who wants to learn something*. Now shift roles: you are an instructor whose main role at the moment is *to help the writer learn more about being effective*. Use the detect and diagnose steps. Write a paper on what you observed from this comparison, using your revision notes as examples.

5 Revise these sentences using the key-word editing technique.

☐a. The thing that tended to bring about the manager's decision to stop hiring was the crisis caused by the sudden departure with company funds of the accountant.

☐b. The key factor in the inflation of the cost of health care in the United States at this time would appear to be the unnecessary duplication of medical services.

☐c. There has been an increase in the number of publications of pornography that sell at newsstands from zero in 1953 to a number well over thirty in the last five years.

☐d. Although a great many of our citizens do not have any wish to see pornography that is of a soft-core nature in our public drugstores, the dictates of the "high percentage" rule allow the storeowner to be paid extra sums of money by the distributor to enable the display of magazines of this nature.

6 For each passage below, figure the noun/verb ratio, note the heavy nouns and negative expression, and locate any linking or passive verbs. Then rewrite each paragraph to make it as forceful as you can. Score your results and compare them to the original paragraph.

☐a. Wanda Stevens, secretary, called public attention Friday to the organization of a demonstration to be held by the Walton Community Council. The demonstration is planned as a protest against the slowness of the city's clearance effort in a vacant lot in the Walton area. Usage of the lot as a playground by local children is not unusual, although it is filled with trash and garbage, and rats and other vermin are often reported there. A clean-up of the vacant lot is expected to be triggered by the demonstration.

☐b. An announcement was made by Rhoda Brown, secretary, of the resumption of operations by the Consumer's Lobby. The decision of the lobby to increase concentration on local issues was noted in the announcement. Enrollment of members is expected to be encouraged through the elimination of previous office locations at some distance from local neighborhoods. In dealing with future legislation, legal recognition of neighborhood rights will be the intention of the lobby, Ms. Brown asserted.

IF YOU WOULD LIKE TO READ MORE

If you would like to know more about editing for style and editing with a reader in mind, see:

Farb, Peter. *Word Play: What Happens When People Talk.* New York: Knopf, 1974. / This book provides a fascinating discussion of how people use language.

Gibson, Walker. *Tough, Sweet and Stuffy: An Essay on Modern Prose Styles.* Bloomington, Indiana: Indiana University Press, 1966. / This book shows the connection between a person's writing style and personal style: whether he or she appears tough, sweet, or stuffy.

chapter twelve

Editing for
a Clear Organization

STEP 9   EDIT for connections and coherence

Edit your paper to ensure that the relationships between ideas are clear and that the logic of your structure is evident to the reader.

Strategy 1   TRANSFORM LISTLIKE SENTENCES

Strategy 2   REVEAL THE INNER LOGIC OF YOUR PARAGRAPHS

Everyone wants his or her writing to be well organized, to have a clear, logical structure. But what makes a structure clear to a reader, and how can you tell if yours will indeed be clear? In this section we will focus on one of the most important things you can do to organize and structure your writing: Make connections between ideas explicit in the text.

STEP 9   EDIT for Connections and Coherence

One goal of a writer is to present his or her message so clearly that readers can build in their minds the same (or nearly the same) structure of ideas that the writer had in his or hers. However, writers often have important relationships in mind that they simply don't express in their words. Take, for example, this passage on how to take care of old pocket watches:

(1)   (2)
Old pocket watches are delicate instruments. It's fun to look at the
                    (3)
mechanism working, but don't open the case very often.

For the writer the connection between the ideas I've numbered
(1), (2), and (3) is absolutely clear. Is it to you? Could you explain
it? In the writer's mind there were meaningful connections between all of these ideas, but in her message there is only one important hook, the word "but." Here is how she revised it to clarify:

(1)   (2)
Old pocket watches are delicate instruments. *Although* it's fun to *un-*
                    (3)
screw the back and watch the mechanism working, don't open the case

very often *because even fine dirt can damage or stop the moving parts.*

Notice how the revisions work. In the first draft there was indeed a connection between idea 2, "it's fun to look at the mechanism working," and idea 3, "don't open the case." However, the
focus of the sentence was on the idea of "fun," whereas the passage was intended to be about watch care. By adding the word
"although," the writer indicated that idea 2, having fun, was subordinate to her main point, the warning about not opening the
case. Then by adding the "because . . ." clause at the end, she
spelled out why that connection or recommendation was reasonable, since opening the case can damage the watch. Here she had
to add information that was missing from the first draft.
    Finally, the writer added the phrase "unscrew the back" when
she realized that some readers might not make the connection
between having a pocket watch and watching the mechanism unless they knew the back could be opened. So the revision made
that information, which previously could only be inferred, explicit in the text.
    Editing for clarity means making the hidden relationships in
your own thinking clear in your prose. Major points should stand
out as important or inclusive; subordinate ideas should be put in
their place. When you don't make these relationships clear, you
leave part of the work of writing up to your reader. He may find
your material hard to follow and end up feeling confused (or, more
likely, assume that it is you who are confused). Perhaps even worse,
he may fail to see your point and build a very different structure
from the one you had mind. In either case you are asking the
reader to draw inferences and make the right connections between
your ideas. As can be seen from the pocket-watch revision, clear

writing not only is more informative but is more persuasive because it often tells the reader the "hows" and "whys" behind your assertions.

Let us look now at techniques for testing your prose and making relationships explicit in both sentences and paragraphs.

⬅ *Strategy 1* TRANSFORM LISTLIKE SENTENCES

In editing sentences for clarity, look for two things. Does the sentence itself emphasize its main point? (Are powerful words in powerful places?) And are the underlying connections between sentences made explicit in the text?

One common irritant to readers is a sentence that reads like a list. For example: "The thing about a sentence with a listlike form is that there are a number of tiny points with independent bits of meaning that are set out in the sentence in a line so that the series of words and phrases read like so many pieces of popcorn strung out on a string." (Compare this to: "A listlike sentence, with its many independent points, lines up words and phrases like popcorn on a string.") Although easy to write, listlike sentences tend to be wordy and boring to read. Furthermore, like a list, they reduce all details to the same level of importance and make it hard for the writer to highlight what is significant.

TESTING FOR A LISTLIKE STYLE

To test your draft for a listlike style, look for an abundance of connective words (*that, which, and, plus,* etc.) and prepositions (*in, of, from, for, by, over, with,* etc.). Consider this sentence:

> The demand (on the part) (of students) (for a greater number of films), (in addition) (to increases) (in film rental fees) (of most) (of the companies), has led us to request an increase (in the Film Society's allocation) (from the Funding Committee).

This sentence is weakened by two things. First, the grammatical subject of the sentence, "demand," is not the real actor (see Chapter 11). Second, the strings of prepositional phrases bog down the sentence. When you write a phrase such as "on the part," you create an independent little unit of meaning. A string of such independent units makes a weak sentence because it doesn't distinguish between major ideas and mere subordinate details, nor does it show their connections. A complex logical relationship is blurred into a simple list.

To transform listlike sentences, do three things:

1. Mark the prepositions (as was done in the preceding example), then promote key words to grammatically powerful places.

   We request that the Funding Committee increase . . .

2. Put subordinate information into a subordinate clause.

   Because students want more films . . .

3. Transform less important nouns into modifying words, and eliminate unnecessary prepositional phrases.

   . . . in addition to *increases* in *film rental fees* of *most* of the *companies*

becomes

   . . . and most companies' film rental fees have increased

Revised sentence:

Because students want more films and most companies' film rental fees have increased, we request that the Funding Committee increase the Film Society's allocation.

Here is another way to combine elements of a sentence. Many sentences contain more than one "simple sentence," that is, more than one subject-and-verb unit. When you review your writing, ask yourself two questions: (1) Have I made the connections between my simple sentences or ideas explicit? (2) If not, how else can I combine them?

In English there are three major ways people combine simple sentences or ideas: by making them parallel or coordinate to one another, by making one subordinate to another, or by adding one to another as a modifier. Each way of combining simple sentences asserts a specific logical relationship between ideas. Furthermore, our language offers a number of devices (grammar, punctuation, and signal words) for indicating this relationship and making it more explicit. Here are some familiar patterns for combining simple sentences.

Coordinate Pattern

This pattern sets up two equal simple sentences in parallel or in contrast with one another. Like all sentence patterns, it has signals that tell you to look for a coordinate structure.

EXAMPLE: Mac is our accounts manager, *but* he works out of London.

SOME SIGNALS: *and, but, or,* :, ;

Subordinate Pattern

This pattern lets you show a subordinate relationship between two ideas by making one grammatically subordinate to the other.

EXAMPLE: *Although* he works out of London, Mac keeps a flat in Paris. *Since* Mac does keep the books, he will know the answer—*if*, of course, anyone can find him.

SOME SIGNALS: *if, although, because, since, when, where, after*

Modifying Pattern

This pattern lets you pack additional information into a sentence by turning one simple sentence into a modifying phrase or clause.

EXAMPLES: Mac, *who never did pass math methods,* manages our accounts.

(Simple sentence: Mac never did pass math methods.)

Managing our accounts from London, Mac drinks dark ale at the Stewed Horse.

(Simple sentence: Mac manages our accounts from London.)

Our accounts, *ineptly managed by Mac in London,* are going to pot.

(Simple sentence: Mac manages our London accounts ineptly.)

SOME SIGNALS: Relative pronouns *(who, which)*

Verb phrases that tie the expression to the main part of the sentence (in this example, *managing, managed by*)

PLACEMENT OF SUBORDINATE OR MODIFYING MATERIAL

As we have seen, an independent simple sentence can be reduced to a clause or phrase and inserted somewhere in another sentence. The next question is, how do you decide where to place it? For example, say you have the sentence "Doggy Odor-Eater powder is now on the market," and you want to add the idea, "It was developed in the last ten years." You have three major alternatives:

243

Left-branching sentence	*Developed in the last ten years*, Doggy Odor-Eater powder is now on the market.
Mid-branching sentence	Doggy Odor-Eater Powder—*developed in the last ten years*—is now on the market.
Right-branching sentence	Doggy Odor-Eater powder is now on the market, *after being developed for ten years*.

Here are comments on the different types of placement.

Left-Branching Sentence

This pattern places the modifying clause at the beginning. Setting up a reader's anticipation with background or qualifying information placed first, left-branching sentences rely on the strong clarifying effect the subject has when it comes. But the longer the reader has to wait without knowing your subject, the more he is likely to become confused. Reread the second sentence in this paragraph, which was a left-branching one. Did you become impatient waiting for the subject, "left-branching sentences"?

Mid-Branching Sentence

This pattern—inserting modifying material between the subject and the verb—tends to create suspense, even to the point of taxing the reader with perverse demands on his attention. (The sentence you just read was a mid-branching one.) If the interruption is too long, the reader is forced to hold major ideas in suspension until the sentence is completed. Used more discreetly, the mid-branching sentence begins with a grammatically powerful element, shepherds modification into the middle—often isolating it with dashes—then makes the mind accelerate toward a tie-up idea and closure. For example: "Clearly, multinational corporations—the giant conglomerates that have covered the globe and permeated many foreign economies—are often the source of a country's economic stability."

Right-Branching Sentence

This type of sentence is developed by adding material: creating a structure that follows a natural pattern of the human mind just as this sentence does, with a series of qualifying phrases added one after another. Right-branching sentences are easy to write and easy to read—to a point. Their weakness is that the writer may tend to ramble on and create listlike sentences without sufficient force or emphasis.

THE SIMPLE-SENTENCE TEST

In editing for connections, watch out for paragraphs made up of a list of simple sentences. Here is an easy diagnostic test you can use to see if your paragraph reads like a list of ideas and if you need to add more cues to help the reader see connections between your phrases and sentences. Consider the paragraph below:

> Rescue dogs are often specially trained. They work in areas where a bomb or earthquake has buried people in debris. There job is to locate where the persons are buried. Rescuers can dig them out before they suffocate or die from other injuries. The dog must guide rescuers to the spot and be willing to sit and bark until help comes. Some dogs can be easily trained for rescue. Collies, shepherds, Airedales—in fact, most working breeds—will happily bark. Spaniels, setters, pointers, and some hounds refuse to bark once they have found their person. They will bark at home if someone comes to the door, but not while they are working. These breeds have been selectively bred not to bark while working and not to scare the game.

To test his first draft of the paragraph, we can look for three things:

1. How many sentences *begin* with the main subject and verb (such as "dogs are," "they work") rather than with a signal word or a subordinate or modifying clause? If all of your sentences start right out with the main subject and verb, your paragraph probably will read like a list of unrelated assertions. In Figure 12-1, the main subjects and verbs are shown in boldface; 10 out of 10 sentences have the initial pattern of main subject plus main verb. This helps explain why each sentence reads like one more item on a grocery list.

2. Next, count up all the additional simple sentences that are embedded within each sentence and that function as modifying or subordinate material. In Figure 12-1, all of the subordinate subject and verb combinations (or embedded simple sentences) are underscored. Add this number to the number of combinations you found in Step 1.

Now compare this total to the total number of sentences. How many simple sentences (including embedded simple sentences) did you average per sentence? The example has a ratio of 17:10—almost two simple sentences per sentence. This is not bad, but could be improved given the closely related ideas in the paragraph. As

Figure 12-1   *An application of the simple-sentence test*

1 main S/V	Rescue **dogs are** often specially **trained.**
1 main S/V, 1 subordinate S/V	**They work** in areas (where) a <u>bomb</u> or <u>earthquake has buried</u> people in debris.
1 main S/V, 1 subordinate S/V	Their **job is** to locate (where) the <u>persons are</u> buried.
1 main S/V, 1 subordinate S/V	**Rescuers can dig** them out (before) <u>they suffocate</u> or <u>die</u> from other injuries.
1 main S/V, 1 subordinate S/V	The **dog must guide** rescuers to the spot and **be** willing to sit and bark (until) <u>help comes.</u>
1 main S/V	Some **dogs can be** easily **trained** for rescue.
1 main S/V	**Collies, shepherds, Airedales** — in fact, most working breeds — **will** happily **bark.**
1 main S/V, 1 subordinate S/V	**Spaniels, setters, pointers,** and some **hounds refuse** to bark (once) <u>they have found</u> their person.
1 main S/V, 2 subordinate S/V's	**They will bark** at home (if) <u>someone comes</u> to the door (but) not (while) <u>they are working.</u>
1 main S/V	These **breeds have been** selectively **bred** not to bark (while) working and not to scare the game.

discussed before, combining simple sentences into more complex sentences is an effective way to make more explicit connections.

3. Finally, count the number of signal words (they are circled in Figure 12-1) that tell the reader you are using a coordinate, subordinate, or modifying pattern. The example has 9 word or phrase signals and no punctuation signals.

In the following revision, the writer tried to vary the simple-sentence beginnings, combine more ideas per sentence, and increase the number of signals to the reader. In the revised paragraph, only 3 of the 6 sentences have simple, main-subject-plus-verb beginnings. The ratio of simple sentences (including embedded sentences) to total sentences is now 17 to 6, or nearly three simple sentences per sentence. And the passage now contains 14 signals to the reader.

Rescue **dogs are** often specially **trained** to work in areas (where) a bomb or earthquake has buried people in debris. Their **job is** to locate (where) the persons are buried (so that) rescuers can dig them out (before) they suffocate or die of other injuries. (Since) the dog must guide rescuers to the spot, **he must be** willing to sit and bark (until) help comes. (As a result) some **dogs,** (including) collies, shepherds, Airedales, and, in fact, most working breeds, **can be trained** for rescue; **others can't. Spaniels, setters,** and some **hounds,** (for example), **refuse** to bark once they have found their person. (Although) they would bark at home (if) someone came to the door, these hunting **breeds have been** selectively **bred** not to bark (while) working (because) it would scare the game.

Remember that there are no set rules for how many sentences you should embed; simple sentences can be very effective. Nor will you always want to go to the trouble of counting up subjects and verbs. But this simple diagnostic test can help you focus attention on three common writing problems. It encourages you to make as many connections and give as many signals as seem reasonable in view of what you have to say. The final self-test in editing is always: Does my style fit my purpose and reflect my underlying meaning?

⮘ Strategy 2   REVEAL THE INNER LOGIC OF YOUR PARAGRAPHS

A paragraph is a working unit or functional part of a paper designed to accomplish something for you and the reader. Before editing a paragraph, you need to know two things: What is the point you want this paragraph to make, and how are your ideas actually connected? Then, when actually editing the material, you apply the test: "Have I indeed been able to make my point and connections clear in the text?"

Many people, however, rely on a weak editing test. They simply read the prose to see if it seems to "flow" or "sounds right." But what does that really mean, and how can a writer test effectively for these qualities?

Because "flow" is such a subjective concept, it is hard to test your own writing for flow as a reader would. What seems clear to you may not seem clear to a reader. The problem is that in rereading your own prose, it is easy to unconsciously supply the missing verbal and logical connections and happily conclude that the paragraph is indeed clearly organized. Flow, it seems, is a quality that rests in the eye of the beholder. Your organization may be logical to you as writer, but it is only clear if the reader sees the connections that lead from one idea to the next. As editors, then, we need a more practical, operational definition of "flow" in order to test our writing from a reader's perspective, not our own.

BASIC PATTERNS READERS EXPECT

One of the simplest ways to test your paragraph organization is to see if it matches one of the basic patterns readers expect, such as topic sentence-revision-illustration, problem-solution, cause-effect, or chronological order. Patterns such as these have a special claim to fame because they are general patterns readers have learned to expect in expository writing. They are not necessarily the best patterns for every purpose, or ones you *should* use, but they are patterns your readers will expect and therefore can easily follow.

The TRI Pattern

Probably the most familiar way of developing a paragraph is to present the topic in the first sentence, refine or restrict it in some way in the next sentence, and use the rest of the paragraph to develop or illustrate the point. A shorthand name for this pattern is the TRI pattern (topic-restrict-illustration). If the paragraph is long or complicated, writers will often return to the topic at the end with a concluding statement that sums up the discussion. The pattern becomes a TRIT.

The paragraph above that began with "Because 'flow' is such . . ." is a good example of a TRIT pattern. The first sentence sets up the topic, "flow is hard to test," and the next sentence refines or restricts the meaning of "flow" as clarity. The rest of the paragraph illustrates why the assertion in the topic sentence is true. Finally, the last sentence makes some restatement of the topic, while also reaching a new conclusion based on points made in the paragraph.

This pattern requires a topic sentence at the beginning. However, for dramatic effect, writers occasionally want to save their point and lead up to it at the end of a paragraph. Sometimes this can be done with great impact, especially in literary or dramatic writing where readers expect to be pleasurably surprised. However, whenever your paragraph begins without a topic sentence or a preview of your point, ask yourself these two questions. First, will my discussion be so interesting or dramatic that I can risk keeping the reader in the dark—violating the reader's topic sentence expectation—and still have him with me when I do make my point? Secondly, will the paragraph be so clearly developed that the reader will be building the same idea tree I am, even though I haven't given him the top-level idea at the beginning? Topic sentences are only a convention, it is true, but they are powerful ones with sound, practical reasons for their existence.

The Problem-Solution Pattern

A second familiar paragraph pattern has only two parts, a problem and a solution. Paragraphs that start with rhetorical questions such as "How did earlier societies build such monuments as the pyramids?" often take the problem-solution pattern.

The Cause-and-Effect Pattern

This pattern is equally familiar. When a paragraph starts out "If the university chose to raise tuition by 10 percent . . . ," the reader automatically expects a discussion of the possible effects.

Chronological Order

If a paragraph starts out, "The first step in training a horse is . . . ," the reader is immediately primed for a chronological organization. He may expect a series of detailed steps for what to do first, second, and third, or he may anticipate a more general organization based on importance (for example, the first thing is to gain the horse's confidence, then worry about breaking it to lead).

The advantage of using one of these patterns is very simple: Readers know and expect them. By building on your reader's expectations, you increase comprehension and make your prose easier to follow. By the same token, when you use another pattern because it would better fit your purpose, you should increase the cues that tell the reader how ideas are related. Phrases such as "for example," "on the other hand," and "a final point" let the reader see your plan.

THE UNDERLYING LOGICAL STRUCTURE

This second test is both more rigorous and more helpful since it lets you see if the paragraph is logically developed around its main point. The test itself is merely an extension of the issue tree that can be used to organize ideas. In a hierarchically organized paragraph, there will be one top-level idea, which we can label level 1. (Generally speaking, this will be the first or topic sentence of the paragraph.) In the rest of the paragraph every sentence should be *related to* this level-1 sentence. It should also be either *parallel or subordinate to* the sentence above it.

There are two ways you could test your paragraph. One is to pull a key word or phrase out of each sentence and sketch an issue tree. The second, which we will discuss here, is the Francis Christensen method, indenting each part of a sentence or paragraph to show its relationship to the elements around it. This can be demonstrated with the following paragraph on creativity. Notice how the level-2 sentences expand or develop the ideas in level 1, the level-3 sentences develop level 2, and so on.

1 The stage of preparation must be taken seriously if one expects to be creative.

  2 Having relevant knowledge does not guarantee creativity, but it is certainly one very important condition.

    3 Van Gogh, while a revolutionary artist, had extensive knowledge and appreciation of traditional artists.

      4 Further, he spent years practicing technical skills, especially drawing, which he regarded as fundamental.

  2 Acquiring the knowledge needed for creativity may require a great deal of work.

3 Indeed, the only trait Anne Roe found that was common to the leading artists and scientists she studied was the willingness to work extremely hard.

1 and 4 Those who plan to relax until their creative inspiration seizes them are likely to have a long, uninterrupted rest.[1]

Note that each idea in this paragraph is clearly and logically related to the ideas that went before it: It is either parallel or subordinate to the ideas above. For the reader this paragraph would "flow" because there are no gaps in the logic and no unrelated ideas to sidetrack the discussion.

A second thing to notice is that this paragraph follows the TRIT (topic-restrict-illustration-topic) pattern. And yet the final sentence is really serving two functions. From one perspective it is a level-4 idea that seems to develop the idea above it, that leading artists and scientists work hard. At the same time the final sentence offers us a more detailed statement of the topic introduced on level 1. It serves to recapitulate the main idea and tie the entire paragraph together.

Checking the structure of a paragraph can often help you detect any sentences that break the logical flow or depart from the paragraph's central focus. Such breaks in logic or focus are often very hard to identify by just reading, because the "unconnected" idea may be clearly connected to something in your own mind even if it does not fit into what you wrote on paper.

The paragraph below has just such a problem. The writer had let the topic and its train of associated ideas dictate what she said in the paragraph. Notice how the two italicized sentences are indeed *related* to the topic she is thinking about but are not clearly connected to the main *focus* of this paragraph, which is to describe, from the tenant's point of view, the possible results of protesting a rent hike. In the act of composing, the writer had simply been sidetracked from the point of the paragraph by her own knowledge.

The primary objective of a rent-hike protest is to have the increase reduced or, ideally, eliminated. In practice there is little chance of either of these occurring. Realtors tend to be unresponsive to tenants' complaints about rent increases. *Some of the most frequent and unannounced rent hikes are found in the tight rental situations around urban universities.* But a protest can have positive results for tenants if it serves to limit future increases or influences the landlord to improve the building's upkeep. Ironically these benefits accrue only to those who remain in their apartments. For tenants who find the rent

(a)

[1] John R. Hayes, *Cognitive Psychology: Thinking and Creating* (Homewood, Ill.: Dorsey Press, 1978).

hike truly prohibitive, the only hope is to inform the realtor that they
(b) are moving out solely because of rent. *Sometimes entire groups of tenants get angry enough to leave in protest.*

Clearly this is a time for the writer to turn editor and evaluate
this paragraph as a functional unit. Is each sentence here pulling
its weight and contributing to the purpose the writer had in mind?
One of the quickest ways to test the fit of each idea is to sketch a
small issue tree of the paragraph, using the key words from each
sentence. As you will see in Figure 12-2, the top idea of this tree
is not an exact phrase found in the first sentence but a key word
"results," that captures the point of the paragraph.

One of the first things this tree tells us is that sentence (a) concerning rent hikes around universities does not develop the key
idea above it (realtors are unresponsive) or the top-level idea (results of a protest). It is really connected only to the term "rent
hikes." At the time of writing, the sentence had probably seemed
to follow, since it does relate to the last words in the preceding
sentence. But to the eye of an editor it is clearly irrelevant to the
larger purpose of the paragraph and should be deleted.

Sentence (b) presents a slightly different problem. Although it
does seem related to the main point of the paragraph, that connection is not explicit enough. The sentence is focused on what

Figure 12-2   *Testing the logical structure of a paragraph*

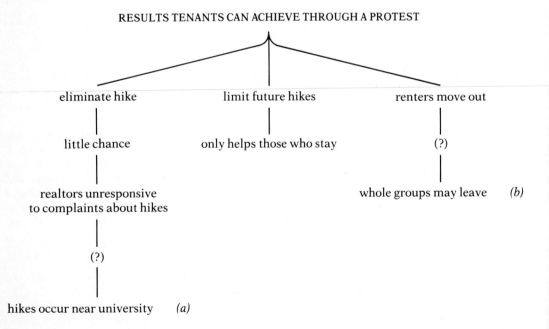

RESULTS TENANTS CAN ACHIEVE THROUGH A PROTEST

eliminate hike   limit future hikes   renters move out

little chance   only helps those who stay   (?)

realtors unresponsive   whole groups may leave   *(b)*
to complaints about hikes

(?)

hikes occur near university   *(a)*

groups do, not on the results that such a protest can bring. By seeing this on her tree, the writer realized that she had shifted focus. Sentence (b) is indeed developing a part of the sentence above it, but it is not connected to the top-level idea of "results tenants can achieve." So she rewrote the last sentence to make it fit her real focus on results: "If an entire group of tenants can decide to leave in a group, this last-ditch effort will sometimes get results."

To sum up, then, checking the hierarchical structure of a paragraph by using either the Christensen indentation method or an issue tree lets you test the logical flow of a paragraph in two ways. It helps you see if each idea is logically related (parallel or subordinate) to other ideas and if all the ideas are logically connected to the main focus of the paragraph.

CUES FOR THE READER

Issue trees and the Christensen method let you see if the underlying organization, or skeleton, of your paragraph is logically constructed. But notice how both of these methods rely on your turning the paragraph into a *visual* pattern with numbers and levels in order to see its structure clearly. Unfortunately, as writers we are usually confined to writing lines of words on a page, which the reader must mentally construct into a hierarchy of ideas as he or she reads. This problem is a real one for the writer, because in the process of reading, people often misunderstand complex discussions and restructure the writer's ideas.

Fortunately, our language also provides us with a large repertory of cues, hooks, and signals that let us make our structure and connections explicit. Some of these devices have been touched on previously. They range from grammatical signals such as conjunctions, to punctuation signals such as colons, to visual cues such as paragraph indentation, to verbal cues such as pronouns and repeated words. Look at the paragraph in Figure 12-3 and notice how many hooking devices the author has used to tie the paragraph together.

Here are some types of devices used:

1. *Pronouns.* The "we" in sentence 4 hooks back not only to "higher animals" but to the readers themselves, referred to in the first sentence with "our."
2. *Summary nouns and pronouns.* The "this" in sentence 6 pulls together the entire paragraph by referring to "experiment" and "play" in sentence 5 and to the "process of learning" in sentence 1. Sometimes a summary noun will do this job. For example, sentence 6 might have read: "Perhaps the nature of a *trial run* is what gives. . . ."

Figure 12-3   *A passage with many word and phrase cues*

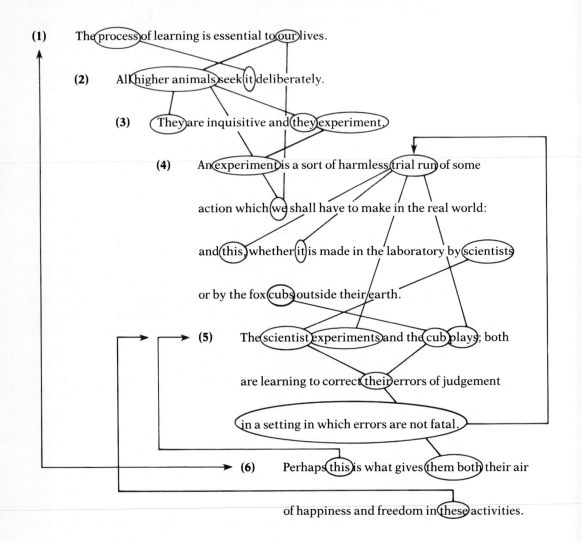

(1)   The process of learning is essential to our lives.

(2)   All higher animals seek it deliberately.

(3)   They are inquisitive and they experiment.

(4)   An experiment is a sort of harmless trial run of some

action which we shall have to make in the real world:

and this whether it is made in the laboratory by scientists

or by the fox cubs outside their earth.

(5)   The scientist experiments and the cub plays; both

are learning to correct their errors of judgement

in a setting in which errors are not fatal.

(6)   Perhaps this is what gives them both their air

of happiness and freedom in these activities.

— JACOB BRONOWSKI

Source: Jacob Bronowski, *The Common Sense of Science* (Cambridge: Harvard University Press, 1953).

3. *Repeated words.* "Scientist," "learning," and "errors" reappear.
4. *Repeated stems.* Bronowski used "an experiment" (the noun) followed by "experiments" (the verb).

5. *Rewording of the same idea.* A "harmless trial run" is later redefined as a "setting in which errors are not fatal."
6. *Punctuation.* Colons usually tell us that an example or a list follows. Semicolons connect two main clauses that generally are closely related.
7. *Parallel construction.* The grammatically parallel construction of "the scientist experiments and the cub plays" (sentence 5) emphasizes the parallel connection Bronowski wishes to make.

The writer's judicious use of repetition is effective because it meets an important expectation readers bring to prose. Normally, readers expect sentences to begin with something they already know about or with a word or topic that was previously mentioned. We might call this the sentence's *old information.* Readers then expect the sentence to add something new, the sentence's *new information.* Notice how this pattern of old information leading to new information works in the following series of sentences.

Shopping for a Turkey

Old . . .   New . . .

The old information was stated in the title. In buying a turkey, you get more meat for your money from a whole bird than from a boned, rolled turkey roast.

Old . . .   New . . .

The reference to "the whole bird" is old information from the preceding sentence. And the bigger that whole bird is, the more meat you will have in proportion to bone.

Old . . .   New . . .

The reference to a turkey's weight is old information, but the fact of one-half waste is new. A turkey weighing less than 12 pounds is one-half waste.

Old . . .   New . . .

"As a result" is old information, referring to the points made previously in the paragraph. As a result, it is more economical to buy half of a large, 20 pounder than to buy a small, 10-pound turkey.

At times this pattern of moving from old information to new information is broken. For example:

Old . . .   New . . .
And the bigger that whole bird is, the more meat you will have in
New . . .   Old . . .
proportion to bone. One-half waste is what you'll get with a turkey

weighing less than 12 pounds.

Figure 12-4   *Common cues for the reader*

<u>CUES THAT LEAD THE READER FORWARD</u>

To show addition:

Again,	Moreover,	
And	Nor,	
And then,	Too,	
Besides	Next,	
Equally important,	First, second, etc.	
Finally	Lastly,	
Further,	What's more,	
Furthermore,		

To show time:

At length	Later,
Immediately thereafter,	Previously,
Soon,	Formerly,
After a few hours,	First, second, etc.
Afterwards,	Next, etc.
Finally,	And then
Then	

<u>CUES THAT MAKE THE READER STOP AND COMPARE</u>

But	Notwithstanding,	Although
Yet,	On the other hand,	Although this is true,
And yet,	On the contrary,	While this is true,
However,	After all,	Conversely,
Still	For all that,	Simultaneously,
Nevertheless,	In contrast,	Meanwhile
Nonetheless,	At the same time,	In the meantime,

<u>CUES THAT DEVELOP AND SUMMARIZE</u>

To give examples: *To emphasize:*   *To repeat:*

For instance,	Obviously,	In brief,
For example,	In fact,	In short,
To demonstrate,	As a matter of fact,	As I have said,
To illustrate,	Indeed,	As I have noted,
As an illustration,	In any case,	In other words,
	In any event,	
	That is,	

To introduce conclusions: *To summarize:*

Hence,	In brief,
Therefore,	On the whole,
Accordingly,	Summing up,
Consequently,	To conclude,
Thus,	In conclusion,
As a result,	

Sometimes the sentence with new information at the beginning is confusing and needs rereading. However, by violating expectations, you can also create surprise and emphasis, as the sentence above did by surprising us with the phrase, "One-half waste . . ."

To sum up, then, you can use various kinds of repetition, in ing the old information/new information pattern, to make connections between sentences.

In addition, you can make explicit connections by using some of the common words and phrases listed in Figure 12-4. These not only highlight the logical connection between your ideas, but often give the reader a preview of what is coming.

ASSIGNMENTS

1 *Checklist: Signals for Diagnosis.* This chapter has presented a number of editing techniques you can use to test your prose.

These techniques help you see whether you have made the connections between your ideas as explicit to your reader as they may be to you. The problem with such tests, of course, is knowing when to use which test. When you first detect a problem, you may know only that "this doesn't sound right." Here are some procedures that can help you decide which test to use and diagnose problems that are really there.

☐a. Learn to listen for any faint sense that the text doesn't flow. Notice, for instance, when you have to rescan a sentence. Like an amplifier that boosts a weak radio signal, try to cultivate your awareness of those signals that say you have "detected" a problem.

☐b. When you have detected a possible problem spot (for example, an unclear connection, a confusing phrase), spend 15 seconds trying to diagnose the problem instead of immediately rewriting.

☐c. If your text sounds long and **wordy** or **unfocused,** then test for a **listlike** style and try other sentence patterns.

☐d. If the text sounds too simple and **choppy,** then try the **simple-sentence** test.

☐e. If a paragraph seems hard to remember or if you cannot see the **gist** of it once you have read it, then you might test for (1) does it have a **topic sentence** and (2) could it fit one of the basic **paragraph patterns?**

☐f. If the text seems to **jump, not flow,** or if you need to **reread,** then test for the **cues** you have given the reader.

☐g. Finally, bear in mind that sometimes the logic of a paragraph or discussion is not explicit in the text because it is not really clear in your own mind yet. Your text is simply telling you to think a little more. When that happens, concentrate on making the connections for yourself first, and on fixing the text itself second.

IF YOU WOULD LIKE TO READ MORE

If you would like to know more about editing with a reader in mind, see:

Becker, A. L. "A Tagmemic Approach to Paragraph Analysis." *College Composition and Communication,* 16 (Oct. 1965) 237–42. / This study includes a discussion of basic paragraph patterns.

Christensen, Francis. "A Generative Rhetoric of the Paragraph." *College Composition and Communication,* 16 (Oct. 1965) 144–56. / This article gives a detailed discussion of hierarchical paragraph organization.

Larson, Richard. "Toward a Linear Rhetoric of the Essay." *College Composition and Communication,* 22 (May 1971) 140–46. / The author studies the function of paragraphs in a developing argument.

O'Hare, Frank. *Sentence-Combining: Improving Student Writing Without Formal Grammar Instruction.* Urbana, Ill.: *National Council of Teachers of English Bulletin,* 1973. / This book gives a detailed discussion of ways of combining simple sentences, or kernels, into complex sentences.

chapter thirteen

Two Case Studies: Research Writing

IN THE CASE STUDY OF Joan (Chapter 3) we watched a writer trying to generate ideas and make meaning out of her own experience. The two writers we will look at here face a different part of the writing problem. They have done a lot of research and have a great deal to say, but they must transform what they know to meet the needs of their readers. For Kate this will mean meeting the expectations of a professor and responding to an assignment; for Ben this means collecting his own data to explore a hypothesis and presenting his interpretation of both the data and his sources. For his paper to succeed it must be both persuasive and well supported. In watching Kate and Ben's papers develop we will see how both writers have to actually rethink and reorganize their ideas in order to design their papers for a reader.

CASE STUDY OF KATE: DEFINING A RESEARCH QUESTION

Kate, a sophomore, is writing her first college research paper and facing that great unknown: "What does the teacher want?" or, more accurately, "What is it academic readers in general expect?" Kate is still making the transition from high school writing to college writing and is trying to figure out how to write a serious academic paper that does more than just display what she knows. This case study describes some of the processes she went through in trying to get an answer.

Kate's assignment, from a course in cognitive psychology, was a relatively open-ended one: "Write a paper on creativity based either on your own experimental project or on a biographical study of some 'creative person.' In doing so, treat some of the theories and principles covered in this course." Papers by other students ranged from studies of Einstein and Shakespeare to one on "Walt Disney: An American Original." Kate had enjoyed her own research on Charles Darwin, and the writing problem really began when she sat down to do a draft of the paper. At this point, Kate had done her homework well, although she felt the research would have been easier if she'd had an idea of exactly what to look for in the first place. Nevertheless, she had accumulated a great deal of information and it even fell into a rather tidy outline.

Kate's plan was to start with a catchy beginning, something like, "Creativity is a thing envied by those who feel they are noncreative. Quite often a noncreative person will marvel at other people's abilities and talents and exclaim on their impossibility and unbelievability. . . ." Then she planned to work through her outline, which is shown below, filling in the material she had found in the library.

    I. Definition of creativity
   II. Darwin's theory of evolution
      A. Social effects—controversy at the time
      B. Main points of the theory
  III. Darwin's biographical background
  IV. Four theories of creativity
      A. Romantic
      B. Freudian
      C. Wallas' stages
      D. Problem-solving

Everything seemed ready to go, but the minute she began to write she knew this was going to be a second-rate paper—boring to write and dull to read. Although it looked well organized, there was nothing holding it together, no reason to write. Kate felt she would simply be plodding through each topic on the outline and writing it up. This method—outline the topic and fill in the blanks—had worked well enough in high school, but she feared it wouldn't produce an effective academic paper. It was hard to imagine a good reason for anyone to read it—or write it.

Here was the dilemma: Kate had worked hard on the course and on Darwin, and had learned a lot, but her paper wouldn't show that she could *do* something with her information. Perhaps a "flash of inspiration" could have saved the paper, but the more frustrated and helpless she felt, the less likely she was to become inspired. Kate felt stuck.

It's hard to say whether frustration, common sense, or the lateness of the hour was responsible, but the next step in Kate's writing process was a return to the basics. She and three friends sat down one night to figure out what the reader's expectations really were, or, as they put it, "If I were the professor, what would I want?"

JAY: Well, I can tell you what I *wouldn't* want. I wouldn't want someone to recite the textbook back at me and feed me another summary of creativity theory. There are 25 papers to read from this class. I'd climb the walls if everyone just repeated the ideas back to me.

ANN: I don't think I'd be so keen on reading large chunks of straight biography either. I'd keep asking myself, "What's the point?"

KATE: O.K., I agree, but you've just demolished two-thirds of my paper. What did I do all that research for if I can't use it? And the assignment says to treat some of the principles of the course. You have to work that stuff in to show you've learned something.

CHEN: Well, if *I* were assigning this paper, here's what I'd want. Naturally I'd want you to show me you know the course material, but what I'd really want to see is if you can *use* those theories—not just repeat them. I'd expect you to *apply* the theory to some new problem like explaining what made Darwin or Shakespeare creative. The exam will show if you've read the text; I think a paper like this should show you can *think*.

ANN: I agree with that. I'm working as a grader for a freshman history class, and we were told to look for two things: if the person can discuss the readings well, that's a "B" paper; but in order to get an "A," they have to come up with their own ideas and be able to support them. That's what a real historian has to do, of course. So we're supposed to treat these papers as if they were going to be submitted to a magazine or journal. I think what Professor Howard wants is for everyone to learn the material and then be able to think like a historian and really *use* it.

KATE: All right, but how do I use creativity theory? What is there to analyze about Darwin? He made a huge splash—though, of course, come to think of it, he wasn't the first person to talk about evolution; Lamarck was. Would you still call him creative? . . . You know, what I could do is use the theory to test Darwin—was he truly a "creative" thinker—and at the same time test the various creativity theories. Do they really account for a person as important as Darwin?

JAY: Now I think you're getting somewhere. Chen was right about applying the theories, not just repeating them. It sounds as if you've come up with a real problem or issue to analyze here. The paper is even starting to sound interesting. I think it would meet the professor's expectations because you'd be using the material in the course to support your own thinking.

Actually, talking this over may help me with my own paper I'm doing for the course, on Thoreau. I was working up sort of a straightforward informal outline, but maybe I should pursue a thought that kept occurring to me when I was doing my research. One of the most perplexing things about Thoreau is that today everyone thinks he's a genius, but in the 1860s no one thought he was creative at all. The botanists thought he was incompetent, and the poets thought he was just imitating Emerson. I think I could tie this contradiction into some of the creativity theories we've been studying.

According to Kate the discussion went on for another hour, but the main ideas that emerged were relatively simple ones:

1. Professors who read academic papers have two very clear expectations. Naturally they want to see that you are learning, but they also expect you to show your ability to think: to use your knowledge to *create* and *support* your own ideas.
2. One important way of coming up with new ideas is to identify a problem, conflict, issue, or contradiction associated with your topic. Papers that merely "cover" a topic are often only school-room exercises. But once you define a real problem or issue within that topic, you have created a real-world writing problem: You have a reason to write and your reader has a reason to listen to you.

Example 1 shows the new plan and introduction that Kate developed. Compare it to her old outline and notice these two differences: First, Kate's paper is no longer a survey of information. Instead, it is organized around a problem or question that the reader (and Kate) will find compelling. Darwin's biography and theory no longer sit in a section of their own. Instead Kate *uses* the information she found in the library to support her own ideas about Darwin's creativity.

Secondly, the paper now has a hierarchical structure. Kate's old plan was a list of topics. Now she states her two top-level ideas in the first paragraph and organizes the paper around them. Notice too that Kate isn't using a traditional topic outline. Her new outline is more a plan for what she wants to accomplish in each section and a reminder of what information she should use to do that. What follow are the first draft of her problem/purpose statement, which sets up the issue she intends to address, and a plan for what she wants to do in the rest of the paper.

KEY FEATURES OF RESEARCH WRITING

Essays are often based on the writer's own experience and thinking; memos and short reports are often written when the author has special knowledge to pass on. Research papers, however, are a form of investigative reporting. The writer not only tracks down new information but tries to test and support these new ideas in the paper itself.

Example 1   *Kate's Goal-Directed Plan*

THE CREATIVITY OF CHARLES DARWIN

Introduction

In 1859 Charles Darwin, a British naturalist, published <u>The Origin of Species</u>, and its impact on the world was tremendous. Indeed, <u>Origin</u> is probably the most influential biology book ever written, and some historians even go so far as to claim that this book ranks second only to the Holy Bible. And yet, Darwin's ideas were not strictly new; he did not actually ''create'' the notion of evolution. Was he just a controversial thinker rather than a creative one?

In this paper I will look at the creativity of Charles Darwin by asking two questions. Does Darwin's work support or contradict current psychological definitions of creativity? And secondly, what is the best way to account for Darwin's own kind of creativity? Which of the major theories best fits the facts of Darwin's life and work?

Discuss point 1: Is Darwin ''creative''?

Define creativity. (Use Hayes, p. 215: ''a novel, surprising, and potentially useful act.'')

Does Darwin fit? Yes, because

1. He contradicted the theory of the special creation of man held by the church and the general public.

2. His notion of natural selection raised a controversy in the scientific community as well.

3. While Lamarck proposed the idea of evolution before Darwin, Darwin was the first to make the theory scientifically plausible. (Use quote from Farish, p. 333: ''No one had ever presented evolutionary theory so forcefully and so well documented.'') Back this up with description of Darwin's biological knowledge and research methods.

Sum up answer to point 1

Discuss point 2: Which theory fits Darwin?

1. Romantic inspiration. No.
   Discuss the 20-year development of Darwin's theory and cover his four key principles here.

Example 1 (*continued*)

2. Freudian sexual energy theory. Possible.
   Mention limited biographical evidence from
   Darwin's 5-year voyage on the <u>Beagle</u>.

3. Four-stage theory—Wallas. Partially true.
   Discuss the biographical information that
   fits this pattern, but note the misfit with
   the third stage.

4. Problem-solving theory. Best fit.
   Show how Darwin spent years of study and
   slowly pieced his ideas together, trying to
   fill in gaps in order to form an integrated
   theory.

<u>Sum up answer to point 2</u>

Many of us are familiar with a watered-down version of a research paper done in grade school—the library paper that was mostly a string of quotations and paraphrases, lightly glued together with transition sentences. My memory is that the goals of such papers were usually to collect a lot of note cards, say ten pages or more on some **topic,** and get the footnotes right. I didn't enjoy them.

A *bona fide* research paper, however, is genuinely exciting to do. To begin with, it is based on a problem or question in which you are already interested, not on a **topic** picked out of the blue. People choose to write research papers because they have a vested interest in knowing the answer. (Most of the books and articles cited in the bibliography of this book were written by just such people.) The "research" behind a researched paper can be done in many ways—in a library reading original manuscripts or reviews and criticism, in a medical laboratory running experiments, on the computer calculating alternative effects, in the field collecting notes and taped interviews, or in experimental conditions as you watch people trying to solve a problem.

Researched writing is a kind of detective work that rests on two premises:

1. A number of good heads are better than one (so that's why you consult other sources, run experiments, or base your own conclusions on a collection of ideas and results from varied sources).
2. People are more likely to read and believe good ideas if your analysis is supported by evidence you can document and/or by data you can show.

But the excitement of research is that investigative urge to answer a question worth answering or to solve a problem—even if your question starts out as wide open as:

What really happens when . . . (people argue, learn to run 20 miles, and so on)?

Why is it that . . . (some tennis rackets are better than others, this novel is called a "romance," and so on)?

How did this strange thing come about . . . (the Texas cattle drives, the changes in computer software, and so on)?

Investigative drive is probably the key to good research writing in most fields. This goal-directed use of research is part of what it means to "think like" a historian, a physicist, a psychologist, or a critic. Here is how a historian once described it to me. He said, "When I write a paper, I start already knowing a lot about my subject, the Korean War. And I have a hunch, a sense that I have something new to say. So I go after the data to find out what *did* happen—to prove or disprove my hunch—and I write to argue and prove my point. By contrast, it seems that some of my students use what I call the "grocery cart" approach to history papers. First they pick a topic, go to the card catalogue, find there is nothing on it, and then begin to wander down the appropriate library shelves, picking out the new-looking books—like dropping oranges in a grocery cart—looking for "good quotes."

Although the grocery-cart process has a certain appealing simplicity, it is unlikely to produce a good paper; it won't give you any experience in thinking like a researcher; and it certainly isn't a very exciting way to spend time. If you are interested in doing research—not just doing a "research paper" with footnotes—the first step is to put yourself in the place of that historian, or as close to it as you can get. Start with an area you know something about or care enough to find out about. I often set aside some time simply to read, refresh my memory, get the big picture, and just think. But most of all, try to locate a question, a problem, or an issue that will reward your effort and guide your research. Be flexible, because your notion of the problem itself is likely to change. But Minsky's Maxim applies: Any plan is better than no plan.

Finding Information

Doing research-based writing presents you with two tasks: (1) finding information (which we shall consider now) and (2) arguing with evidence (which we shall consider later). Rather than try to outline a single procedure for finding information, let me offer you some rules of thumb experienced researchers use.

1. Go to "expert" sources. One of the best-known techniques for doing good research is to ask another expert. If you have good questions, you will usually find that people are quite willing to share their knowledge. Some good sources are (a) a teacher in the subject area who can often send you to the major books and sources first, (b) a practitioner who may have practical knowledge not found in books, (c) a research librarian who is a professional whose job is to help you find the best sources, including indexes and guides you may not know about. Don't wander aimlessly in a library when an expert can point a better way. The bibliography in the major books you consult is another expert source—the author has already done some of the searching for you.

   "Expert" sources can also be defined as those best adapted to the job. If you are trying to decide what to read, look for an annotated bibliography that comments on sources. If you are investigating an established area, look for books that give an overview and synthesis. But if you are working on a recent development or a current question, consult up-to-date periodicals and scholarly journals.

   Finally, a full-size standard handbook like the *Harbrace College Handbook* will give you detailed information on standard library sources and on standard procedures for documentation. You should probably own a handbook for other reasons, but they are also available in the reference section of libraries.

2. Good questions get good answers. Like any detective, you need a good cover story when you begin a search for information. Try to write this script for yourself:

   a. The question/problem on my mind is _____.

   b. I want to review the scholarly debate on _____. Who are the major sources?

   c. Or, I am interested in applying ____(this theory)____ to _____(my question)_____. How could I learn more about it?

   d. Or, I have a hypothesis that _____ is relevant to _____(my problem)_____. How could I test that idea?

   e. The key words associated with my topic (which might appear in library guides and in book indexes) are _____. Where can I learn more?

   Use these "loaded questions" when you consult your expert sources and when you review books.

3. Be pragmatic. Define a problem or question you have the time and space to handle. A fifteen-page paper is only about 30 minutes of talk (less than half a class session). If the question is too large, you will be left making broad, airy generalizations (discussing the nature and history of "romance," for example) when you could be saying and supporting something specific (showing how one kind of romance tradition works in this novel). The problem is that readers quickly begin to skim these grand but unsupported statements—even if they agree—because they are looking for evidence in the text. So give yourself the kind of focused problem that will let you do solid, intelligent work that can stand on its own, even with a reader who doesn't agree.

4. Leave a clear trail as you work. There are certain tricks of the trade researchers use, because the extra minutes they take in the beginning often save hours in the long run.

   a. Write down basic bibliographic information on each book or source you consult when you use it: call number, author, title, publication date and source for books, and the beginning and ending page numbers for quotations.

   b. Keep separate ideas and topics on separate pieces of paper or cards. The order in which you find ideas and take notes will not match the logical order you will want to impose. It helps to be able to physically sort and shuffle all of the information.

   c. Keep track of the sources of any information—whether it is a quote, a paraphrase, or an idea—on the note. Don't count on finding that place again if you don't. And take any quotation down exactly as you find it, including underlining and punctuation.

   d. Think before you take a note. Where it is possible, make your notes show a gist, or main idea, from your point of view; annotate as you go along. Most important, don't just collect information and plan to figure it all out later. It is a lot faster in the long run to do your thinking and planning as you search.

   e. Finally, as you read, look for the facts, data, or arguments that support any ideas you find. Remember that the other researchers you read, even published ones, are like you; they can be wrong and they certainly could be argued with. If it is an important issue, you are likely to find that your sources disagree with each other. That is normal and healthy, but it means you must read with a critical eye, not only for good ideas but for the evidence that supports them. Your paper will be stronger if you argue from evidence rather than merely cite authorities.

At heart, a research-based paper is no different from any other analysis—you must define a central problem or issue, think it through, and try to present and defend your conclusions. But because a researched paper also tries to provide evidence in the form of other sources or data, it has some special conventions. If you examine them, they are actually quite sensible ones.

Using Documentation. Accurate documentation, in the form of footnotes and a bibliography, allows other people to use your research by going back to original sources and to evaluate the strength of your argument by seeing its foundation. If you use an idea, a paraphrase, or an exact quotation, document its source. Do this, first of all, because it is honest; give other researchers their due. Secondly, do this because such support is evidence for your own argument. The reader is more likely to believe you if you can show that people already agree about much of the issue and that you are adding knowledge or clarification. Readers are naturally more skeptical of writers who set up weak straw men only to knock them down or who suggest that everything they say is original. Research is, in part, the art of building upon what other good minds have created. Documentation is one way you can convince the reader and build a foundation for yourself.

Using Format. A researched paper does not have to be a single, flowing argument, the way a short essay does. You can use different sections with headings to do different kinds of work for you. Here are some optional sections found in many research papers:

Introduction. This sets the stage, creates a context, or provides background if the reader needs it.

Problem/purpose statement. This section may run from a paragraph to a page or two long. It is the initial statement that defines the problem, presents your question or thesis, and gives the reader a road map for reading the rest of the text.

Review of research. Data-based studies sometimes move from a concise problem/purpose statement to a review of the relevant previous research or theories. This then leads into a discussion of the writer's own study.

Research methods. For reporting studies based on data you have collected, this is a necessary statement about how you collected that data, what methods or research design you used, and who your subjects were. It should be quite concise but detailed enough to let someone else duplicate your study. Data-based papers may also use separate sections titled "Results" and "Discussion."

Sometimes journal editors and teachers will request specific formats or methods of documentation (such as MLA or APA style). Your handbook will show you the details. But in general you can look on format as a tool. In organizing a paper, use whatever format and headings will fit your purpose and present your material. Here are two general formats often used:

Argument-Based Papers	*Data-Based Papers*
Problem/Purpose Statement	Problem/Purpose Statement
Discussion	Review of Research
Section Headings based on	Research Methods
the argument	Results and Discussion
Conclusion	Conclusion

 ## CASE STUDY OF BEN: DOING RESEARCH

The following case study of a research paper by Ben Craft gets us a bit closer to the process itself. These excerpts from his process log show some of the decisions, plans, and problems that go into doing a researched paper.

Process Log

In keeping this log of his own composing process, Ben said his goal was to discover something about the kinds of choices and decisions he had made at the major turning points in his writing process—that is, what had he done and why. The design and content of the log reflect his goals.

Ben Craft
Process Log for Research Paper

DAY	ACTIVITY	OBSERVATIONS AND COMMENTS
Oct. 8	Discuss in class	I didn't come away from class with a topic. No ideas leap out. Massive lack of excitement. I don't think I have much to say on anything. Listed topics, photography, logic, argument, sportscasting techniques. All seem enormous.
	Reread assignment	Noticed phrase in assignment, ''think about problems noticed in your own experience or reading.'' That puts me on a different track. Thought of problems like trying to have a reasonable discussion with my roommate. But how do I turn that into a paper?

Oct. 9	Trying on ideas	Keep coming back to a mental image of 2 people in front of library arguing. Want to work on argument somehow I think.
	Checked card cat. after lunch	Discouraging. The topic doesn't hang to-gether. Plato, debate, rhetoric, linguistics, legal, history of, how to win, family arguments . . . Can't turn my mental image into a topic.
Oct. 10	Prof. Enos said something about ''power of the printed word''	Chance comment. It kept sticking in my mind. That's the question: are written arguments more powerful just because they are written? <u>Powerful</u> <u>arguments.</u> Felt very clever!
Oct. 11	Spent about 20 minutes listing features of argu-ments	This was one of several not very systematic ef-forts to get a handle on the question or to get a hypothesis. Kept feeling stuck. Not sure just what I should be doing, because I don't know the answer to my question. And yet how should I know it? Decided to talk to Prof. Stratman who teaches argument.
Oct. 13	Looked at 2 in-troductory books	Talking to Stratman and reading 2 books he men-tioned is a great boost. Realize now I felt blank because I needed to read. Got really hung up for a while on reading about the oral vs. written language—a big controversy. Was going to come up with a theory about oral vs. written argument. But finally realized it would just end up being another one of those speculation papers.
Oct. 15	Still reading	Breakthrough. Have an image of my problem as people arguing in the dorm, but the argument always seems to go in circles. Yet written ones seem to go forward. Reading to find out why, but no one talks directly about it. Ended up realizing it was the form or structure of the argument itself that seemed different. I remember being excited about this, and in-stead of scanning the books for answers or just speculating, I started writing down all the examples I could think of, of actual arguments and the moves people made. Then went to the Union to eavesdrop on real arguments and test my ideas, made more notes. Felt I really had something solid.

Oct. 16	Went to the library	Had some ideas now, but realized reluctantly that I needed more info on the form of argument. Yet felt when I went to the library that I was procrastinating and should have stayed at home writing. But reading turned out to be the correct decision. Used to think that that blank feeling was just a block that would go away. Why is it so hard to realize it when that blocked feeling really means ''go read''? Felt sleepy and overwhelmed by the info while reading. But told myself I would wake up and sketch out a new plan tomorrow from 8–10 A.M.
Oct. 17	I did it! Have a real problem now	Now I am starting to work systematically. Is it supposed to take this long to really know what you are doing? Talked to Stratman again, this time about how to collect some data on my own. I'm psyched.
Oct. 20	Collecting data	

Nov. 2	Doing a draft. Actually putting pieces together	Didn't realize how undisciplined my writing process was! For example:
		    3:15 fell asleep
		    3:30 went out for coffee
		    3:50 got up to take a walk and get a plan
		    4:15 got coffee and stopped to talk
		    6–7 went to dinner; talked about argument, got a buzz, and was taking notes on the napkin
		    7–12 wrote draft; didn't look back
		In retrospect I realize how much real work got done when I wasn't legally ''writing'' but was walking around thinking and talking about it.

Nov. 4	Tried to explain my ideas to two other guys	Found out they kept thinking of all arguments as fights. Had to explain the idea of argument as it comes out of logic and rhetoric. That gave me my introduction.
Nov. 7	Doing a second draft	Change I am most pleased with is changing from a sort of boring description in some places to a more persuasive style.

Some of the problems, decisions, and breakthroughs Ben described are unique to him and this paper. But some are common to the process of research writing. Let me note just three.

Ben seemed to be trying two different strategies for finding a research question. One was to fish for a topic and go through the card catalog for subtopics, a version of the grocery-cart tactic. The other way was to think of a problem that interested him and use a combination of reading and mulling it over to define a researchable question—that is, a question or hypothesis he could really test or answer.

Another major decision Ben made was to drop his grand theory in favor of a more limited, solid, supportable idea. Research writers sometimes *do* propose grand theories, but they usually spend some years testing and supporting those theories, and their papers are based on evidence. From your experience, what is the logic behind the grand-theory strategy when students, who don't have the time to support such claims, use it?

In rereading his log Ben said he was surprised to see how many times he had felt blank, confused, or stuck. But he also noted that the breakthroughs came when he took that feeling as a signal to change his strategies—to read more, talk to someone, think of concrete examples, or actually collect some data. This is not an uncommon situation. People often get blocked when they are writing because they really need to do some thinking or reading. The fact that words don't flow is just a symptom. Yet, as Ben says, it is often hard to recognize that feeling as a signal to change strategies or learn more before you write.

Look over Ben's log for evidence of other common problems and breakthroughs you recognize. How would you say Ben handled his problems? What led to his breakthroughs?

The Final Paper

Below is an excerpt from Ben's final paper. I find it particularly interesting to note how his process log entry on November 4 turned into the problem/purpose statement that begins his paper, and to see how he has organized his reading and research around the ideas that begin to emerge on October 15–17. In fact, the paper shows how extensively he has *re*organized the material he read around *his* problem; that is, he *uses* his reading and research to provide background for his question, to present some alternative hypotheses, and to offer various sorts of evidence for his own conclusions. If we could have somehow glimpsed Ben's inner, mental representation of what he knew about the topic "argument" on October 10th or 13th or even 16th, it would have been very different from the structure of ideas we see in the paper. The research writing process that led to Ben's paper is that of a detective rather than a bricklayer. Instead of simply piling up layers of facts—

bricks of information from various sources—the research writer turns information into clues and evidence for the case he or she is building. In reading Ben's paper, notice what he has done with the Toulmin theory he read about and with the research he conducted himself. And notice the various ways he tries to signal this idea structure to the reader. Is he successful?

EVERYDAY ARGUMENTS: USING STEPHEN TOULMIN TO UNDERSTAND ORDINARY ARGUMENTS

Students who study logic learn to construct syllogisms such as:

> All men are mortal.
> Socrates was a man.
> Therefore, Socrates was mortal.

They look on these syllogisms as challenging games. However, they usually don't see a strong connection between these logical puzzles and ordinary, everyday arguments that go on in the dorm, at ball games, or even in writing papers. Recently, some people in education, philosophy, and psychology seem to be agreeing with the view that ordinary argument has its own logic.

In both ordinary argument and ''critical thinking'' people talk to themselves or to someone else. They use this as a way of ''checking over or testing ideas as they are presented in everyday encounters.''[1] Some philosophers argue that thinking in ''natural language'' can lead to better, richer inferences than thinking that goes on in ''formal languages'' or abstract systems of formal logic like the syllogism. Gilbert Ryle is a major critic of these formal systems. He objects to the way they reduce meaning to a ''carefully wired marionette of formal logic.'' He goes on to say:

> Of those to whom this, the formaliser's dream, appears a mere dream (I am one of them), some maintain that the logic of the statements of scientists, lawyers, historians, and bridge-players can not in principle be adequately represented by the formulae of formal logic.[2]

Formal logic attempts to reduce words to mere abstract patterns. However, some philosophers and logicians, siding with Ryle, argue that the meaning of words is in their use. J. L. Austin, in <u>How to Do Things with Words</u> (J.O. Urmson, ed, Cambridge: Harvard University Press, 1962) sees the meaning of words in terms of the use to which they are put--such as making a promise or a request. Stephen Toulmin, in <u>The Uses of Argument,</u> makes a similar point. An argument is not simply a matter of logic and definition, but it is an act people perform in order to support or test a claim.[3] Toulmin says that an argument is made up of three basic elements: the claim you make, the data you have, and the warrant that lets you go from the data to your claim. This system for describing arguments offers a way to analyze real arguments that occur in ''natural language'' and to evaluate how complete and effective they are as persuasion.

How do people really use argument in discussions of the kind heard in the library or the dorm? Do they always supply the warrants or data when they make claims? In particular, I was interested in why these ordinary arguments often seem so inconclusive. Everyday conversational arguments seem to go in circles, repeat themselves, and often no one is convinced. Written arguments often seem to move forward, to answer questions, and to reach conclusions that seem persuasive, at least at the time. Would an analysis of the elements of the arguments help account for these differences?

This study is based on the hypothesis that Toulmin's analysis of written arguments could help track out an ordinary oral argument and evaluate why and how it succeeded or failed. In the first section of this paper I will discuss Toulmin's system and use it to analyze an argument from a textbook used in a university course. In the second section I will use the system to evaluate an ordinary oral argument that I tape recorded between two college students.

I. Toulmin's Pattern of Argument

Although Toulmin is a logician, he says that when people argue, they do not use formal logic. Instead, they think more like lawyers in a courtroom. They make claims and then try to justify or support them with evidence. Listeners test (and accept or reject) arguments in the same way. They look at the evidence that supports the claim.[4]

According to Toulmin, the layout of an argument includes three major elements (claims, warrants, and data)
and two minor ones (backing the warrant and qualification of the claim). The Toulmin layout shows how you go
from data to claim with the support of your warrant (or
back the other way if you are testing an argument). See
Figure 1.

I will illustrate each of these parts of an argument
by using them to analyze some of the claims made in a
textbook chapter on creativity. The authors, Hayes and
Bond, make a global claim that starts by recognizing that
women have a lower record of productivity in highly creative achievements (they have only won 5% of the Nobel
prizes). But, they claim, this is because of cultural

Figure 1. Toulmin's Pattern of Argument

If the CLAIM needs to be qualified or the WARRANT needs
more support, the argument would look like this:

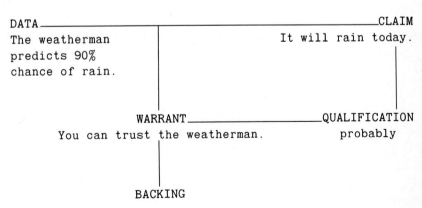

influences, not nature.[5] To support this claim they make a number of subclaims and arguments in the chapter. I will apply Toulmin's system to two of these arguments, which I will paraphrase from Hayes's book. (See Figure 2.)

CLAIM

Arguments begin when a person I will call the Claimer makes an assertion or claim about something, and another person I will call the Tester disagrees or is not immediately convinced.

Claim 1: Creativity demands an investment of an enormous amount of time. (See Figure 2.)

Figure 2. The Pattern of a Written Argument

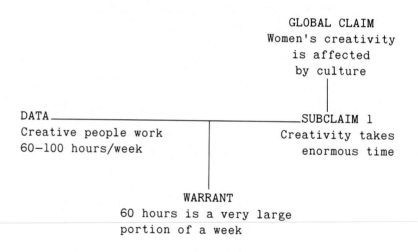

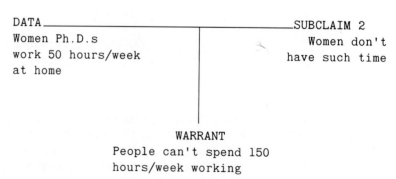

DATA

People disagree about the claims in an argument. But one thing both sides agree about is the data or evidence. This means the Claimer must be able to refer to some neutral data, facts, or observations as the evidence for the claim.

Data for Claim 1: University of California professors average 60 hours/week on teaching and research. Nobel Prize winner Herbert Simon spent about 100 hours/week in the years he was doing the work that won the Prize.

WARRANT

The warrant is the crucial logical step between objective data and a claim. It is the ''since this is so . . .'' statement that says, ''if you accept the data, then you should also accept my claim, because . . .'' If you think of a claim as an inference someone makes from data, then the warrant is the ''license'' to make that inference. It is like a fishing license; it shows you have the right to do certain things. Some warrants or licenses seem to be based on common sense, such as the assumption that you can believe what the weatherman says. As a result, they are often not stated by the Claimer. But sometimes they are really important assumptions that need to be said, since the Tester might not automatically come up with the same assumptions about weathermen or might even disagree.

Warrant for Claim 1: Since there are only 168 hours in a week, it is obvious that intense creative work of this type takes precedence over everything else—including sleep!

Table 1 summarizes my main points about these three key elements of an argument.

Sometimes arguers add two other elements to an argument.

QUALIFICATION

Sometimes a Claimer wants to qualify a claim either to soften or to increase what Toulmin calls its ''force.'' This seems to be what Young, Becker, and Pike would call showing the ''area of validity'' or just how far this

DATA	WARRANT	CLAIM
What does it offer?		
Evidence	Logical link	Assertion
Do people agree?		
Both parties agree	Some or most people agree	Two parties disagree
What are cue words?		
If this is true . . .	Since it is reasonable that . . .	Then . . .
Is it stated?		
Sometimes	Often not	Usually

Table 1. Features of Data, Claims, and Warrants

claim holds.[6] Words such as _perhaps_, _maybe_, _probably_, _we must believe that_, and _unless x happens_ show that a qualification is being made.

Qualification for Claim 1: Even that much time and effort might not be enough for creative achievement.

BACKING

Sometimes the Claimer needs to give some sort of backup or support that makes the warrant itself believable. However, in my example the warrant for Claim 1 is based on such obvious common sense that there is no need for any backing.

The written argument in this chapter is typical of the arguments Toulmin and others describe. It uses more than one subclaim to support its major claim, and the subclaims are themselves linked in clusters and chains.[7] The following example is one of the subarguments in Hayes and Bond that supports their claim.

Claim 2: Our social expectations make it hard for women to invest that amount of time and energy.

DATA: 95 percent of women marry. Married female Ph.D.s typically spend about 50 hours/week doing housework, their male counterparts, 10 percent.

WARRANT: People who spend 100 hours a week on research and 50 more on housework won't survive long, let
alone win a Nobel Prize!

BACKING: The authors give no explicit backing, but if
someone said to them ''Why do you assume your warrant is
reasonable?'' they could offer a case study or a calculation that showed that 168 hours in a week minus 150
hours of work equals 18 hours, divided by 7 days a week
yields 2 hours a day to sleep, eat, and see movies.

II. Predictions About Oral Arguments

Section I outlined the structure of an effective
written argument. But what happens when people engage in
ordinary oral arguments? What makes these arguments seem
incomplete or less persuasive? Based on my reading of
textbooks and the research on ordinary argument already
cited, I think we can make certain predictions:

1. The data or evidence is likely to be based on informal, personal observation (not the systematic and experimental observation that goes on in science). Or it
will be based on someone's testimony (on the fact that
''Charlie said so'' rather than on facts, statistics, or
logical inferences).[8]
2. The arguers will drop the attempt to make logical
arguments and will resort to ''nonargumentative'' forms
of persuasion such as insults, yelling, and unfair re-
marks.
3. Some parts of the argument, especially the warrants, will be missing.
4. The missing warrants will create a problem because the Tester in the argument will not see why or how
the data are significant (the Tester won't come up with
a warrant on his own) or the Tester won't agree that some
implied warrant actually makes the logical step from
warrant to claim. In other words, the people don't really
agree on the warrant, but they don't know they disagree
about that.

RESEARCH METHODS

My research was designed to do three things: (1) to
try to apply Toulmin's theory to ordinary oral argument,

(2) to see why and where that kind of argument was weak, and (3) to test my predictions. My method was to tape record an argument in the dorm without letting the people know I was doing so. Then immediately afterward, I told them why I had recorded and I asked for their written permission to transcribe the tape. I also told them that names, etc., would be kept anonymous. I then analyzed the transcript, coding it for data, claims, and warrants (so the first claim for speaker A would be coded A-C-1). The coded transcript is found in Appendix 1.

PROBLEM AREAS IN THE ARGUMENT

The argument I chose to analyze is a very common kind of friendly but serious argument--two guys discussing the record of Franco Harris, star running back for the Pittsburgh Steelers. His lifetime rushing record for yards gained had just broken the previous record held by Jim Brown of the Cleveland Browns. From a rhetorical point of view this is a definition problem. Should we define Franco's record as ''awesome'' or nothing? Is he as good as Jimmy Brown?

In the argument, the major claim is pretty clear: Franco is (is not) as good as Brown. Both A and B stick pretty close to that issue throughout the argument. As seen in the transcript, both A and B offer many pieces of evidence for the major claim, as well as evidence that later changes into claims. Warrants, however, are rare. Both people assume that yardage and game time are considered criteria for judging running backs. But they seem to be drawing different inferences from the same facts.

Their warrants or assumptions about what high game time means are in conflict. This problem keeps coming up in the argument. For example, A feels that because Franco has lasted so long in the league, Franco is a good player. B feels that this only gave him more playing time and explains Franco's high yardage. If A were to explicitly state the warrant for the evidence--''Only a durable, skillful player can last as long as that''--B would have had more difficulty undermining A's argument. Similarly, B could have made it clear why he feels that the duration of Franco in the league is the reason for his high yardage and not his skill.

Unlike some ''friendly'' discussions of this kind, the data are not simply testimony (such as ''everyone says he's great'') but include statistics on yardage, games and seasons played, and other players. However, they do resort to some nonargumentative tactics. When B says, ''without his line he wouldn't do jack shit and you know it!'' we can see two examples of nonargumentative persuasion. First, there is the use of very strong words. Saying ''jack shit'' instead of ''very few yards'' or some other substitution shows how B is trying to intimidate A. He is subtly insulting A with the use of such terms as a response. And then the statement ''and you know it'' is unfair. I see B as saying all of the following with that statement: ''You're lying, you're uninformed, you're ignoring the truth, etc.'' The same thing occurs when he says, ''That's not what I mean and you know it.''

Another feature of this argument . . .

CONCLUSION

Ordinary arguments can't be reduced to a syllogism. But they do have their own logic and structure. Stephen Toulmin's theory of argument can be used to evaluate the structure of both written and oral arguments. It reveals that . . .

FOOTNOTES

[1]R.R. Allen, Jerry D. Feezel, and Fred J. Kauffeld, A Taxonomy of Concepts and Critical Abilities Related to the Evaluation of Verbal Arguments, (Madison: University of Wisconsin Center for Cognitive Learning, 1967), p. 1.

[2]Gilbert Ryle, ''Ordinary Language,'' in Philosophy and Ordinary Language, ed. Charles E. Caton, (Urbana: University of Illinois Press, 1963), p. 108.

[3]Stephen Toulmin, The Uses of Argument, (Cambridge: Cambridge University Press, 1958).

[4]Toulmin. This analysis will be based on Chapter 3 of the book.
. . . .

Allen, R.R., Jerry D. Feezel, and Fred J. Kauffeld. <u>A Taxonomy of Concepts and Critical Abilities Related to the Evaluation of Verbal Arguments</u>. Madison: University of Wisconsin Center for Cognitive Learning, 1967.

Ehninger, Douglas. <u>Influence, Belief, and Argument: An Introduction to Responsible Persuasion</u>. Glenview, Ill.: Scott, Foresman, 1974.

Hayes, John, R. <u>The Complete Problem-Solver</u>. Philadelphia: The Franklin Institute Press, 1981.

....

APPENDIX 1: Coded Transcript of Oral Argument

      A: Wrong!

B-C-1 B: Franco isn't even in the same class as Jimmy Brown!

A-D-1 A: No, he just has 11,000 yards rushing . . .

B-D-1 B: Yeah, on 10,000 carries!

A-C-1 A: Bullshit. Franco's awesome; look, he is still playing after 12 seasons. Jim Brown only lasted 9, or something like that.

B-W-1 B: Which is why he is so great! Franco has been running for more years but he still has more yards than him.

      A: But . . .

B-W-1 B: And do not forget that Jim Brown only played like 9 or 12 games a season. Franco plays 16.

A-W-1 A: But that just proves what a good runner he is! He has durability.

B-W-2 B: That is because he runs out of bounds before he gets hit, or else he falls down.

      A: Right! That is why he has lasted so long!

      B: Well then how can you say he is better than Jim Brown?

      A: Woooo! I did not say that he was better than Brown. I said he was in his class.

B-C-2 B: Still though, no way Franco is in his class even. He stinks!

      A: Oh, you do not even know what you are talking about.

(PAUSE)

B-W-2   B: If he is so damn good, then why does he have to carry the ball more than anyone else?

A: Well if you want yards you have to carry the ball, right?

B: What about Walter Payton?

A: What about Walter Payton?

B: He's right up there with Franco and he hasn't been playing nearly as long.

A: He's good; I'm not saying he isn't.

B: But if Franco gets the ball so much more than he does and he only has a few more yards, then how can he be great?

A: Because he . . .

B: And what about his offensive line? Payton doesn't even have one but he still gets the yards.

A: So does Franco!

B: But that's because he has an offensive line. If he played for Chicago he wouldn't get half the yards he does!

A: Oh bullshit. He'd get his yards playing for any other team.

B: But his line . . .

A: Just because he has a line doesn't mean that, well, he gets his yards by himself.

B: Without his line he wouldn't do jack shit and you know it!

A: Oh yeah, Mike Webster carries the ball for him, does he?

B: That's not what I mean and you know it.

A: Everybody has a line. It's the runner that gets the yards.

B: But the offensive line means everything. If there are no holes then the runner isn't going anywhere.

A: But Franco finds his own holes by ducking and stutter-stepping.

B: Yeah, and all that does is give the other team time to catch up with him.

A: Then he turns on the speed and the moves and he's gone!

B: What moves? He never jukes anybody.

A: Which is why he has 11,000 yards!

B: Because he carries the ball so often.

A: Oh, let's not start that again! Regardless of whether he gets the ball . . .

Ben's process log gave us a glimpse into some of the ways he developed and reorganized his ideas during the process of writing. For many writers much of this thinking and restructuring is often done in revision, once they have a first draft in hand. Trying to make a first draft more focused and effective for the reader can often lead the writer to breakthroughs in his or her own thinking. Here is a section of Ben's first draft, which shows how revision affected a short segment of Section II. (The small numbers in circles refer to the comments which follow, and the brackets enclose material Ben added in his second draft.)

Revised Section of the First Draft

~~Hypothesis~~ 6

~~Conversation and Argument~~ 6

Predictions About Oral Arguments ①

[Section I outlined the structure of an effective written argument. But]② ꓷhat happens when people engage in ordinary oral arguments? [What makes these arguments seem incomplete or less persuasive?]③ Based ~~on my~~ ~~reading, I think~~④ on my reading of textbooks and the research on ordinary argument already cited, I think ~~it~~ ~~is possible to~~ we can make certain predictions:

    a. The data or evidence is likely to be based ~~on~~ ~~personal statements,~~⑤ [on informal, personal observation (not the systematic and experimental observation that goes on in science). Or it will be based on someone's testimony (on the fact that ''Charlie said so'' rather than on facts, statistics, or logical inferences).⁸]

    b. The arguers [will drop the attempt to make logical arguments and] will resort to [''nonargumentative'' forms of persuasion such as] insults, yelling, and unfair remarks. ~~Many political arguments use what are called ad hominum arguments (i.e., against the man) which try to personally discredit the opponent~~⑥

Ben's changes on this short section are a good example of how you can use a second pass to make a paper more substantial by going back and making clearer connections between your ideas, by elaborating important points for the reader, and by packing in specific information where your first draft was general. Note some of Ben's changes:

1. The headings in his first draft indicate only a fuzzy relationship between his two topics: his own study and Toulmin's theory. Ben didn't write a good heading until he had actually worked out the relationship by writing about it. (People often have this problem writing topic sentences and introductions. It is often best simply to lay the framework in the first draft and return to clarify it in the second.)

2. In the final version of this paper, Ben added an introductory sentence that makes his transition from written to oral arguments more explicit. Getting this top-level structure clear (and clearly expressed) is one of the chief ways revision can make major improvements in a paper.

3. On rereading, Ben realized that this was really the point of the previous sentence. He hadn't stated it originally, because—at the time—it had seemed too obvious to say. On the second day he realized it was obvious only because he had been thinking it.

4. Ben wrote this, thinking about the books and papers lying right there on his desk, then realized that the reader, who didn't have them to look at, might want to know what sources Ben, the writer, had in mind.

5. In writing this sentence Ben said he suddenly drew a blank. It said what he meant and he couldn't think of anything else to say. Yet he knew he hadn't said enough. It was too short for such an important point and it felt incomplete. His solution was probably one of the best ones a research writer can use: He turned around and asked himself, as a slightly skeptical reader might, "What do you mean by that? Can you give me an example, show me some evidence?" This led him back to his data and some concrete examples that not only supported his point but made it a more explicit, two-part idea.

6. This is a sentence that got off the track. It was true; it was interesting; and it was connected to the sentence just before it. But after 10 minutes of trying to fit it in, Ben realized that it simply didn't support the main point he was trying to make. It was leading him down the garden path.

This case study of one student's experience writing a research paper is an appropriate conclusion to this book. For one thing, it illustrates how writing often begins with trying to define and explore a problem in one's own mind. Here that exploration led to a thesis and ended in a paper which tried to support that thesis with an argument and evidence. The formal features of the research paper were used in order to support what really mattered—helping the writer and the reader consider an interesting problem.

Secondly, the process log and the revisions let us glimpse a goal-directed writer who is aware of his own writing process. He uses that awareness to give himself choices and alternative strategies as he works on planning and revising, and, as he does on October 16, to learn from his own experience. In fact, the most interesting thing about this case study may be the way it shows a learning process and a writing process which are inextricably intertwined. The strategies which helped Ben write an insightful paper are the ones which helped him define and understand an interesting problem. And the strategies which helped him structure and revise this paper for the reader are also the ones which helped him develop and organize his own thinking. He has turned his own writing process into a serious and powerful tool for thinking.

PROJECTS AND ASSIGNMENTS

1 Part of the argument transcript from Ben's paper has been left uncoded. From reading his discussion of Toulmin's method, can you now code the rest of the transcript?

2 Based on your analysis of the transcript, what points would you advise Ben to add to his paper, either to support his main point or to add new ones?

3 Given the argument of the paper and your own analysis, write a Conclusion for the paper as you would do it. The Conclusion should show the link between the initial problem, the writer's predictions, and the actual results of the analysis. Use it to sum up what you and the writer have learned through your research and reading.

4 Use Ben's report as research reports are meant to be used. Treat it as a theory you can test and/or a research method you can use to do your own research. Do your own study. Does your analysis of a written and/or an oral argument support Ben's? Remember to cite him as a source.

5 *Checklist:* The Overall Evaluation of a Paper—from a Reader's Point of View. This checklist covers the major features readers look for in any well-written analysis or report. Notice that it includes a number of features we have looked at throughout the book.
   ☐ *The problem analysis:*
      Is there an effective problem/purpose statement? Does the paper define a real problem (instead of just describing a situation or recommending a new program)? And is this problem centered

around a shared goal? *(or)* Does the writer state a clear issue or thesis that the research paper will explore?

☐ *The overall structure of ideas:*

Is the paper organized around an issue tree that is focused on the problem or thesis?

Does the paper provide cues, such as headings, that help the reader see this top-level organization?

Is the overall structure reader-based rather than writer-based?

☐ *The structure of sentences and paragraphs:*

Has the writer chunked his or her ideas and provided organizing ideas for the reader? Is the function of each paragraph clear? Has the writer provided *cues* for the reader, such as overviews and transitions, that make the relationship between paragraphs or sentences clear?

Do the paragraphs have a reader-based organization?

☐ *Editing:*

Does the paper use vigorous prose?

Does the writing make the underlying relationships of ideas clear?

Is the writing proofread and free of errors?

☐ *Overall academic or professional quality:*

Does this paper show the overall attention to research, analysis, and presentation that you would expect from a professional researcher, consultant, or academic writer?

Will this report have a real intellectual or functional value for its intended reader?

Index

composing process (*continued*)
  case studies of, 53–57, 259–62, 269–73
  getting started, 35–39
  methods, 40–45
  planning, 65–71
  problem-solving approach to, 43–45
  problems with, 33–40
  strategies for, 1, 35–39, 40–46
  strong and weak approaches to, 37–39
  see also creative thinking, strategies for; organizing ideas, strategies for
concepts, *see* ideas
conclusion, open-minded, 141–42
conference, student-teacher, 54–55
conflict, critical, 30–31, 135–37
constructive strategy for operational planning, 91
consulting report, case studies of, 194–97
context, providing a, 137–38, 170–72
conventions of a discourse community, 21, 23, 153
conventions, writing, *see* text conventions
conversation of a discourse community, 21–23
coordinate sentence pattern, 242–43
creative process, Wallas's four stages of, 43
creative reader, 166–83
creative thinking, strategies for:
  free writing, 103–104
  rest and incubate, 108
  systematically explore one's topic, 105–108
  talk to one's reader, 104
  turn off the editor and brainstorm, 102–104
    see also ideas
creative writing, *see* writing tasks, personal
critical conflict, 30–31, 135–37
cues by writer, 172, 202–206, 253–56

D

debate, as form of argument, 206–210
designing for a reader, *see* reader; reader-based prose
development, and issue trees, 119–21
diagnosis, checklist for, 257
discourse communities, 20–23, 150–52
  conventions, 21, 23, 153
  entering the conversation, 21–23
  member of, 21
discourse community checklist, 26–27
documentation in research writing, 268

E

"Eagle, The," 64–65
editing, 2, 227–35, 239–57

for connections and coherence, 239–57
for economy, 228–31
for a forceful style, 231–35
key-word, 229–31
to reveal a paragraph's inner logic, 248–57
reviewing, 214–17
of sentences, 241–47
strategies for, 241–57
techniques of, 215–26
see also revision
editor:
  internal, as cause of writer's block, 40
  turning off, and brainstorming, 102–104
evaluating one's writing, 2
  awareness of one's own composing process, 31–33
  checklist, 286–87
  editing, 227–35
  reviewing, 214–17
explaining an assignment to yourself, 82–85
exploration of a topic, systematic, 105–108
expository writing, 4–5
expressive writing, *see* writing tasks, personal

F

forceful style, 231–35
formal features of academic discourse, 78
formal report, case study of, 269–86
format for papers, 204
  for research writing, 268–69
freewriting, 103–104

G

generating ideas, 102–108
  see also creative thinking, strategies for
getting stopped during writing, 39–40, 103–104
Ghiselin, Brewster, 140
gist, 67, 70, 94, 169–70, 173, 215–16
  and list strategy, 90–91
global revision, 215, 217
goal-directed thinking and brainstorming, 30–31, 54–55, 86, 259–62
goals, 4–5
  operational ways of creating, 89–92
  reviewing one's own, 186–87, 215–16
  setting of, 1, 55, 66–67, 71, 82
  shared, 188–90
Guitton, Jean, 79

H

habits, writing, 34–35
heavy nouns, 232
heuristics, 44–45
hierarchical organization, 10–12
  in issue trees, 117–29
  in reader-based prose, 201–202
  readers' creation of in text, 173–74
  in real-world writing, 10–12, 15
  see also organizing ideas, strategies for;
    paragraphs
History of Western Philosophy, 190
hooking devices, *see* cues by writer

I

idea, top-level, 13, 119–21
  see also hierarchical organization
ideas:
  finding missing parts of, 114–15, 120
  main, 94, 175
  nutshelling and teaching of, 116–17
  subordinate in paragraphs, 250
  see also creative thinking, strategies for; or-
    ganizing ideas, strategies for
illumination, as phase of inspiration method,
  43
image of rhetorical problem, 76
images, mental, *see* mental representations
imaginary reader, 221–22
imagination in generating ideas, 101–108
incubation, as strategy for creative thinking,
  43, 55, 108
inferences, 166–68, 169, 176–83
information:
  chunking, 168–69
  finding for research writing, 265–68
inspiration:
  myth of, 41–43
  as strategy for writing, 36, 43
  waiting for, 38
institutional prose, 228–29
internal editor, as cause of writer's block, 40
intuition in planning, 92
issue analysis, 127–29
issue trees, 117–130
  examples of, 11–12, 15, 71, 118–23, 126,
    128, 130, 252

J

James, William, 79, 91
jobs and writing, *see* writing, practical

K

key-words:
  editing for, 229–31
  in assignments, 84
knowledge:
  different ways of representing, 65–66, 68,
    70–71
  reader's, 159, 161–63
  usable, 84
  ways of knowing, 61–65
"Kubla Khan" and myth of inspiration, 41–43

L

Labov, William, 192
Lakein, Alan, 132
Latinate endings to nouns, 232
Linde, Charlotte, 192
linking verbs, weak, 232–33
listlike style, modifying a, 241–42
local revision, 215
Lowes, John Livingstone, 43

M

main idea, 94, 175–76
  see also top-level idea
McCarrell, Nancy, 170–171
meaning and the creative reader, 166–74
member of a discourse community, 21
memory:
  dump, 83–84
  network, 68–69
  and readers' needs, 168–71
mental representations, 61, 65, 68, 70
Miller, Thomas, 203–205
Minsky's Maxim, 67, 86, 265
modifying sentence pattern, 243–44
myths about writing, 2, 41–43

N

narrative, 197–98
needs of reader, 1–2, 10, 160–63, 259–62
negative expressions, transforming, 233
notation techniques, as strategy for writing,
  36, 39
nouns:
  noun-verb ratio, 232